A Very Private School

Charles Spencer

A Very Private School

WILLIAM
COLLINS

William Collins
An imprint of HarperCollins*Publishers*
1 London Bridge Street
London SE1 9GF

WilliamCollinsBooks.com

HarperCollins*Publishers*
Macken House, 39/40 Mayor Street Upper
Dublin 1, D01 C9W8

First published in Great Britain in 2024 by William Collins
First published in the United States by Simon and Schuster in 2024

1

A catalogue record for this book is
available from the British Library

HB ISBN 978-0-00-866608-8

Set in Adobe Caslon Pro
Printed and bound in the UK using 100%
renewable electricity at CPI Group (UK) Ltd

MIX
Paper | Supporting
responsible forestry
FSC™ C007454
FSC
www.fsc.org

This book is produced from independently certified FSC™ paper
to ensure responsible forest management.

For more information visit: www.harpercollins.co.uk/green

For Buzz

One of the luckiest things that can happen to you in life is, I think, to have a happy childhood.

– Agatha Christie

I am not writing to solicit any special sympathy. People survive much worse and never put pen to paper. I am writing in order to take charge of my childhood.

– Hilary Mantel

CONTENTS

Preface		1
Introduction: For the Empire		11
1	Early Misgivings	19
2	A Place Called Maidwell	35
3	New Boy	55
4	Judging Jack	79
5	At Arm's Length	101
6	A Day in the Life	117
7	Willing Henchmen	141
8	Potential Saviours	163
9	Blood on the Floor	179
10	Bullying	189
11	Please	201

12 My Parents   217

13 Leaver   231

14 Looking Back   241

15 Facing the Past   247

16 A Different Generation   255

    Epilogue   267

    Acknowledgements   291

PREFACE

This is a look back at how things too often were, fifty years ago, in the English private educational system.

Maidwell Hall, the school at which I boarded from the age of eight to thirteen, was built on a lie common to institutions of its type: on the cock-and-bull notion that children were better off under its roof, learning to be biddable, influential members of society, rather than living as we should have done, as nature intended – with our families.

This book is a blend of chronicle and memoir that's intended to stand as a piece of modern history – a record of a time, not so far back, when things were quite different for children in these most privileged of English academic settings.

There were no emails or mobile phones in the 1970s, of course, and we boys at Maidwell had no access to a landline. During the three annual terms, each of some twelve or thirteen weeks, contact with our parents was a Sunday letter home, written under supervision.

But it's not just the tools of interaction that were different. Privileged parents back then tended to devote less direct energy to their children than is expected, and considered normal, now. The limitations set around communication, and the nature of our family relationships back then, made abuse possible – indeed, more likely – and hard to detect.

Maidwell was typical of the boarding schools of its time in being, effectively, a closed community. It attracted staff who were drawn to this blend of quiet and secrecy. Some of them welcomed power, and status, and the ability to cut with the outside world. Many of these adults weren't there for the boys' best interests, but to meet their own darker needs.

While abuse in boarding schools is impossible to eradicate, owing to the flaws of humankind, we can hope that modern-day victims have greater recourse to help than what was previously available. Now, there is a general understanding of the importance of having those who act in the parents' stead trained and vetted. It's no longer acceptable to subcontract the crucial business of bringing up children to unregulated amateurs with unknown tendencies, as happened in my time.

During the years that this book has taken me to contemplate and complete, various of my Maidwell contemporaries have re-entered my life. We first knew one another as boys, but have become reacquainted in late middle age. One of these faces from the past came to visit me a couple of years back, on business, at my family home, Althorp. We had last seen each other back in 1978.

'It's so good to see you,' I said, starting gently: I knew from his wife that this kind, quiet man refused to discuss his time as a pupil at Maidwell with her, or with anyone else. It was a subject that, if raised, made him stare at the floor, in silent desolation.

My greeting was left hanging as we sat on either side of a fireplace, taking in the changes in each other's appearance. But then I suddenly remembered how much I'd liked him, four decades before, and this spurred me to jump in.

'I'm writing a book about Maidwell ... What do you remember most about the place?'

He paused before answering, then opened up to me about his experiences and the impact they have had on his life ever since. I jotted down what he said, in ten pages of my notebook, as we shared and compared our recollections.

When I told him that I had been sexually abused at Maidwell, he immediately named the member of staff responsible.

'Yes – goodness. You're right ...'

'I always knew,' he said.

'But how?' I replied. We had been friendly as boys but, being in separate years in a rigidly hierarchical place, never confidants.

'I just did. It was obvious.' Then he named others who had been victims of the same predator. Three I knew about, while the other was a new entry to The Preyed Upon, a dire club whose membership nobody would seek.

To my horror, he told me of his being sexually assaulted at Maidwell three times, when aged nine, by someone who was meant to protect him. His assailant threatened him with terrible retribution if he ever told anyone about it. He remembers feeling troubled that other boys within earshot must have heard his struggles as he was overpowered, and this added a further layer of humiliation to the ghastliness of his violation.

His main memory of Maidwell, he told me, was of being made to feel worthless, every day of his five years there. He was badly bullied, particularly by the headmaster. 'I was petrified of him,' he said. 'He took me to a place inside myself that I didn't want to go to.

'I have never got over it,' he continued. 'I don't have anger, I don't want justice – whatever that would be – but I do know that my life never had a chance, once I'd been so badly scarred by that school.'

At the end of a harrowing hour, I set down my notebook, declaring that what he'd told me was too terrible to be committed to the page. I promised that I would never betray his confidences by naming him in this book, or by disclosing the breadth or detail of his suffering. At this he became animated for the first time and leaned forward. 'But someone *has* to tell our story!' he pleaded.

I've had several similar reunions since, with Maidwell contemporaries who suffered terribly. Four years ago, as I arrived to speak at a book festival, a tall, lean man approached me and his features called to mind someone I'd briefly known, as a boy.

'Charles Spencer?' he asked, holding out his hand in greeting. 'You won't recognise me, but a very long time ago …'

'Yes, I actually *do* recognise you,' I replied, naming him. 'We were at Maidwell together.' He looked surprised: we'd only overlapped at the school during my first ten months there.

'Tell me,' I asked, 'when you think of Maidwell, what's the *one* word that comes to mind – the one that really sums up the place?'

He stopped and stared into the distance. 'Fear,' he said.

He sniffed, apparently surprising himself at having revealed so much in one, stark word.

I pushed him: 'And what was at the root of that fear?'

He sniffed again.

'Waiting to be beaten yet again, for God knows what.' He blinked hard, a successful professional in his sixties, unexpectedly reconnected with the vulnerable child he had been, caught in the tendrils of unfathomable sadistic rituals.

I've learned of other contemporaries who have died, accompanied to their ends by deeply painful memories of their time at that school. The cumulation of all this hurt and damage persuaded me to write this book – my record of what it was like for us, as boys, to live in a beautiful place, under a dark power.

I hope that this account might lead to some form of closure for those who, it's clear to me, are still bearing the emotional scars of a regime that was so very harsh and gruelling.

There were bright spots of happiness and comradeship in those years, and they are celebrated in what follows, too. But these were despite, not because of, the fundamental nature of the place. Meanwhile the resilience that such a tough upbringing can impart has been bought at the cost of sensitivity being trampled, and sometimes eradicated.

I've frequently witnessed deep pain, still flickering in the eyes of my Maidwell contemporaries. The snarled root of that hurt trails back to not being cherished, encouraged or valued, as we might have been at home, but belittled, scolded, beaten or – if lucky – merely tolerated. This, while being moulded into end products that were not only damaged but outmoded, even back then.

Others appear to have survived intact, some even to have enjoyed their time in the school, while acknowledging its severe shortcomings; but many of us left Maidwell with demons sewn into the seams of our souls.

While writing my story I have inevitably taken a good look at what I believe is a fascinating aberration: the boarding school system as a whole.*

It's a fact that many of the leading figures in British public life today – from prime ministers to royalty – have received the privilege of just such a private, boarding school, education. While some thrived under benevolent headteachers, others have been wounded by wretched treatment during formative years. Some of this poisonous legacy they've unwittingly passed on to society. As Diogenes said in the fourth century BC: 'The foundation of every state is the education of its youth.' If that education system is flawed, the state's foundations will be, too.

I have to say – without wanting sympathy, but because it's important to know the context to what follows – that it's been an absolutely hellish experience at times, this chronicling of casual cruelty, sexual assault and other perversion from long ago. As I wrote this book, the crushing migraines that often felled me back

---

* While many girls suffered similarly back then, of course, this book is my eyewitness account, with historical context, of the male system that I was an involuntary part of; it therefore – inevitably – focuses on the male side of the issue.

then returned. This, after forty-odd years of welcome absence. I've also had dozens of Maidwell nightmares. Fenn traps have gone off in my mind as I retraced the footpaths of my early schooldays. I have come to accept that they have snared part of my psyche forever.

The events I describe in the following pages all happened as written, and the character sketches are, I believe, accurate. The reported speech is as near to the truth as I can remember, and certainly conveys the meaning of what was said at the time. I have changed all the boys' names – even though many said they were happy for their true identities to be used.

I wrote the body of this manuscript from my extremely clear recollections, which were seared into my brain as a child. The psychotherapists I have seen over the decades say that trauma at this age often leads to memories being expunged; but it can go the other way. Recollections can remain with the abused, vividly and forever, as they have with me. In addition, I have drawn on contemporaneous sources from my Maidwell years – my school reports from each of my fifteen terms there, as well as my diaries and my letters home.

Clearly, what I endured during five years in one of the most expensive private schools in England, during a time of solid political and economic stability, is not at all comparable with the terrible suffering of so many other children – now and in the past – forced to struggle to survive in landscapes of total despair. There is only the most tenuous of links between my privileged experience and the experience of those facing economic adversity and social exclusion: that of childhood trauma.

I've read avidly about childhood trauma, particularly those elements that are connected to emotional attachment. This area fascinates me because I experienced abandonment before being sent off to Maidwell. This was in the mid-sixties, when I was two, and my mother left home for a man she had fallen in love with.

Back then the discipline of a boarding environment was often thought to provide a stability that a 'broken home' was believed to be incapable of. But I loved home, and most definitely did not want to leave it, even when it lacked a mother. Being transplanted to a strange and repressive place was the last thing I needed – especially as a child of divorce.

As a historian, as a product of the system and as a man, I am fascinated by what on earth was going on at schools such as the one I attended. Why were parents blithely sending us away, to live with adults and children who were total strangers, in a clear rejection of family? Why replace this natural unit with an environment of often marked harshness?

There remain 630,000 boarders in 2,500 boarding schools in England now, but few of those institutions would have survived if they hadn't evolved significantly from the time I write about.

If you look at Maidwell's website today you will see there is a head of pastoral care, who has a deputy to assist. The recently appointed headmaster declared, on taking up office: 'I have been dedicated to education – education in its fullest sense – to seeing the whole child and their potential and helping them to achieve this.'

This was not the Maidwell that I knew. There was not one person in the structure of the place who had any responsibility for us young children beyond the tight confines of bookwork, discipline, the sports field, hygiene and nutrition. The emotional wellbeing of the child was not considered a specific need.

Our softest nerve endings were crushed by an experience that was irreversible in its distress. While a small number of boys, sadly, came from abusive homes, and were arguably better off in this harsh place, the rest of us had to learn to live without the comfort and protection of home. What we suffered was not just a separation from all that we knew and loved, but an amputation from it.

While this book describes a world of privilege alien to most, I hope it will resonate with anyone, anywhere – from all walks of life – who was ever made to feel frightened, powerless and abandoned as a child. For Maidwell, in the 1970s, was meant to serve as a surrogate home. But it lacked the most important quality of a home: it was without love.

Introduction

For the Empire

The upper echelons of English society have long subjected their sons and daughters to the forced abandonment of boarding school. Such exile from home has been seen as a worthwhile sacrifice: in return for a broken heart, the discarded child was launched down a narrow chute that ended in the soft landing of an adulthood where privilege and power lay all around them.

I can trace this trend through the past three hundred years of my own family's history, and see that my being sent away to boarding school at an early age was simply part of an ancestral tradition. My parents weren't being deliberately cruel; they were simply being true to the customs of their class.

In 1716, my ancestor John Spencer went to board at Eton College with his brothers. John was, like me when I started at boarding school, eight years old. But John's maternal grandmother, Sarah, the Duchess of Marlborough, was unhappy about the decision. She was a force of nature who had been Queen Anne's favourite at court, captivating the plodding monarch with her charisma and vitality, until the two fell out forever. Sarah's free thinking had seen her absorb the works of the philosopher John

Locke. In *Some Thoughts Concerning Education*, Locke insisted that the next generation of England's ruling class must be taught practical and useful disciplines – mathematics, the sciences and modern languages – instead of being burdened with the dead tongues and academic disciplines of ancient Greece and Rome. More enlightened learning, Locke insisted, would benefit not only the individual child, but also the nation as a whole.

John Spencer's father died in 1722, when he was thirteen, and his duchess grandmother swung into action straight away. She removed John and his brothers from Eton and installed them in her favourite residence, Windsor Lodge, where they were home-tutored by James Stephens, a brilliant mathematician. This rare escape from conventional boarding school for one of my distant forefathers was brought about by their grandmother's educational prejudices rather than a hatred of sending children away to learn. The nineteenth-century Spencer boys were less fortunate.

On 13 May 1808, my great-great-aunt Sarah Spencer wrote to her grandmother about the impending fate of her youngest brothers, Frederick and George, who were aged ten and eight: 'Next Wednesday our two dear little boys go to Eton. I won't allow myself to think of it in as melancholy a way as I am inclined to do, for I know my regret at it to be very selfish; they will be most satisfactorily situated in every way; and are I think too young to dread the event much. They have no conception of what it is to leave home, poor things …'

In middle age, this George Spencer, a devout Christian all his life, would look back on his Eton years as having been spent 'in an enemy's country', one where he had been 'obliged to guard against danger on all sides'. His tutor, the Reverend Richard Godley, was so worried by the bullying George suffered outside the classroom that he withdrew the boy from the school's everyday life.

However, George's parents felt sure that their son would benefit from Eton's customary rough and tumble, and so transferred him, aged eleven, to a boarding house with other students. But the boy's devout Christianity saw him relentlessly bullied by other pupils. After ten days of their spite, he felt compelled to hide the faith that would remain central to his life.*

In the early twentieth century, my widower great-grandfather, Robert 'Bobby' Spencer, also sent his sons away from home. The younger ones went as boys to Dartmouth, the Royal Navy's officer training college. When the youngest, fourteen-year-old George, was about to leave for Dartmouth, the boy confided in his private journal: 'I do not want to leave my lovely family circle ... It is lovely here [at Althorp], and father and everyone are *so* nice and kind.' He wrote of how much he'd miss the particular joys of his home life: playing tennis, table tennis and cards with his older siblings; riding his horse, Redwing; and playing with his father's incorrigible dog, Swift, who stole from the table. And he felt quite sure that Dartmouth would have no food to match his favourite home dish, chocolate custard.

But my family had a tradition of naval service, and of children doing as they were expected. 'How miserable it is,' George

---

* George would convert from Anglicanism to Roman Catholicism, before joining the Passionists – a strict religious order. In 2021, the Vatican announced that George Spencer was to be termed 'Venerable', so setting him on the path to possible sainthood.

concluded, shortly after being sent on his way. 'I must work awfully hard & please father ... How I wish I could please everyone here. "May the Lord help me to do my duty and keep all my resolutions".'

Meanwhile Bobby took his eldest son, Jack (my grandfather), for his first day at boarding school when he was eight. Bobby recorded in his journal how awful he felt, committing this innocent, trusting son to an institution where he had, in his turn, been so utterly miserable. He consoled himself with the thought that young Jack, fortunately, had no idea how ghastly his boarding school life was going to be.

Sarah and Bobby Spencer, writing nearly a century apart, separately identified a timeless truth: children cannot possibly anticipate how harsh the reality of life alone, outside of their family unit, can be, when they are not simply learning but also sleeping, playing and eating with strangers. Many of them are traumatised by abandonment. This is the lot of the orphan, but in this case voluntarily foisted on them by their (mostly) well-intentioned parents.

Such a harsh tradition only becomes fathomable once you accept that the English boarding school wasn't created to meet the child's educational or emotional needs. Indeed, it wasn't a system designed to serve the individual at all. Rather, it was nurtured in the strong rays of the British Empire, to populate and replenish the ranks of those who administered, controlled and expanded that global mission.

At its peak, the British Empire covered thirteen million square miles and demanded loyalty from a fifth of the world's inhabitants. Such a gigantic dominion required an officer class, to exert control on London's behalf: men nourished from an early age on a concept of Britishness that the private schools packaged and released, year after academic year.

Lord Curzon, a former viceroy of India, told the Imperial Press Conference at Oxford, in 1908, 'We train here, and we send out to you, your governors and administrators, and judges, your teachers, and preachers and lawyers.' This was a process rounded off at university, but it began with little boys being deposited at the hundreds of boarding schools that dotted England.

These institutions were never designed to be pleasurable. In 1904, Lord Meath introduced Empire Day as an annual celebration in the United Kingdom. Schoolchildren spent the morning examining their colonial heritage and venerating the national flag, before having the afternoon free. Meath believed education needed to be rigorous if it was to be effective. 'If the white men and women of the British Empire are idle, soft, selfish, hysterical and undisciplined,' he asked, 'are they likely to rule well?'

To be effective in their imperial roles, the sons of the empire needed to have the instinct of pining for home snuffed out, early and forever. The tightly wound 'Brit' of caricature often had his stiff upper lip cast in the furnace of English boarding school life, where his emotions were cauterised. The resultant, desensitised functionary could be reliably deployed far from home – whether in Calcutta, Cape Town or Calgary.

These psychologically hobbled victims would invariably perpetuate the madness, unthinkingly condemning their children to the fate they'd painfully endured, sending them to the same schools they had hated in their time. In this way, they gave the wheel of imperialism yet another spin.

English boarding school children were raised with resilient service in mind, and they were programmed to believe that their country, their Christianity and their school formed a blessed Trinity – one that demanded total loyalty. The War Cloister erected by prestigious Winchester College to salute the 500 of its old boys slain in the First World War asserts:

> In the day of battle, they forgat not God, Who created them
> to do His Will, nor their Country, the stronghold of freedom,
> nor their School, the mother of godliness and discipline.
> Strong in this threefold faith they went forth from home and
> kindred to the battlefields of the world and, treading the path
> of duty and sacrifice, laid down their lives for mankind.

Preparation for such martyrdom began at boarding school.

In the century and a half before I started at Maidwell, the ailing British upper classes – hit by increased taxation, while their traditional, agricultural incomes were strangled by cheap wheat and meat imports from the Americas – surrendered power and influence to the wealthier element of the middle classes.

The two social blocs intermingled, trading in status and cash, with boarding schools forming an essential staging post for the children of the socially ambitious. George Orwell* wrote, in an essay of 1941, of how the aristocracy, rather than accepting its

---

* George Orwell was the pen name of Eric Blair.

time had passed, 'simply intermarried with the merchants, manufacturers, and financiers who had replaced them, and soon turned them into accurate copies of themselves. The wealthy ship owner or cotton miller set up for himself an alibi as a country gentleman, while his sons learnt the right mannerisms at public schools* – which had been designed for just that purpose.'

Orwell was typical of those raised to serve the cause of the ruling classes, and their empire. His father – employed in the Opium Department of the Indian Civil Service – brought his family back to England for the children's education, before leaving them behind and returning to his work overseas.

Orwell never forgot the shock of being sent, in 1911, to board at St Cyprian's, one of a cluster of boarding schools on the English south coast. Aged eight, he found this uprooting so traumatic that he started to wet his bed – a developmental stage that he had outgrown, at home, four years earlier. The headmaster beat him for this with his bone riding whip, spitting out 'you dir-ty lit-tle boy' in time to a hail of blows that could last for several minutes.

Orwell moved from St Cyprian's to Eton, after which he was ready to serve the empire. Being from the right boarding school background guaranteed rapid promotion: by the age of twenty, he was an assistant district superintendent in Burma, overseeing the security of two hundred thousand people around Rangoon.

During the Second World War, Orwell wrote *Such, Such Were the Joys*, a chronicle of his misery and mistreatment at St Cyprian's.

---

* Confusingly, the English have traditionally referred to their private schools as 'public' schools.

It ended on a note of optimism: surely, he concluded, a place like St Cyprian's could no longer exist in the 1940s, three decades after he'd left the place? Given the societal shifts of the previous generation, he asked: 'Does a child at school go through the same kind of experiences nowadays? ... it is obvious that the present-day attitude towards education is enormously more humane and sensible than that of the past ... Clearly there has been a vast change of outlook, a general growth of "enlightenment", even among ordinary, unthinking middle-class people. Religious belief, for instance, has largely vanished, dragging other kinds of nonsense after it ... Beating, too, has become discredited, and has even been abandoned at many schools ... The real question is whether it is still normal for a school child to live for years amid irrational terrors and lunatic misunderstandings.'

Well, 'normal'? – no. But did the traditional, harsh mould of boarding school education continue beyond the world wars, even though the first of these drew the teeth of the British Empire, before the second put it to sleep?

My experiences at Maidwell, thirty years after Orwell wrote on this theme, would suggest the answer is, sadly, yes. All you needed were the right conditions to prevail, with the wrong people in control, and the abuses rife in previous generations could continue on.

1

Early Misgivings

There is always one moment in childhood when the
door opens and lets the future in.

– Graham Greene

I put food on my fork. Convivial lunch. Elegant, old-fashioned
dining room. Immaculate serving staff. Concise but confident
menu. Most importantly, exceptional company: round the table
sat men, in various hues of ripe middle age, who shared something profound and indelible – their distant past.

We had settled in to one of our occasional get togethers,
decades of familiarity spiralling back to the five years when we
had lived at boarding school like brothers.

'What was I like at Maidwell?' I asked.

'Angry,' came the cheery reply, without a pause.

'Really?' I stopped, shocked. I had no idea.

'Yes – my memories are of you being very angry. All the
time.'

This from one of my oldest friends, who had started at Maidwell with me on the same day. We'd first met in the summer of 1972, when he was seven and I'd just turned eight, on a sunny afternoon in a beautiful, rural corner of the English Midlands. We were both guests at the new boys' tea party at Maidwell Hall, an exclusive private boarding school for seventy-five eight- to thirteen-year-old boys.

While my father made small talk with the other parents over teacups and finely sliced sandwiches, we dozen sons of the wealthy were beckoned away by some smiling man connected to this strange place. He reassured us that our tour of the school would only last a short while. I looked quickly up at my father, who gave a nod of encouragement, his eyes feigning excitement on my behalf.

Our Pied Piper took us on a merry dance through the enormous grounds. The sunlight played through the trees, while our guide pointed out new features that have long since been, for me, the unforgettable landmarks to a precious yet painful chapter of childhood.

There was a long walk round Maidwell's lake, bounded by banks of bulrushes that were speckled with vivid wildflowers – red and yellow campion, ragged-robin and marsh marigold. My young mind thrilled at the slowly shifting shapes of fish in the water – plump golden orfe cruising at a stately rate, as they skirted round lilies and knots of weed. Meanwhile coots briskly bobbed across the surface, shrilly alarmed by our intrusion.

We spent half of this new boy tour negotiating woodland called 'the Wilderness', a name that conjures up images of loss and abandonment. The ground under the Wilderness's canopy of trees was shrouded with dog's mercury, a poisonous plant that thrives in the shade.

Some of the other boys seemed giddy with excitement, thrilled to have a fresh audience to show off to. Two of them, from one of the country's wealthier families – the younger of whom had, I assume, joined us because his parents didn't want him bothering them during the adult tea party – twisted and turned like animated dragon flies. I was intrigued by their brashness, and marvelled that our adult guide tolerated it. His frozen smile never cracked.

A clumsy quiet hung over most of us. We trudged forward, beginning to size one another up with sideways glances. Our attempts at conversation were infrequent, short-lived and awkward. Often, when we looked up, we saw from a fresh angle the huge, imposing building that was to be our surrogate home for the next five years.

Only after I had left the school did I realise that there were two contrasting sides to Maidwell: the handsome outer skin of the hall, with its glorious grounds; and the inner, beating heart of the place, which contained something sinister in the lining of its critical valves.

The original manor house had been erected in 1637. A fire in 1895 carried off much of this structure, and the bulk of what I saw for the first time, that summer day, was designed at the end of the nineteenth century by John Alfred Gotch, a local architect with a national reputation. Gotch built to impress. He planted a tower at each of the hall's four principal corners, every one topped with hammered lead, tapering up to spired tips, giving the hall's silhouette a stately air. You can just detect at Maidwell a muffled echo of the Tower of London. A construct of wealth and power, the hall adapted into a seat of learning for the sons of the wealthy and powerful only when its original purpose, as a family's magnificent country seat, fell away.

What little I knew of this place at the time made me distrusting and anxious. This wasn't a school such as the one I was then attending, where pupils went home at the end of the day. Rather, I had learned to my horror, this was somewhere that you were sent to stay, for weeks at a stretch – away from your family, your home, your pets, your toys; from all life as you knew it. It was such an alarming thought that I simply couldn't comprehend it.

My father had explained that I would be coming here – so far from home, and where I knew nobody – for five years. He shared with me some of the lexicon of the privileged. Maidwell was to be my 'private' or 'prep' school, preparing me for the entry exams for Eton, the 'public' school that he and so many of our male forebears had attended in their time.

What little I knew of boarding schools came from a recent BBC TV adaptation of *Tom Brown's School Days*, the nineteenth-century novel by Thomas Hughes based on his chastening experiences as a boarder. I had watched horrified as this classic English tale of brutality, set in a harsh, Victorian school, unfurled over several weeks.

Tom Brown's school, Rugby, was presided over by a cold, aloof headmaster who caned boys' buttocks hard and often, with tight-jawed enthusiasm. His creed – 'First religious and moral principle, second gentlemanly conduct, third academic ability' – was based on a muscular Christianity, where concepts of masculinity and faith reconstituted in hard form to fit a narrow prejudice.

Tom Brown existed in an institution where retribution was short, sharp and painful. Meanwhile, in the emotional void that attended the headmaster's authoritarian rule, bullying among the boys flourished, unpunished. At such a school, terror was everywhere: it came from above, but it also attacked from the flanks.

I watched for signs that, underneath the forced camaraderie of the new boys' tea party, Maidwell Hall might be harbouring similar terrors. While nothing obvious struck me during my visit, I returned home that evening deeply troubled. I had been dreading the idea of Maidwell for as long as I could remember; I was already ticking off the days that lay between me and the incomprehensible terror picked out for me by my parents.

But now I had a picture of it, and of the faces that would surround me there. From that point on, Maidwell took on a tangible reality – one that was coming my way, on a collision course that would destroy the world I knew and loved.

My schooldays up to this stage had been wonderfully gentle, part of a happy early childhood spent in the lyrical countryside of North Norfolk, on England's east coast. Home was Park House, a handsome, sprawling country house built in the 1860s, set in parkland that stretches out to envelop Sandringham House, one of the royal family's rural escapes.

In the 1930s, Queen Elizabeth's father, the future King George VI, offered the rental of Park House to my mother's father,

Maurice, Lord Fermoy. The two men were good friends, thanks to my grandfather's charm: his wit and gift for mimicry took the shy, stammering king out of himself, and they enjoyed playing tennis together in the summer, as well as shooting partridge and pheasant in the colder months. My grandfather was a trusted figure who taught Queen Elizabeth how to skate, on Sandringham Lake, when she was a girl.

He must have struck his royal neighbours as somewhat exotic: an Irish American, he'd grown up in Manhattan, attended St Paul's School in New Hampshire, and graduated from Harvard, before coming to know Europe when fighting for the US infantry in the First World War. Two years later, on his father's death, he had inherited the Irish title of Lord Fermoy, moved to England, established British citizenship and been elected Member of Parliament for the political constituency that included Sandringham.

In his mid-forties Maurice met Ruth Gill, a beautiful Scottish concert pianist half his age who'd been dating his twin brother, Frank. 'Frank was always saying, you must meet my brother, Maurice – he's so much nicer than me,' Ruth would recall. 'And – well – he was!' She managed an amicable break-up with Frank, and married Maurice, after which she would become a courtier and confidante to George VI's queen, Elizabeth – later the Queen Mother. Maurice and Ruth had two daughters and a son. The younger girl was my mother, Frances.

My mother entered the world on 20 January 1936 – the same day that George V departed it. Her birth in Park House and his death in Sandringham House took place less than a mile apart.

My mother later learned that nobody celebrated her arrival because they were consumed with grief at the king's loss.

In the summer of 1955, at the age of seventy, my grandfather suffered a stroke that, three weeks on, proved fatal. Soon afterwards, my parents – married for a year – settled into Park House. My mother was famously stay-at-home, the young fulcrum to a burgeoning family: she gave birth to Sarah when only nineteen, Jane a few weeks after turning twenty-one, Diana (a home birth, in Park House) when she was twenty-five, and me, her final child, when she was twenty-eight.

Park House was a wonderfully happy family home that became the hub to a network of Norfolk friends. There were horses in the paddock, as well as hard-fought matches on our tennis court and on the village cricket pitch over the garden fence. At my father's memorial service, his eulogist would note that these Park House years were the happiest of his life, and my stepmother graciously nodded at that truth.

My parents' marriage was gravely rocked by the events of 12 January 1960, the day on which their third child – my older brother, John – was not only born, but also, within twelve hours, died. I suspect this family tragedy torpedoed my parents' relationship, leaving an imperceptible hole beneath the waterline, through which water entered, unstaunched.

Six years after their elder son's death, my parents went on a skiing holiday with two couples, and my mother and one of the other husbands fell in love. They left their families and moved for six months to Australia, where they enjoyed life far from judgement. When my mother's older sister Mary pointed out that such a protracted time away would weigh against her in a custody battle, my mother replied, 'But when you think about it, what does it matter? All four of my children will be in boarding school in five years' time – when Charles goes away. And then I will have equal time with each of them, in the holidays, anyway.' It's a calculation that makes sense when your brain is drunk with love, and when your standard for parental engagement is based on the traditionally distant model of the British upper classes.

I can remember when I first realised that my mother was gone. One morning Mrs Petrie, the cheery, red-faced cleaner, showed me a postcard. She said it was from my mother and pointed to the picture on its front: 'Look! Mummy's in Australia – on holiday ...' Mrs Petrie's tone was, as ever, upbeat and kind. But when she added 'She will be back soon', a switch turned off inside me, for I detected the lie at once: my mother, I knew with a thud in my chest, wasn't coming home, even though I had no idea why.

Shortly before my fifth birthday, my seven-year-old sister Diana and I got off the train at London's cavernous Liverpool Street Station and saw our mother approaching, in an open-armed swoop. She was with a stranger – a broad-shouldered man – and they both looked deliriously happy. The man wore a dark suit and she a modish 1960s dress. They both had unusual speckles of colour scattered over their shoulders – confetti. My father's lawyers had stopped my mother from introducing her new man to us when he had been her lover. But now he was her husband, the law stopped respectfully outside the marital door.

'This is your stepfather,' my mother announced, excitedly. 'Peter Shand Kydd!' It was perhaps the first time I had heard that word 'stepfather'. We had no idea how to address such a being, and the question mark must have shown on our faces, for the tall stranger looked down, still smiling from the heady excitement of the day, and said, 'Just call me Peter.' This was a delicious novelty: in the tiny world that we inhabited, no adult asked a child to call them by their first name. We headed to the taxi stand, and I learned that my family structure had sprouted new struts out of nowhere: for I now had two stepbrothers and a stepsister. The three of them were away at boarding school, so it would be months till we met.

My mother and Peter bought a three-floored flat in Cadogan Place, in London's Belgravia. There they had a housekeeper, Mrs Pierce, from Putney in south London. She had a loud, lilting voice, and her comedy heroes were Frankie Howerd and Benny Hill, who made her laugh raucously. When she babysat, she left her false teeth in a glass by the kitchen sink.

We'd come to see my mother at Cadogan Place every fourth weekend in term time, and then would stay with her at her country house during the half of our school holidays that was allotted to her. She and Peter rented a house called Hilliers, an hour west of London. My sole memory of the place is a manmade pond, with a plentiful population of common newts. We were at Hilliers only briefly, but it must have been long enough to include the newts' mating season – I remember admiring the crest on the males' backs, a seasonal flourish that lent them the air of medieval warhorses, decked out for battle.

But Peter was a man of the sea, who'd served in mini-submarines during the Second World War. Soon after marrying my mother, he decided to find a new home on the coast, so they could sail regularly. They moved, when I was six, to Itchenor, a harbour in Sussex whose voice was a cacophony of shackles on halyards, beating against metal masts.

Their home there was Appleshore, a comfortable (if plain) modern house whose finest features, from a child's perspective, were its kidney-shaped swimming pool and its pets. We had two dogs at Appleshore: Qantas, a thickset yellow Labrador, named after the airline my mother and Peter used for their annual get-away to Australia; and Carnaby, a Jack Russell who took his name from the street in London that had been the epitome of 1960s cool.

I remember being in the front garden at Appleshore, one sunny afternoon during the summer when I had turned eight, shortly before setting off for Maidwell. We'd been cycling and swimming before enjoying a barbecue. I recall looking around slowly, absorb-ing the perfection of the moment, and thinking, with a dark flutter in my heart, This is all too good to last.

At that moment, from beyond the tall trees that shielded us from the lane at the end of the drive, there came a crunching thud followed by the tinkling high notes of shattering glass. We rushed down to find a man lying shocked and bruised beside his motorbike. He managed to tell us that our two dogs had chased and caught up with him, and that the Labrador had jumped up and knocked him to the ground. My stepfather called an ambu-lance.

The felled motorcyclist had escaped serious injury, but my mother decided on drastic action. While we were distracted by the drama, she had Qantas jump into her car and they disappeared together. On her return she was alone. She had, she explained, been to the vet and had Qantas put down.

That evening, while up in my bedroom struggling to make sense of the agonising loss of Qantas, I heard my mother downstairs phoning friend after friend. To each she described the upending of the man on the motorbike, then recounted the decisive course she'd taken. 'I couldn't have the children having one last night with the dog,' she said, in each call, with conviction and some pride, 'and then have them crying as they said goodbye to him in the morning. It was better this way.'

I felt, even then, that Qantas could surely have been trained not to chase people, instead of being put down. But that horrifying option was selected because of a skewed but sincere view as to what was in the children's best interests.

I've often wondered since if this deeply distressing episode, which took place weeks before I was despatched to boarding school, gives a clue as to why children like me were sent from home for our education: our mothers and fathers knew there would, inevitably, be keen pain. But, despite that, in our parents' judgement, 'it was better this way'.

When young, my mother and later my three older sisters had been home-schooled at Park House by a governess, Gertrude Allen. 'Allie' was gentle yet cheerful, with a clear voice, white hair, fine skin and an open smile. Perhaps because of Allie's advanced age, I was never entrusted to her classroom. Instead, in the autumn of 1968, when aged four, I was enrolled at Silfield School, in King's Lynn.

Before I set out on my first day, my father photographed Diana and me side by side on the top of the stone steps that led from Park House's gravel border to the lawn below. I was resplendent in a piercingly scarlet blazer, my breast pocket and cap emblazoned with the school's intricate black and gold crest of intertwining *S*'s. I wore baggy grey shorts, pulled up socks, new school shoes and a shy but excited smile on my face.

The headmistress of Silfield was Jean Lowe, a patriotic, unmarried intellectual who had founded the school in 1953, the year of Queen Elizabeth's coronation. My parents knew Miss Lowe slightly, as she helped at the charity fundraisers that they hosted from time to time at Park House. She was tall, white-haired, dark-eyed and slightly stooped; her billowing white blouse and shin-length skirt the dress of an old-fashioned governess. Her rich and husky voice had a sing-song tone that became fluty when animated. She crackled with emotional and academic intelligence, and possessed a natural, benevolent authority. Both her manner and her clothes harked back to an age when deference was expected and given.

Although she could be strict, Miss Lowe saw that the children committed to her care were treated with kindness. This was a quality that danced in her eyes. She was quick to smile, or even to tip over into a throaty laugh.

Miss Lowe's Silfield was safe, warm and fun. I was included in a school run of close friends, half a dozen of us bundled into a car like a litter of puppies, seatbelts never considered. After being dropped off on Gayton Road, where a gap in high fencing denoted the start of the passage that led to the school, we would march up the path each morning, swinging our brown leather satchels, at ease with whatever the day might present.

The layout of Silfield was reassuringly compact for a small child. Its backdrop was a stark, six-bedroomed house that belonged to the Pages, Miss Lowe's sister and brother-in-law. We children entered their home only for lunch, which we ate on long benches at low refectory tables, in a dark back room.

The school itself comprised three buildings: Miss Lowe's classroom for the senior years, which was accessed up some steep stairs; a timber framed assembly hall, with a high ceiling; and a glass and steel classroom that was the domain of Silfield's other mistress, Mrs Lacey, whose daughter was one of my classmates. We could play on Hipkin's Lawn (named after the school's flat-capped gardener) at the back of the property; in a large sandpit; and on a tennis court next to the assembly hall. The paths linking these various parts consisted of chunky gravel so deep that it smothered our sandals.

Miss Lowe wrote the school play every year, with parts for each of her boys and girls. In one of these – a folk tale called *The Happy Man* – I played a shipwrecked sailor. Eventually, my turn came to take to the stage, and the lead, playing a prince, asked me if I was that seemingly elusive figure, a happy man. 'Me, sir?' I replied, 'A happy man? I have no ship – I have no money. Nay, sir, I am not a happy man.' I then shrugged my shoulders and exited stage left, my clumsy cameo concluded.

Miss Lowe believed that education shouldn't be confined to textbooks: we were at Silfield to prepare for life. One dank morning she announced to my class: 'Right, I want you all to walk in pairs round the school – follow me!' We poured down the steps behind her, chattering excitedly at this unexpected break with routine. As we passed the sandpit, I was surprised to spot a blue plastic sports sash rising out of a puddle, its corrugated surface encrusted with mud. I thought about picking it up, but the moment passed and I left it where it had fallen.

Back inside our classroom, we returned to our desks and Miss Lowe turned on us in a voice quivering with anger: 'I'm very disappointed in you all!' We looked up at her, bewildered. 'There is a sports sash lying on the ground out there. Every single one of you had the chance to pick it up and bring it in. But *none* of you did so! It's *selfish* not to have helped in such a simple way. I'm thoroughly disappointed in *all* of you!' We were crestfallen. Miss Lowe wasn't someone we ever wanted to disappoint.

Equally, Miss Lowe's praise meant everything to us. I have her school reports, which looked for the positives. 'Charles clearly has a real love for History,' she wrote, when I was five, spotting a passion that's lasted a lifetime. My appalling maths was clearly and fairly noted too, but with encouragement, not ridicule.

Above all, Miss Lowe was sensitive to all her children's needs and addressed them with thoughtfulness and tact.

Diana and I were among the very few Silfield children with divorced parents. On every fourth Friday during term time, we went with our nanny on the lengthy train journey from King's Lynn to London, to be handed over to my mother so we could spend the weekend with her.

Rituals sprung up around these monthly treks. The bespecta-cled porter at King's Lynn Station, immaculate in his British Rail uniform and peaked cap, would greet me with a smile and give me a wodge of cards – of dinosaurs, flags or sports stars – gleaned from his packets of tea and cigarettes. This kindness dampened my dread of the slow, rattling journey to London through a series of stations whose names I can recite now, decades on, without consulting a timetable.

The slog from Silfield to my mother's Cadogan Place flat took three and a half hours. To get there by bedtime meant leaving school early. During the penultimate class of those handover Fridays, Miss Lowe would catch my eye and silently nod. While my classmates remained hunched over their books, I'd slip out, the headmistress leading me to the empty assembly hall. Here Diana would join us, fresh from her senior classroom, and we'd change out of our uniforms into regular clothes. It was all done without fuss and with dignity, so we wouldn't feel different or embarrassed.

As was normal, I left Silfield soon after turning eight. I still see three of my friends from the school a couple of times a year, more than half a century on. They all continue to live in that same part of Norfolk where we overlapped in early childhood. We remember Silfield as warm and happy, with no bullying. We remain in awe of Miss Lowe – a sort of loving awe, underpinned by respect and gratitude. I've checked with all three to see if I'm guilty of looking back at our Silfield days with the fantasy that nostalgia can foster. They're unanimous that I'm not: this is how it was.

I last saw Miss Lowe when she was in extreme old age. Her eyes and legs were failing her, but not her memory. She remembered so much, all with relish, and shared it to the accompaniment of her rich laugh – halting, yet still spirited. She loved to talk about the old times at Silfield, the school that had been her life. 'Your very first day,' she recalled, 'Diana was in my classroom and just wouldn't settle, so I said to her, "Go on, go and check on him, then!", and she rushed out to your class, to see how you were coping. She returned a couple of minutes later, with a beaming smile, and said to me: "Thank you – Charles seems to be doing fine!"'

When Miss Lowe died, aged ninety-five, in 2009, the announcement in the *Lynn News* recorded that she was a 'loving and much-loved aunt, great aunt, and great-great aunt'. Her family asked that no flowers be bought for her funeral, but that any gifts in her name be donated to her favourite charity, Save the Children.

2

A Place Called Maidwell

Childhood is a very, very tricky business of surviving it.
Because if one thing goes wrong or anything goes
wrong, and usually something goes wrong, then you
are compromised as a human being. You're going to
trip over that for a good part of your life.

– Maurice Sendak

When friends of my father asked me where I would be
moving on to after Silfield, I would at first reply, 'Maidwell Hall.'
But since nobody in the proudly self-contained county of Norfolk
seemed to have heard of the place, I got used to producing a more
complete answer: 'I'm going to a place called Maidwell – it's in
Northamptonshire.'

For some time, my move to this new school seemed so far off
in the future as to be of no immediate concern. But during the
Easter holidays of 1972, my father casually mentioned that he
knew the exact day, later that year, on which the utter transformation of my life would occur.

'When?' I asked, not really wanting a reply.

'On the twelfth of September.'

From that moment, the date became a dread spot on the horizon, constantly in view even when my eyes were closed. My nanny later told me that, because of gnawing, escalating anxiety, I didn't have an uninterrupted night's sleep during the six months leading up to the day of my departure.

Knowing how distraught I was at the prospect of boarding school, my father looked into employing a governess, so I could be taught at Park House. This was a bold piece of thinking, since it was a given in my father's privileged circle that the education of young children involved being sent away. Other parents quickly stifled his plan, persuading him that my being home-schooled would be eccentric and unacceptable, and guarantee ridicule for us both.

My despair only deepened when I realised that all my Silfield friends would be moving on to other Norfolk schools while I was to be despatched so far from home.

Maidwell stood a hundred miles west of Park House, in a little-known part of the Midlands, and seemed a random destination for a boy raised near the Norfolk coast. There were a few, tenuous associations between the school and my family, however. My Spencer grandfather knew Lady Margaret Loder and her husband Reggie – a former army officer, who became an amateur explorer and African big game hunter – who had been Maidwell Hall's last private owners before it became a school.

My grandfather remembered Maidwell from its days as a grand country house: he and his siblings dined and danced there often, in their youth. He told me how, one evening in the 1920s, Reggie Loder invited him and other friends over, to witness the wonder of his new-fangled acquisition, a 'wireless' radio set. 'But to be honest,' my grandfather told me with a smile, 'all we could make out was a series of wails, pings and scratches – it was a god-awful racket! But we told our host it was marvellous, of course.' I smiled back, quite unable to imagine the rambling, intimidating school as a hospitable family home.

My father liked to claim that he chose Maidwell for my education because it was ten miles from Althorp House, where our family has lived since 1508. He said that my grandmother (his mother, Cynthia) would therefore be on hand, to take me out from school to tea. But as soon as I got there, this ceased to ring true: I quickly learned that Maidwell forbade boys from leaving its grounds, except over the two or three set weekends each term when parents briefly reclaimed their sons.

I suspect my father's choice of Maidwell came down to a practicality that was hard for him to admit without looking somewhat calculating. He had, I believe, supposed that his overweight father, born in 1892 and wounded in the First World War, would most likely be dead by 1972, when I would start at the school. On my grandfather's death, my father would inherit Althorp, and the short distance between the ancestral home and Maidwell would be a welcome improvement on the two-and-a-half-hour trek between North Norfolk and Northamptonshire.

But my grandfather was still very much alive as 12 September hove ever closer into view. Home was not going to be down the road from my boarding school, as planned, but a very long way away indeed.

After my mother left home, my father was bereft. Whenever I passed the open door of his study, I saw his seated silhouette against the long window, his shoulders collapsed in despair. He seemed devoid of energy or purpose, and I now suspect that he suffered from undiagnosed – and therefore untreated – depression. My father's face seemed only to light up at the sight of his four children.

To oversee the day to day running of Park House, my parents had employed Mr and Mrs Smith, an elderly couple with thick Norfolk accents who occupied an upstairs flat on the other side of our back yard. Mrs Smith, the housekeeper, full of warmth, bustle and quiet affection, was a constant in my home life. Her silver-haired husband, Ernest, looked after the garden. He mowed the lawn with stiff-backed precision, wearing a knitted, grey, sleeveless sweater, no matter how hot the day, a packet of Player's No. 6 cigarettes always to hand. He also tended the swimming pool, as well as the greenhouse whose fat tomatoes had the taste of summer baked into them.

The Smiths formed such an inherent part of my life that I included them in my nightly prayers, alongside family, close friends and pets. I would sometimes lie awake dreading the day when Mrs Smith might die, as she seemed unimaginably ancient, though I suppose she was in her fifties and sixties when in my life. But she was almost like family, a solid presence in a house where my two elder sisters Sarah and Jane – nine and seven years older than me – were frequently away from home, mainly at boarding school and at other times with our mother.

For a couple of years from when I was six or so, my father retained a butler. Mr Betts – trim, pale and waistcoated – had slicked-back white hair and thick-rimmed spectacles. He liked to walk briskly, with nose in the air, face clenched, his eyes fixed ahead; as if engaged in a never-ending egg and spoon race, the finishing line always just over the horizon.

Park House, though decidedly large, probably wasn't quite grand enough a habitat to satisfy Mr Betts. But he was prepared to make do, given the scarcity of options at a time when the British aristocracy was taxed hard (my grandfather's income tax peaked at 98 per cent) and struggled to survive, even in reduced circumstances. My father had a title, after all, and Mr Betts wove 'my lord' and 'your lordship' into their verbal interactions as often as he could. In return, my father appreciated his butler's loyalty and deference, and called him 'Betts'. Theirs was the bond of two characters in a nineteenth-century play.

Having no perceptible interest in other people's children, Mr Betts seemed a curious major-domo for a family home. My direct contact with this standoffish figure was confined to the evenings when, with barely a word, he'd bring me my supper on a tray while I watched TV. After I turned seven, with all three of my sisters at boarding school, I would often be the only child living at Park House. From that point, during term time, I'd eat by myself in one of the large armchairs in the drawing room, while my father would also eat alone, later than me, in the dining room across the hallway. Although he was a loving parent, old-fashioned notions of a child's place in the home persisted – as I now realise, to both our cost.

I ate with my father only at lunchtimes on those rare days when close family members came to visit. Otherwise, in a tradition that harked back to Victorian times, I was delegated at breakfast, lunch and teatime to my nanny's care.

My father, if at home – and he usually was, unless performing his duties as president of a youth charity, the National Association of Boys' Clubs – would visit my bedroom after the nanny had watched me bathe, brush my teeth and comb my hair. As the day drew to a close, and I lay ready for sleep, he would kindle my imagination with a chapter from *The Jungle Book*, *Doctor Dolittle* or *The Lion, the Witch and the Wardrobe*. We'd also play chess, after which I got up and knelt beside my bed to say my prayers, out loud. I began with 'God, bless Mummy and Daddy …' before moving further through the rollcall of those that I loved.

One evening my father's obvious unhappiness permeated my bedroom. As I knelt to say my prayers, I felt I must send him some sort of loving message, so I upended my prayers' opening, starting instead with 'God, bless *Daddy and Mummy* …' I had put him first. I looked up, smiling, sure that he'd understand the significance of what I'd done: I was telling him that, at this time of particular sadness, he came first in my world.

He hadn't heard me, though, in his haze of dejection, and my instinctive urge to comfort him went unnoticed. His face remained a study in torment. When he saw me peeping up at him with a grin on my face, he started. Unsure as to what was going on, he smiled back at me with brave but cheerless eyes. As I got into bed again, he placed a hand on my shoulder and bent down to kiss me goodnight, as he did every night.

My father tried to lessen the wrench of my pending departure by strengthening a slight bond I'd formed with another child who'd been at the new boys' tea party earlier that summer. William Purefoy came from a family that had fled religious persecution abroad. His enterprising ancestors had prospered in England, and William's branch of the dynasty owned a country estate two hours from Park House.

William and I hit it off from the moment that his jovial parents dropped him at my home. My new friend had a rich repertoire of tall stories. He claimed that his family had a swimming pool in their garden that was filled to the brim with the sloshing blood of Roman soldiers. Also, that his bed at home was a stack of mattresses, with a hidden hollow into which he burrowed when it was time to sleep. It was harmless fantasy, born of a lively imagination, and it formed part of a cheery zest for life that I warmed to straight away.

We spent many hours swimming in Park House's pool, where we were joined by my Silfield friends. Figures from my past and future worlds played happily together in the water as my life approached its dreaded crossroads.

When William's parents reappeared to take him home, I was meant to go back with them for a few nights. But, when the moment came, and I was standing in the hall with my suitcase by the door, I heard myself say out loud the words that had been circulating in my mind for hours: 'I'm not going.'

The thought of being away from Park House was too much. I'd come to know William a little, and I liked him a lot, but his family and home were alien to me: I'd never stayed under the roof of strangers by myself, and the idea of doing so terrified me.

My father was flustered by my blunt refusal to go, fearing I'd be seen as rude and ungrateful. He hurriedly ran through all the fun things I'd be doing at my new friend's home, but no amount of encouragement could make me change my mind. William's parents realised that I wasn't for turning and headed off without me. If my father had been in any doubt before, he now knew for certain that I was not cut out for boarding school.

It was around this time that I started to have a recurring nightmare. Its roots could be found in my terror of Maidwell, and its expression stemmed from a visit I'd recently made with my father to a wildlife park. There, I'd been intrigued by a pack of wolves – secure behind a high, meshed fence, but menacing, nonetheless.

At night, reality fused with foreboding to whisk up a demonic brew that swirled in my mind. The setting was always the same: I was walking beside my father on a trip to a zoo – an old-fashioned place, with a grid of red-brick barrack-block buildings, locked away behind high iron gates. In this recurring vision, as in life, my father was immaculately dressed, in a hand-cut tweed suit, cotton shirt and crisp tie. His receding hair was slicked back, and he was clean-shaven, as if he'd just received the attentions of

Johnson, the Cypriot barber who tended him at Trumper's in London.

In my nightmare my father looked straight ahead, smiling trustingly, while talking to me in his customary calm and loving tone. I realised with alarm that, for all his gentleness and charm, this kindly man was failing in his key duty: he couldn't see that, in this landscape of suppressed danger, what I urgently needed was not his tender words, but his watchful eye and protective arm.

I glanced anxiously back at the wolf pen and was horrified to see the pack's alpha male alone at the gate. He was standing tall, on hind legs powered by rippling muscle. This creature was looking at me with keen eyes that shone out above a wicked smile, while his slavering tongue dangled, expectantly. The predator had noted my vulnerability and was poised to exploit it.

The wolf stretched out one of his front legs, like a human proffering a handshake. As I watched, transfixed with terror, this mottled, wiry limb took on a supernatural air, extending telescopically towards me. My father continued on his gentle amble, oblivious to the threat behind us – talking, but not listening. He carried on, eyes still set forward, an English gentleman on a stroll with his boy. Meanwhile I was mute with terror.

The wolf's arm reached me, as I knew it had to. It hooked round my rib cage with bracing force, before silently reeling me in. I knew what must follow, in this nightmare that haunted me throughout the summer of 1972: I was going to be devoured.

* * *

When 12 September at last arrived, I was in a state of exhausted shock, unable to make sense of what was happening to me.

I'd woken up in the small bedroom where I'd slept since I was a toddler, in a corner of the house reached by a staircase at the rear of the nanny's bedroom. My wallpaper hadn't changed since my infancy: playful puppies and fluffy chicks the colour of egg yolk, sitting happily together in an endlessly repeated pattern of animal innocence, while on my white headboard were stickers of Donald Duck, Cruella de Vil, *The Aristocats* and other cartoon favourites. This had been my sanctuary since my earliest days and I realised that, on this day when childhood as I'd known it was at an end, I would be leaving it behind for a very long time indeed.

My father marked this distinctive milestone in my life with the gift of two suitably sober books: a navy-blue Bible and a maroon leather Common Prayer Book, whose cover was embossed with a thin, gold cross. He inscribed each, in the impeccable hand that he brought to his fountain pen writing, with:

Darling Charles,
With much love,
Daddy
September 1972.

After a lunch that I couldn't eat, I put on the clothes of a Maidwell boy. Surprisingly for such a traditional establishment, there was no set uniform – just parameters of acceptable dress that had to be observed: tweed sports jackets, ties, cotton or woollen shirts, sensible trousers and leather shoes.

The Prince of Wales check jacket, thick green corduroys and black lace-ups that I put on that first day were solidly in tune with the Maidwell code. My shirt and tie echoed the blue that threaded through my jacket. As I dressed, I was alone with my nanny for the last time.

Over the previous six years, a string of women had been employed to fill part of the void left by my mother's departure. My favourite nanny, by some distance, had been Sally Percival, who fortunately stayed for the longest stretch. She was wonderful to be with – warm, fun and lively   but also perceptive and calm. Sally understood the psychological upheaval of travelling between parents' homes at weekends and was a soothing presence when things, inevitably, got fraught.

There had been six or so others in this role, as well as a succession of Scandinavian au pairs. Nanny Forster, the oldest of our many nannies, had been terrifying, with an attitude as starched and unyielding as the apron she chose to wear to work. Her tightly puckered mouth gave a hint of her inner unhappiness. When no other adults were present, she veered between lazy unkindness and focused cruelty.

While in charge of the nursery, Nanny Forster introduced fear and hurt into our pampered lives. Even though I was, I believe, four or five when she worked at Park House, there was no escaping the harsh corporal punishment that she meted out. For minor misdemeanours, I'd have to hold out my hand to her for firm strikes from a wooden spoon. If she deemed the offence to be more serious, she would grip my hair tightly and bang my head hard against the plain, whitewashed wall of the corridor leading to the nursery loo. If Diana and I were both seen to be at fault, she banged our heads sharply together. The impact of these blows was shocking, the deep, misty pain taking an age to clear. I remember her with a shudder.

Janine, a Walloon Belgian, brought a younger, kinder aura to the nursery. Tasked by my father with teaching me a little of her native French, Janine cut out paper squares that she illustrated with objects in vibrant felt pen – a slab of golden butter, a scarlet-handled knife – with the French translation for each image beneath. She pinned these on the nursery wall, above the table where I ate with her, day to day.

I remember the faces of several other nannies who came to live at Park House during my earliest years, including Nanny Richardson, who was unkind, and Madeleine, who was perhaps too timid to handle spirited children.

Apart from Sally, they tended to stay for a few months before suddenly being gone. This was a relief in Nanny Forster's and Nanny Richardson's cases, but it was otherwise deeply unsettling. Up until the age of six, I could go to school at Silfield in the morning with one, established primary carer and come home to Park House in the late afternoon to be greeted by someone entirely new, with no chance to say goodbye to the former or to prepare for the latter. My father for some reason believed it was less traumatic for a young child this way, since no notice of the change avoided tearful farewells. But it was destabilising and, with the departure of my mother when I was two, it made me view emotional attachment as a particularly dangerous business.

In the lead-up to my departure for Maidwell, my nanny was Mary Clarke. Mary – who had Canadian ancestry – was tall, athletic and young: she turned twenty-one days before she started at Park House. My father liked that she came from a happy home – he'd insisted on going to meet her parents before offering her the position. He explained to Mary that with Diana about to begin at her own boarding school – Riddlesworth Hall in Norfolk – the focus of her nannying role would be preparing me for Maidwell. Mary committed to stay till the day I set off for life as a boarder, thus breaking, as she once wrote, 'the endless succession of au pairs and nannies passing through' Park House.

Mary, who had an affinity with animals, understood how much I adored my Dutch Barge Dog, Gitsie, a black, white and grey fur ball of intelligent, snuffling nonsense. When even younger, Mary had taught children to ride, and she held my lead rein when I rode my bay pony, Teddy Tar, through Sandringham Park after school and at weekends.

My trust in Mary was total. She was the only one I told of the first, innocent kisses on the cheek that I exchanged with my Silfield 'girlfriend', who was two weeks my junior. 'Today I kissed her ten times,' I announced proudly at bath time, when aged seven, and Mary snorted into my towel, eyes twinkling at the delicious ridiculousness of my romantic update.

Mary had been looking after me for eighteen months when the wolflike arm of Maidwell finally reached out for me. She had helped me prepare for the move in practical ways, sewing CHARLES SPENCER name tags into my new school clothes and teaching me how to tie a tie by myself. A few days before I left Park House,

Mary took me to the hairdressers in King's Lynn: my thatch of red hair was tidied up so I could be handed over in good order to the alien habitat selected for me.

Years later, I worked out that Mary must of course have known that my leaving for boarding school meant the termination of her employment at Park House. No more cutting me a teatime slice from the chocolate cake in the stacked tins in the kitchen. No more supervising my evening bath times, when I'd slide down from the top of the tub into the water with a whoop, a swoop and a mighty splash. No more watching over me as I cantered Teddy Tar along Brancaster Beach.

I wandered around Park House in a daze, saying my goodbyes. I knocked at the door of the Smiths' flat and when Mrs Smith opened it, I felt unable to speak without crying. She threw out her arms and, for the first time in my life, held me tight in a warm, wordless embrace while I sobbed.

I walked across the garden, pushed at the paddock's rusty gate and went up to Teddy Tar for a final hug, fretting how he'd fare without our daily rides. It was even harder to part from Gitsie, who bounced around, inviting me to play just one more time. I asked Mary to care for her while I was gone, not understanding that the redundant nanny's suitcases were already packed and that she'd be heading off to her own home as soon as I left.

There were no more ways to delay the journey. I walked out of Park House's front door, looking blankly at the familiar setting before me: the grassy turning circle at the centre of the gravel drive, the bushy rhododendrons, beyond which a thick belt of trees screened Park House from the world beyond.

My father's dark Jaguar was ready to go, its bulbous nose pointing towards my new beginning. Out there lay a crisscross of roads through which, I knew, my father was going to pick an unwavering route, to that place called Maidwell. He would then leave me there, before returning home, alone, and resuming his life. It seemed impossible that things could go on at Park House without me. But, somehow, this was how it was going to be.

I was crying openly now, breathing hard through my tightened throat. Raw misery and fear had me in their grip. My eyes puffed and prickled with tears, both shed and suppressed, as I tried to regain self-control.

My father insisted on capturing my departure for a new phase of life with his ever-present camera. I wiped away the tears, determined to present the brave face that I sensed all those around me wanted to see, and stood for him.

When I look at this photograph today, I'm drawn to the sadness and shock engulfing my eyes. There I am for eternity, my shoulders frozen in disbelief at what is being done to me, while wishing with every fibre that I was merely held in a wolf-filled nightmare that would be dissolved by the solace of daylight. Mary, to my left, performs her final nannying duties, looking down at me with an anxious smile, checking that I'm composed enough to navigate this prelude to the day's true ordeal. In front of us, Diana sits on my trunk, smiling, in home clothes and her old Silfield sandals, the day before she had to return to her own boarding school, while Sarah and Jane were already back at theirs.

My trunk has a solid navy-blue frame with gaudy brass buckles. Below its lock, 'C. SPENCER' is painted in bold white letters. This chest contains the clothes demanded by Maidwell's school list: a second tweed jacket and tie, further pairs of corduroys and of shoes; a grey flannel suit, for Sunday church services; a dozen white handkerchiefs; vests, socks, underpants, shirts and sports clothes for the winter term to come – for rugby, a sport I've yet to play, and for the school gym.

On top of the trunk lies a plain suitcase. The contents of this 'overnight bag' are to tide me over till my trunk can be unpacked. It contains the wash bag, hairbrush and comb, pyjamas, slippers and dressing gown I will need for the first night, along with a set of clean clothes for my first full day as a Maidwell boarder.

After the photograph, I was enveloped in hugs from my nanny and Diana and, weeping quietly now, took my seat in the Jaguar, my feet not quite reaching the floor. A sense of horror over-whelmed me: the dreaded moment to leave had finally come, as I'd always known it must, despite my many prayers for deliver-ance.

The drive to Maidwell took forever. Norfolk is a destination county, jutting out into the North Sea, on the way to nowhere. Its inhabitants are used to tortuous roads, none of them a motorway. We wound along our route, the silkiness of the Jaguar's progress at odds with the turmoil tearing at my innards. Once my father appreciated that light conversation wasn't going to distract me from my gloom, we hardly spoke. To make the silence between us less awkward, he played his eight-track cassettes. After two hours we crossed into Northamptonshire, Maidwell's county. A few miles in, my father broke our silence with a gasp: he had, to his astonishment, spotted a familiar figure walking at the side of the road. Stopping our car, he called out and the man turned, walked over to the Jaguar and leaned down to chat about this and that – the weather, the harvest and mutual friends. I found it incomprehensible that the two of them could carry on as if all were normal, while my world was in freefall.

My father's acquaintance suddenly noticed me sitting, tense and silent, in the passenger seat. He smiled and offered a friendly hello. I whispered a reply. 'I'm taking Charles to his new school today,' my father explained. 'It's his first day – he's starting as a boarder at Maidwell.' The man nodded, understanding the enormity of my unfolding rite of passage, and gravely wished me well.

Soon after passing the village sign for Maidwell, we entered the school's front gate, rumbled over a cattle grid, and my father drove so slowly along the drive that I couldn't help but register how enormous this place was that was about to claim me.

As we swung left, past a tall, thick yew hedge, we arrived in the front courtyard. Here we slowed, to join jumbled columns of parked cars which were disgorging boys, parents and luggage on either side of an oblong lawn. This had a massive concrete ball at each corner (to protect the grass), and a classical statue at its centre. I would soon learn this wing-heeled figure was Mercury – the Roman god of communication.

Two of Maidwell's backroom staff were on hand to heave the boys' trunks out of the cars and carry them into the school's entrance hall, where they stacked them high. My father thanked the pair for their assistance, before carrying my suitcase into the school, with me walking silently beside him.

I felt exhausted and sick. I knew that, however inconceivable the prospect seemed, my father was on the point of abandoning me. My sister Diana had countered her first-day despair on reaching boarding school with the heroic challenge: 'If you loved me, you wouldn't leave me here.' But she had been a girl of ten and I was a boy of eight, and I lacked the words or the maturity to express the shocked sense of betrayal that was chewing at me from within.

My father pointed out an elderly lady standing assertively in the middle of the hall, her silver hair pulled tight in a rigid, surprised, perm. Her skin was sallow and worn, laced with liver spots that dappled the wrinkles between her chin and temples. When she turned away the thick knots of varicose veins bulging in her calves reminded me of the bunches of black grapes that occasionally graced Park House's fruit bowl. Her expression was at once quizzical and contemptuous. She had a hand to her hip and a jut to her jaw. Her bespectacled eyes darted in every direction, missing nothing. She exuded a chill authority that marked her out as the queen bee of this boisterous hive. She snapped instructions at the two men hefting the boys' trunks and occasionally flicked a thin smile of recognition at a parent.

My father led me over to this cocksure figure and introduced himself, then me, to her. 'I'm Mrs Ford,' she replied, 'the *senior* matron.' Having emphasised the particular importance of her role, she went on to explain the breadth of her power: 'I'm in charge of all of the domestic staff here – and that includes everything to do with the kitchens; as well, of course, as all matters pertaining to the laundry.'

My father caught the distinct accent wrapped around the feeble boast and, hoping to find common ground to build upon for my benefit, offered: 'And what part of Scotland are you from, if you don't mind me asking, Mrs Ford?'

'From Edinburgh,' she replied, haughtily. She seemed to think this provenance added further gilding to her rank. The surprised inflection in her response hinted that this was all the private information she would be divulging.

My father changed tack, returning to the business in hand: 'You'll remember my son, Charles, perhaps, from the new boys' tea party?' Mrs Ford fixed me with a look that suggested strongly that she'd never set eyes on me before, her right eyebrow arching so high that it disappeared behind the upper rim of her metallic spectacles.

My father continued hopefully, keen to secure for me some special protection from this guardian of Maidwell's gates. 'Charles has never spent a night away from home on his own before,' he confided, in a low voice, 'and I was wondering – only if it's not too much bother, Mrs Ford – if perhaps somebody kind from among the older boys might keep an eye on him till he finds his feet?'

Mrs Ford seemed amused by the request. Her voice soared, in mock delight: 'But of course!' she trilled, as if such a plan was one that she would have offered up herself, if my father hadn't beaten her to it. She searched the hall with lively eyes, which soon settled on a distant figure. 'Miles!' she shouted, her voice cutting through the general babble like the boom of a deck gun.

In the distance a thickset boy with bright red hair stopped, seemed to contemplate turning a deaf ear to the call, then turned slowly to look at the senior matron. He had surly little eyes pushed deep into a wide, pasty face. Mrs Ford ushered him over with impatient swishes of her right hand, while her left remained cocked on her hip like the hammer on a duelling pistol. As the redhead reluctantly approached us, scuffed heels dragging across the floor, I noticed that the pallor of his skin accentuated the yellowness of his teeth. He looked up at Mrs Ford with smug defiance, his gaze letting her know that he would listen to her request but not necessarily obey it.

'Miles, this is Charles Spencer – a new boy, no less! His father here would be ever so grateful if you could keep an eye on his son "till he's found his feet". And, Charles Spencer, this is Miles Corbet. He's nearly twelve years old – a big boy! He's been with us here at Maidwell for four years now, so he knows the ways of this place … I'm sure he'll look after you, right enough!'

Relieved that I seemed to be in safe hands, and eager to leave while I was distracted, my father bent down and kissed me quickly on the cheek, wishing me luck in the term ahead and promising to write soon. He then walked speedily from the room towards his Jaguar, without a backward glance.

I followed Miles Corbet, my new guardian, with a stone in my heart. After a few paces, he looked back over my shoulder, his dead eyes sparking to life as he noted that my father was gone, and that Mrs Ford was immersed in another conversation. Sure of his moment, he looked me up and down with icy contempt. 'You're on your own!' he spat.

I walked to a window and saw that my father had already left for Park House, the home where I no longer belonged.

3

New Boy

You go through something which, at that age, defines
you and your ability to cope. There's a sudden lack of
intimacy with a parent, and your ability to get through
that defines you emotionally for the rest of your life.
It's a very violent experience in those first few weeks.

– Damian Lewis, actor and former
boarding school pupil

The headmaster would write to my parents at the end of
my dizzying, stomach-churning first day in his school: 'Charles
was a bit tearful as he came in, but the anticipation was worse than
the event, for after his father had gone, he accepted that term had
started …' While it was, of course, this man's professional duty to
make parents feel better about the life-changing decision they'd
made for their child, his reassurances on my behalf were a lie.

I found myself dropped into an alien world, without map or
guide. Immediately abandoned by Corbet, I was clueless as to

what to do or where to be. While nearly everyone else seemed to be part of a richly choreographed routine, I felt awkward, exposed and alone. I was consumed by a thudding pain deep inside, at the loss of family, and of home. I now recognise that this was grief.

Poet Cecil Day-Lewis,* a schoolmaster in the 1940s, remembered watching his eldest son Seán enter life at his new boarding school, when aged seven, and

… like a satellite
Wrenched from its orbit, go drifting away
Behind a scatter of boys.

I felt a similar violent detachment from my familiar path as I watched the older pupils around me pick up with one another again after eight weeks of summer holidays. I understood at once that I had entered a community far removed from that showcased three months earlier at the new boys' tea party. The veneer of gentle, smiling kindness was gone, and nobody seemed to have a moment for the fresh intake.

That first evening I found myself upstairs in 'Pink', the most junior of the eleven dormitories that I remember at Maidwell. This was, I learned, the communal bedroom where four of the six other new boys and I would sleep for the next thirteen weeks.

'Pink' was an incongruously soft designation for such a grimly Spartan setting. The room derived its name from the colour of the

---

* Father of actor Daniel Day-Lewis.

rough woollen blankets that were pulled tight over each of the dormitory's metal beds and folded under their hard, thin mattresses. The other dormitory names included Rose, Blue, Mauve, Primrose, Camel, Gold and Green – in theory, a kaleidoscope of comforting hues; but, in reality, basic sleeping quarters, suitable for soldiers, yet packed with very young boys.

From the ceiling of Pink hung the dormitory's sole light bulb, beneath a pale, ceramic shade. A wooden chair stood next to each boy's bed, while one chest of drawers served us all, with our hairbrushes and combs on top.

My bed was directly behind the dormitory's only door, and my surname was written in large letters on a piece of white paper taped round the top bar of the bedstead. One of the succession of shocks that hit me as a new boy was learning that given names had no place at Maidwell. In a calculated stripping away of identity that was common to English boarding schools then, I was no longer 'Charles', but simply 'Spencer', to staff and pupils alike.

I saw 'PUREFOY' written on the dormitory bed next to mine, and it was consoling to have William, who'd come to stay with me at Park House that summer, so close in such joyless surroundings.

The bed beyond him was made over to George Fleetwood, one of two seven-year-olds in the school. I'd seen this tiny, elfin figure with unruly auburn hair arriving in a Mini driven by his tall, stout father. Fleetwood looked too young to be away from home, even to us eight-year-olds. He sucked his thumb, said little, smiled gently and – while the rest of us had arrived at Maidwell with a teddy bear each – he liked to busy himself at bedtime with a veritable menagerie of stuffed animals. Nobody teased him about this, for it seemed reasonable that one so young needed more home comforts than the rest of us.

One along from Fleetwood was John Hewson, a kind boy with an angular, expressive face. Hewson probably struggled as much as any of us with being away from home, but he carried his torment quietly. He would drift into daydreams, his huge brown eyes locked in a distant, melancholy daze.

The other seven-year-old to start in Pink that same night was Thomas Scot. His strong-jawed mother hailed from Charleston, South Carolina. While Scot had inherited her broad smile, several years in England had left him with few traces of his mother's Southern accent. He had an older brother who'd been a pupil at Maidwell for three years – as was the custom of the school when brothers coincided there, the senior of the pair was now known to the school as 'Scot I', while my fellow new boy was 'Scot II'. The Scot brothers were the only Maidwell boys who wore metal braces in their mouths, reinforcing the customary American perception that the English and dental care rarely overlap.

It was a good cohort of contemporaries to start off with – they were each kind-hearted and friendly and, like me, they were doing their best to find their feet in this overwhelming setting where we were due to spend the next five years of our lives, because our parents thought it best.

The next day I wrote to my mother, concluding my letter with a commonplace sentence that was, in this case, laden with yearning: 'I can't wait till I see you again.'

* * *

New boys were expected to fit in with Maidwell's ways from the start. I entered the school's dining room for breakfast my first morning and was motioned by Mrs Ford towards a dark wooden chair that would, she told me, be my place for all my meals, for the term ahead. It gave me a clear view of the blackened, Victorian fireplace, above which stood a silver statue of a soldier – a parting gift from troops billeted on the school in the Second World War – which I found exciting, as Airfix model soldiers were my most prized toys.

My introduction to Maidwell fare, that day, was porridge. It was slopped out in glutinous lumps from a huge metal cauldron, the steaming contents starting to congeal as soon as they plopped into our cold white bowls. After a few disbelieving chews, I put my spoon down in disgusted defeat. 'Spencer!' bawled Mrs Ford, from the end of the table. I looked up to find her staring at me ominously over the top of her glasses. '*Everyone* at Maidwell eats whatever is put in front of them. We make *no* exceptions.'

She paused for effect, delighting in my flushed embarrassment. Unsmiling and unblinking, she continued, more slowly now: 'So … you … will … *eat* … your … porridge. Every … last … spoonful … And you will do it *now!*' I retrieved my spoon and slowly waded through the contents of my bowl, chomping on slug-like nuggets that had evaded the cook's stirring spoon.

When I was done, I added my bowl to a stack of others in the centre of the table and looked up to see that a further culinary test was coming my way: a charred sausage.

I wasn't a fussy eater, generally, but that first breakfast posed substantial challenges. When bitten into, the black crisp on my sausage's exterior cracked, releasing the mild spice of its filling in a spray of hot grease. My mouth was quickly cloyed in smoky, perfumed fat. Knowing that the sausage had to be eaten (Mrs Ford's unrelenting stare made that clear), and desperate not to stick out in this unforgiving landscape, I got it all down, in an ordeal of endless repulsiveness.

An older boy who'd seen me squirm under Mrs Ford's unkind attention that morning told me, 'We call her "Granny" Ford rather than "Mrs" Ford – not because she's nice, like a grandmother should be, because she isn't like that at all – but because she's so old.' It was a comfort to know that others found her just as awful.

There were further new boy hoops to jump through that first day. For the simpler administration of the school, we were each allotted a unique number, inherited from a boy who'd left Maidwell the previous term.

'Your number is sixty-four, Spencer,' Granny Ford told me. 'It was Shepherd's number before becoming yours. A nice boy, Shepherd …' she said, wistful at the departure of a boy she liked, and coming to terms with the regrettable fact that he'd been replaced by one she had already decided she would not. During my five years at Maidwell, '64' was on all my clothes, on the changing room peg where I hung my sports things, on the hook for my towel in the washroom, and also in indelible ink on the plastic mug where I kept my toothbrush and toothpaste.

That first afternoon we were led, in our sports gear, to the school's pool. The master in charge of swimming pointed at the concrete cavity over his shoulder and boasted: 'Seventy thousand gallons of water go into this pool – all piped out of our own natural spring – and we're not so soft at Maidwell as to bother with heating.'

He bent to scoop out the pool's floating thermometer: 'Today the water is – let's see – sixty degrees … And for those of you who think that's cold – the pool remains open for swimming till it gets down to forty-eight.'

He explained that the school viewed us all, on arrival, as 'learners'. 'You'll want to rid yourselves of that *miserable* status and become "swimmers", if you want to be allowed into the pool's deep end,' he said. 'That means you'll have to complete a length, unaided, under my supervision. Now, change, and let's see if any of you can swim that far.'

To my mortification my swimming trunks hadn't been packed. Mary, my nanny, had reasonably assumed that there would be no swimming during the Christmas term, so they remained at Park House. When I nervously shared my predicament with the tall, hard-faced master, he looked at me with cold disdain.

'Well, you'll still have to take the swimming test!'

'But how, sir?'

'I suppose you'll just have to do it in what you're wearing – your rugby shorts,' the master said, crossly, with a snort of disgust bursting from the hairy nostrils of his Roman nose.

The coldness of the water was a shock, but that afternoon I gained my first, lowly toehold in Maidwell's hierarchy by becoming a 'swimmer', along with most of the other new boys.

* * *

During that first week, I wrote to my mother, thanking her for a letter. I put a brave face on things, assuming she must know how terrible my new life was, but not wanting her to worry about me: 'I have settled down alright and William Purefoy is in the same form. This is only a short note. I have made three other friends not counting William.' These were my new dormitory comrades, Scot, Fleetwood and Hewson.

To counter our homesickness, my new Maidwell acquaintances and I tried to keep each other's spirits up. My party piece was imitating Bert and Harold, absurd characters from *The Adventures of Sir Prancelot*, a children's TV series. But it proved impossible to distract ourselves for long from the yearning for home.

Homesickness is a horror that great writers have described with brilliance. George Orwell remembered it as 'The horrible sensation of tears – a swelling in the breast, a tickling behind the nose.' Roald Dahl reckoned that 'Homesickness is a bit like seasickness. You don't know how awful it is till you get it, and when you do, it hits you right in the top of the stomach and you want to die.'

To me, homesickness was as inexplicable as it was inescapable. I found it simply overwhelming – a secret shame that had to be denied, because the first lesson we absorbed at Maidwell came not from the teachers, but from the older boys. They explained that 'blubbing' was unacceptable. 'If you blub, you're "wet",' we were told – and nobody wanted to attract that level of ridicule, whether new boy or older. At the same time, we were all told that we would 'get used to' homesickness. Like so many others, I never did. So I learned to hide my despair, knowing I would never conquer it.

My homesickness combined the agony of a twisting blade with the slow, constant suffocation of hope and reason. It came in waves and – just when I hoped I had it under control – it would crash in on me once more, with colossal force. It could be particularly dangerous at night, when the sound of another child's choked anguish easily set me off.

Pink's light was switched off at the end of each day by Granny Ford, with the sing-song farewell, 'Good night – don't let the bed bugs bite.' Once she closed the door, sobs could break the silence from any corner of the dormitory. Generations of boys had suffered homesickness lying on these same, lumpy beds. I recently spoke to a man who arrived at Maidwell as a seven-year-old, a decade before me. He recalled how bereft he had been at night as a new boy: 'I had a very good cry. I knew nobody there – absolutely nobody.'

Many in my generation experienced the same trauma, after being abandoned so young in such a strange place. Two of my year recall their first day: 'I'd had this beautiful childhood,' the first says. 'Then I was dumped [at Maidwell]. My parents dropped me. I sat on my trunk and cried, asking myself, "What am I doing here?" It was brutal from that point on.' The second remembers: 'I had a sense of abandonment and a fear in the pit of my stomach the like of which I had never experienced – and which I don't think I have ever experienced since.'

At the start of each term, looking at those other faces, white with shock and their eyes red-rimmed with suppressed tears, the trauma was never far away. To survive it, a small but important part of us had to die.

The relentless timetable could distract you from homesickness during the daytime. But the hours of darkness remained silent and empty. No talking whatsoever was allowed in a dormitory between Granny Ford's turning off its lights and her marching into your room again in the morning. Alone with my thoughts, in the dark, I felt the full pain of separation from my family. I wondered what was going on at home in my absence. Sleep provided the sole escape from such difficult thoughts, and it was best reached with a teddy bear held tight – a soft shield against a hard world.

But such mementos of home could carry their own dangers.

Robert Tichborne, four years my senior at Maidwell, recently told me how he chose to leave his teddy bear at home, his first term, because he 'didn't want to look babyish'. At the start of his second term, having seen that younger boys weren't looked down on for having teddys, he opted to bring his to school. But rather than acting as a comfort, it exacerbated his suffering. 'The teddy bear was the thing that did it,' Robert recalled. 'It triggered my homesickness, being such a direct connection with home. It set me off completely. I was in puddles of tears. I had to put it to one side and take it home as soon as I could.'

Each of us had to find his own way of coping with the feeling of abandonment at night-time. One of my fellow new boys in Pink could only get to sleep through rocking his entire body back and forth, rhythmically. He did this for twenty minutes or so each night, hugging himself tight in a self-soothing routine to counter the turmoil tearing at him as he lay in the dark. His rocking would finally slow, then stop, as he was enveloped in the comfort of sleep.

When I'd been at Maidwell for five days, the headmaster sent a handwritten note to my mother: 'The slightly anxious look is leaving Charles' face, and I am now usually greeted with a broad grin. He is moving happily & confidently from one companion to another when they play in the garden, and this shows greater confidence. School porridge finds little favour, but he is coping. I will write again.'

This he did two weeks later, in correspondence of a more formal kind, typed on Maidwell Hall writing paper and addressed to my father. He sent a copy to my mother too, his handwritten scrawl revealing his thoughts about the relative status of the sexes: 'My normal practice is to write to fathers about a boy's work but thought you might like a copy,' he sniffed.

This more considered letter began: 'The time has come for me to write to give you some account of the impression which Charles has made in the classroom.' This was to be a work report, without a nod to my emotional reaction to being removed so abruptly from home.

'I can do this very briefly because it takes very little time to say that all is well. He is a quiet member of the form who has shown himself to be a reliable and a rapid worker. His reading is excellent, and he clearly enjoys it … But when he writes stories, he reveals that he is not as relatively mature as he appears on the surface. However, he shows a lively imagination, and he uses words to convey his meaning very well.'

The headmaster then paid tribute to the quality and range of Miss Lowe's teaching at Silfield: 'This is something which is becoming increasingly rare – and it is very welcome … If the opportunity arises, I hope it will be possible to pass on to his previous school our thanks for grounding him so well.'

The teacher who had taken on the baton of my education from Miss Lowe was Miss Best-Shaw, who taught seventh form, Maidwell's junior class, where all new boys began. Miss Best-Shaw seemed immensely old to me, but I see now that she was thirty-eight when I came under her charge. She was plump, of modest height, with thin, short, wavy brown hair, and glasses of a type that had been fashionable in her teens. She was without vanity and her wardrobe never changed: a navy-blue cardigan, a white ruffled shirt and a grey pleated skirt that she flattened out with open palms when nervous. Another sign of her being flustered was a surprisingly loud sniff.

The Best-Shaws were Kent aristocrats, and her mentor was her childhood nanny, who would live with the family for sixty years. There was something childishly kind about Miss Best-Shaw, which made her well-suited to overseeing seven- and eight-year-olds. She seemed much less assured with adults: I don't recall ever seeing her interact with her Maidwell teaching colleagues.

Miss Best-Shaw's classroom was in an isolated, ugly, modern block, removed from the bustle and beauty of the main school, but she seemed happy in her backwater. It was here that she greeted us, my first morning at the school, with an astonishing announcement: 'Although my name is, indeed, Miss Best-Shaw, you will at all times call me "Please".' Seeing how baffled we looked, she continued: 'All female members of staff here at Maidwell – teachers, as well as the matron and assistant matrons – are called

"Please". It is one of the school's traditions. It's seen as a way of instilling good manners into all of you boys while you're here – addressing a lady as "Please", regularly, will hopefully make politeness a habit that will stay with you forever.'

I remember thinking – even then, as an eight-year-old – that this was deeply odd. There was also the clumsiness of it all: when asking for something from a female member of staff, you had to start 'Please, Please …' It neither seemed nor sounded right then, but it's even more baffling to me now. This strange custom was a sublimation of the individuality of Maidwell's women. Allegedly designed to underpin good manners, the practice instead reinforced a view that each female working at the school was undeserving of specific respect. She was simply to be bundled under the nonsensical classification of 'Please'. There was no similarly idiosyncratic term for the male teachers.

Miss Best-Shaw's seventh form offered a gentle introduction to Maidwell. We had all our lessons in her simple classroom. Alongside undemanding forays into English and maths, we did plenty of 'handwork' – *papier-mâché*, basket weaving, painting and making model planes. We received an introduction to the Greek and Roman myths, while being the only class spared French and Latin lessons. When it was sunny, Miss Best-Shaw occasionally dared to take us outside and read to us, with evident enjoyment, in the shade of one of Maidwell's mighty trees.

While being cared for by a kind teacher, new boys were also granted a period of grace that shielded them from the physical punishments that, I was horrified to learn, seemed to lie in wait all around us. Nobody had warned me that Maidwell would be a place where corporal punishment was not only allowed but rampant.

An older boy in Miss Best-Shaw's class explained to me, during my first week or so, that you were 'whacked' by the headmaster with the slipper for talking after 'lights out' in your dorm, for spilling things, for treading on the flowerbeds, for letting water tip over into your boots, for leaving your clothes on the changing room floor, for barging past masters, for being rude, for flicking ink from your pen, for being late for meals – for all sorts of things. But, being a new boy, you'd have to spill your milk or water at meals thirty-two times in your first term to get whacked, while a senior boy would be beaten for doing that sort of thing just three times.

More serious breaches of the school's discipline – such as stealing or lying, or using sticks or stones when fighting – would, I gathered, lead to caning. There were two canes, so renowned that they had been given their own names – 'the Flick' and 'the Swish' – and they were deployed on boys' bare buttocks.

The Flick, the headmaster's regular choice, was, I heard, a thin, malicious instrument that whipped round the buttocks to nick the top of the recipient's right thigh. This flogging was administered with such force that each lash had the sound of a pistol crack and cut the skin open, leaving blood oozing from tight, agonising lines. These vicious wounds changed from red to bluish-purple in their first week, before billowing into cloudy brown bruising thereafter.

Particularly serious misdeeds saw the headmaster reaching for the Swish – a sturdier, knotted piece that packed a heavier punch.

In fencing parlance, the Flick could be seen as the épée, with the Swish the sabre.

When in the mood for something a little more exotic than this pair of old faithfuls, the headmaster would stroll into the school's grounds and use his pocketknife to cut down a stalk of bamboo for use as a 'one-off' on a specific victim.

From the start of my Maidwell career, I was determined to avoid the pain and humiliation of slipper or cane. At the end of my first term, the headmaster wrote of me: 'Being a good natured and amenable boy, he has no difficulty in keeping our fairly modest quota of rules …' But in truth the rules were innumerable and complex and weren't written down or recorded anywhere. I feared that they'd be impossible to negotiate safely once I was shorn of the leniency afforded a new boy.

The only true safety at Maidwell seemed to lie in being far away from the place, at home. And this was a sanctuary we rarely reached.

There were three terms at Maidwell each academic year – 'Michaelmas' (also known as 'Christmas') was the longest, running for three months from mid-September to December; 'Lent' from mid-January to late March; and 'Summer', which began in late April and closed the academic year when it ended in mid-July.

During each term every boy was allowed out for two weekends, called 'leave-out', which lasted from the end of morning lessons on a Saturday till late afternoon the following day. During the Christmas and Summer terms there was also a week's 'long leave', halfway through the term. I had one leave-out per term with each parent and alternated my long leaves. So, as I worked out carefully at the time, when trying to bring some logic and order to a life so out of control, I spent 67 nights per year with either parent and 230 nights – almost eight months in the year – at Maidwell. It was a calculation that weighed on me, as I tried so hard to fit inconspicuously into a setting that, as the newest of new boys, proved particularly alien and intimidating. It was exhausting, those first weeks, having so many new customs to learn, and people to look up to, when the only kindness stemmed from my fellow inmates of Pink, the self-conscious Miss Best-Shaw, and Francis Allen – a boy three years older than me who, being number 65 in the school list, had his changing room peg next to my number 64. Kind smiles from such a senior boy were a rare comfort in a setting where older pupils seemed determined to inflict on us the same frigid disdain that they had suffered in their own time as new boys.

My initial leave-out that first term arrived on Saturday 14 October, 1972 – a day I had held in focus since before starting at the school. My opening letter to my mother as a new boy had flagged it up, as a longed-for moment of liberation. Giddy excitement built up among the pupils as the day approached. Granny Ford always resented these obvious boosts in morale, and she loudly scolded boys for being 'bumptious', as she peevishly called it – as if we were somehow rude for bursting with excitement at the delicious prospect of a weekend back at home with our families.

Never have I known time go slower than on that Saturday morning, as I watched the classroom clock tick slowly towards the lesson's conclusion. On bursting out into the front courtyard, I ran to my father and hugged him round the thighs.

As we made for his car he gave me the disappointing news that it was too far to make it home, to Park House, when only allowed out for a single night. Instead, we'd be heading to Althorp for lunch with my grandparents, before going on to my father's London mews house. But when we arrived at Althorp, Mr Pendrey, the genial butler, informed us in a sombre voice that my grandmother sent her regrets, but she felt too unwell to join us or to even receive me. My father briefly visited her in her bedroom, while I for the first time experienced Althorp without my grandmother's palpable love.

I'd last seen her during the summer between the new boys' tea party and my first day at Maidwell. Her head had been swathed in bandages, after surgeons had failed to remove a brain tumour that had taken root where she'd been struck hard, long before, in a train crash.

She'd bravely ventured out into her beloved rose garden that sunny day, and let me play with her hosepipe and watering can till the roses and I were drenched. My father would later tell me that she turned to him, as I happily bustled about, and told him: 'Charles will always have friends.' It proved to be the valedictory judgement of a matriarch who knew that death could not long be denied.

My grandfather, father and I lunched together, in Althorp's dining room, an oak-panelled cube swathed in Flemish tapestries portraying rural scenes. A grandfather clock's tick-tock filled the silence as the three generations found they had little to say that could counter the tragedy slowly reaching its conclusion upstairs.

Mr Pendrey, unflappable, carried on as if all was well. First presenting a silver salver, then lifting the lid off a pair of seventeenth-century tureens, he bowed forward so each of the Spencer males could help themselves to the solid English fare typical of that era – overcooked meat and underdone vegetables that sighed in defeat on the plate.

Our lunch had been prepared by Phyllis, a spirited cook with heavy, black-rimmed spectacles that framed darting eyes. Phyllis would engineer a blazing row with my grandfather each mid-December, so she could resign and therefore not have to cook over Christmas, before reappearing in the kitchen, without comment, at New Year. This wily opponent of my grandfather's came from Great Brington, the village on the hill beyond Althorp where fifteen generations of our family were buried and where, the adults knew, my grandmother would soon be laid to rest, for all time, in the chapel built by a pious ancestor who'd been knighted by Henry VIII, in 1519.

With silent gloom draped over Althorp, it was a relief to get in my father's car that afternoon and head for his London pied-à-terre. The next day, almost before I knew it, we were wending our way back to Maidwell, where another long spell away from my family beckoned. My first leave-out was over in a flash, and I hadn't even been home.

My grandmother died at Althorp soon afterwards. I was given the day off from Maidwell to attend the first of her two memorial services, which was held in All Saints' Church, Northampton. My memories of the day are few: of one of the church attendants keeling over in a faint, and of my having an unstoppable coughing fit during the service; but chiefly of breakfast at the start of that day, which was overseen by Mr Pendrey, who had always adored my grandmother. 'Such a lady,' he would say, judging her against his butler's exacting yardstick. 'The way she sat at table, ramrod straight – only real ladies do that ...' He shook his head at how standards had slipped, elsewhere in the aristocracy.

I'm not sure what Mr Pendrey made of my grandmother's brother on that mournful day. My great-uncle Jimmie was an old, mustachioed Irish duke of military bearing. So weighed down was he by the loss of his sister, and so underwhelmed by the prospect of Phyllis's greasy offering, that he left his eggs and bacon untouched and instead lit a cigar. To my delight, he stubbed this out in his untouched half-grapefruit, and an almighty hiss marked its demise. Mrs Ford would have been rendered speechless by such a cavalier breakfast mutiny.

That same new boy term I met another memorable elder from my grandparents' generation. This tweed-suited figure with a large, drooping nose and a florid, wizened face was a visitor to Maidwell. He heard someone say my name and came over to introduce himself: 'Hello, Spencer. I'm Mr Wyatt and I know your grandfather quite well.'

Oliver Wyatt had founded Maidwell as an academic institution in 1933 and he had remained its owner and headmaster until retiring in 1963. The day we met, Wyatt was returning for a ceremony in his honour as the school's founder: a new gate leading from the school to the village churchyard was to be dedicated to him, in recognition of two of his great loves, the school and God.

This was to be Wyatt's last time at Maidwell. Four months later he was leading a service in a church near his sister's manor house, in Suffolk, where he lived in retirement. Addressing the congregation from the pulpit, he suddenly stopped, looked up in pained surprise and said, 'I don't feel very well', before collapsing on the floor, dead.

Wyatt's memorial service was held in Maidwell's church. It was so tightly packed that we schoolboys were made to stand outside in the graveyard, in light rain, listening to the tribute to his life over a loudspeaker. From what I learned that afternoon, and afterwards, Wyatt was the key to unlocking many of Maidwell's mysteries: while essentially a genial figure, liked by most of his pupils, the school's original headmaster had contributed to the dark tone of the place that persisted while I was there.

Wyatt had been decorated as an artillery officer in the First World War. He'd then taught at another school – Shardlow Hall, in Derbyshire – whose finances were sunk by the Great Depression. Looking for somewhere to start again, Wyatt, an avid gardener, judged Maidwell the perfect place for fostering rare floral breeds and noble British bloodlines; its ten-acre garden showed great promise, while there was space in the hall to accommodate seventy boarders. After transplanting the remaining forty Shardlow pupils there, he soon persuaded other aristocratic and wealthy parents to commit their sons to his new nursery for young gentlemen.

The bachelor war hero proved something of an enigma, enthusiastically introducing his boys to boxing, while also trying to instil in them a love of plants and flower-arranging. Many of his Maidwell charges went on to the most famous of English senior schools, mainly Eton or Winchester. Meanwhile, in the gardens, he grew dwarf bulbs and lilies, and introduced a new species of snowdrop, still flourishing today, called 'Maidwell'.

During the Second World War, the American Air Corps built a base for heavy bombers at Harrington, two miles from the school. Their navigators used the gleaming water of Maidwell's ornamental lake as a marker to circle, as they slowly gathered into formation before setting off on missions over Occupied Europe. This nearby military presence brought the war to Maidwell.

Oliver Wyatt was appointed the regional chief air warden, but his safety instructions to his pupils were quirky. Rather than provide underground shelters, he ordered the boys to stay in their beds during night-time bombing raids and take their chances. If German bombers appeared in daytime, his pupils were to gather in the school's central hall and to wait there till they heard bombs fall, at which point they must run in the opposite direction, with, Wyatt insisted, 'hands over ears, lips apart, teeth not clenched – all in the approved style'.

One term this stern, old-fashioned headmaster gave an illustrated lecture to Maidwell's pupils about a trip he'd taken to Kashmir. The highlights of this expedition, he told them, included killing three geese with one blast of his shotgun and learning of a friend who'd established a school there, with 'original methods … to punish his boys'.

Wyatt revelled in his reputation as an enthusiastic deliverer of sharp pain to boys' buttocks. He saw this as an essential part of his leadership, which he termed 'harsh but fair'. It was a theme that was reprised in the school's eulogy to its first headmaster:

> He served his fellow men, and he loved his boys with a clarity
> of vision unclouded by mawkish sentiment: he gave short
> shrift to those who deserved it, but they loved him for it, for
> they wanted his good opinion more than anything else.

This attitude to strict punishment persisted at Maidwell when I arrived there. This fed my fears that, though I was somehow on sufferance as a new boy, the cornerstone values of this place were dangerous.

The report from the headmaster to my parents, at the end of my first term, seemed keen to stress how well I had settled in at Maidwell: 'The only difficulties that he faced were those that arose out of his own apprehensions. He does not like not knowing what is going to happen next, and as the term went on he became increasingly relaxed and confident. He lives on good terms with his companions, and he has a pleasant sense of humour; a twinkle appears in his eye when he sees a joke coming.' It was, I see now, a glib summation of three months when I had, every day, wished myself safely at home.

My heart plunged when the headmaster added that I'd been promoted from the haven of Miss Best-Shaw's seventh form to the next class, where he was the teacher in charge. He wrote: 'I shall be glad to see more of him next term in the Sixth Form –

and he need not start fearing that promotion will bring awful problems!'

But I did fear that, and so much more. I was miserable, being away from home, even though I had forged some quiet friendships. The reassurances that my parents were receiving – that I'd become a happy boarder as soon as my father left me, and that I'd further blossomed as the term progressed – were simply untrue. I was at Maidwell very much against my will. But rather than letting the weight of my sentence close down my senses, I felt them heightened by all I witnessed around me.

From the start, I watched Maidwell extremely carefully. Being extra vigilant seemed the most likely way of staying safe in such a puzzling setting, with its rumbling undertones of danger.

4

Judging Jack

Headmasters have powers at their disposal with which
Prime Ministers have never yet been invested.

– Winston Churchill

Now that my relocation from happy home to boarding
school had come to pass, as I'd feared it must, I studied my new
surroundings and its personnel with unblinking eyes. The headmaster was my focus since he clearly set Maidwell's mood and
tone.

It is time to properly introduce John Alexander Hector Porch,
who succeeded Oliver Wyatt as Maidwell's head in 1963. Mr
Porch was known as 'Alec' to those adults close to him, but the
pupils nicknamed him 'Jack'.

When Wyatt gave up work, the pupils hoped that Maidwell's
era of corporal punishment would join him in retirement. For a
week under Jack there were no beatings, but then things changed.
He caught some boys misbehaving in their dormitory, and, in

what would become his trademark beating ritual, he sat down, flicked up a slipper from his foot, caught it in his right hand, then called forward the mischief-makers one by one for their punishment.

By the time I arrived at Maidwell, nine years later, Jack's headmasterly demeanour had set into unsmiling hardness. He reserved his happy face, such as it was, for Maidwell's parents during their brief forays into his school. They were greeted by an entirely different man to the one who imposed harsh discipline on their sons as soon as they had departed. He beat us – often, and painfully. The threat of such punishment made my stomach clench in terror and fuelled the misery of my homesickness.

Early in my first term I realised with a start that Jack was the Pied Piper figure who'd led us – with an unbreakable smile and limitless patience – round the school on the afternoon of the new boys' tea party. It seemed impossible to me that this most daunting of figures had ever been able to show such lightness and tolerance.

Jack came from a family of financiers; their firm was, at one point, second only to the Bank of England in the production of sterling banknotes. The Porches bought a landed estate near Glastonbury, and provided two mayors for that town, but had to sell up in 1914 when their finances collapsed. They faded into obscurity, apart from the time when Jack's cousin, Montagu Porch, briefly became Winston Churchill's stepfather.

Jack's father, Robert – who, for some reason, was nicknamed 'Judy' – played cricket from time to time for his native county, Somerset. He was a schoolmaster at Malvern College, a leading boys' private school. Jack Porch gained a scholarship to Malvern, then earned a degree at Cambridge, before following his father into teaching. He was an inspiring presence at Abberley Hall, a prestigious boys' boarding school. One of Britain's leading historians of the Second World War, Sir Antony Beevor, was among his pupils there, and he recalls with gratitude how Porch awoke in him a passion for the past. I wonder where and when that good teacher within Porch began to die.

Although I am unaware of any sexual scandal attached to the bachelor Oliver Wyatt's rule, Maidwell's governors insisted that the next headmaster be a married man. Jack wed Ann Aitken, Abberley's matron, in time to be eligible for the job. They had one child, a daughter, who was roughly my age. She joined the school as the only girl, more than holding her own academically and on the sports field, winning the junior 100 yards and the 220 yards at sports day my first summer.

Jack had a formidable intellect, which was a source of understandable pride. At lunch one day he told us that his brain was at its sharpest when most under pressure. 'On the morning the governors were considering me for the role of headmaster here,' he said, 'I polished off the *Times* crossword in half an hour while awaiting my interview.' The memory of this feat made him purr.

Jack was a throwback to the Victorian era, when headmasters were aloof and omnipotent, acting as prince, parliament and police chief in their small state. When I came under his tutelage, I found his power palpable. Pupils and teachers acted differently when he was around: their mixture of fear, awe and respect led to an uncertainty that rendered them clumsy and timid in his presence. He seemed to enjoy having this disabling effect and appreciated that his silent, focused stare caused others discomfort. As a small boy I liked to see people as animals, and in my mental menagerie Porch was a venomous snake.

Jack spotted, from the start, that I was observing him and his regime closely. 'He tends to be rather quietly watchful, but this seems to be his nature,' he wrote to my parents, soon after my arrival. When I was ten, he would note of me: 'He takes in a high proportion of all that goes on about him ...' Eighteen months later, Jack opened my report home with: 'Charles is a shrewd observer of all that goes on here; I am never sure where determination ends and obstinacy begins, but he has a share of both ...' In December 1976, after I'd been under him at Maidwell for more than four years, Jack would pull this all together with: 'He is keenly interested in people, and one of his particular talents is nosing out information on everything that goes on in this place; consequently, he is usually in a position to form accurate judgements.'

In judging Jack, I should start by saying that his was an austere rule, in keeping with his puritanical garb: a drab brown jacket of lightest herringbone, a plain cotton shirt, a muted tie, with cavalry twill trousers above robust shoes by day and silent slippers at night. His belt sometimes had a knotted handkerchief attached; a reminder that some matter required his keen attention as soon as he made it back to his study – the room that was the nerve centre of the school, and where he liked to beat very young boys.

Jack was lean, wiry and (except for a thin comb-over) bald. His face, at rest, had a forbidding air. When he chewed, the fine muscles near his temple could be seen at work, pistons efficiently engaged in the necessary, but apparently joyless, task of eating. He despised expenditure on frivolities, once telling me that going to the cinema was a waste of money, because if a movie was any good, it would end up on television where he could watch it for free.

Christianity provided Jack's bedrock, from which the school's principles were mined, then displayed to the world. I imagine that his pupils' parents found his faith reassuring. His mantra was that honesty trumped all, and he lectured us on sincerity, even explaining his version (which is incorrect, but revealing) of the Latin roots of the word: we Maidwellians were to be solid citizens, through and through, and must be *sine cera* – without wax at our core. Jack's code was, seemingly, a mixture of truthfulness and toil, virtue and self-sacrifice, patriotism and love of God. 'This is Maidwell!' he would declare, as though planting a flag round which good Christians could rally with righteous pride.

Each Sunday Jack oversaw our procession to the local church, where a sprinkling of white-haired widows from the village sat in the front pews to the left of the aisle. These compulsory services were led by the Reverend Hilary Davidson – a wire-haired priest, who walked with his head tilted to one side. The vicar's careworn expression hinted that he hadn't entered the church to administer to the sons of the extremely wealthy. His Sunday rituals alternated between matins and Holy Communion. The former passed particularly slowly, because of the weightiness of its many sung and spoken offerings: particularly dour was the mournful sixth-century hymn *Te Deum*, which we renamed the 'Tedium'.

Jack also officiated a weekly service in the school. Each Wednesday evening, booklets the colour of milky tea would be handed out for compline, an obscure observance that suited Jack's personality perfectly. It begins with acknowledgement of sins committed and a plea for forgiveness. A Psalm or two follow, interspersed with fiery prose from the Testaments, before supplications seeking God's protection from the 'perils and dangers of this night'. Compline yielded a sombre moment in our week, rather than an uplifting one, and was more suited to a monastery than to a school for young boys.

In addition, Jack supervised our daily communal prayers. Before these, he would run through any school housekeeping points before suddenly, without a word, sliding down from his chair onto his knees. We would all follow his lead – facing the backs of our chairs, leaning on our elbows, eyes closed – as he led us through a handful of religious texts, always concluding with the Lord's Prayer. But this outward Christian zeal could be deployed *insincerely*, to bamboozle and snare vulnerable boys.

William Say, a friend a few months older than me, found himself favoured by Jack from his arrival. He was a short, nice-looking boy with blond hair, in whom Jack delighted. The headmaster's general gruffness slipped in a letter to William's parents: 'He's a dear little boy,' he wrote, disclosing more than he intended.

On Sunday nights, while the rest of the school slept, Jack would take William down to his study for one-to-one assignations. The headmaster told William to think of these as his 'Sunday confessions'. Jack would express his great sadness at William's parents' divorce and suggest, with an apparent generosity of spirit, a consoling thought: 'I'm your father now.' Jack explained that, for such an intimate bond to work, they must have total honesty between them. 'This is what I expect of you,' he told William.

Jack also expected the boy to take down his pyjama bottoms. William obeyed, and knelt on Jack's pouf – the soft, tan, circular cushion in the centre of the study – with his naked buttocks in the air. 'What have you done wrong this week?' Jack would ask, in a low voice. This put William in a quandary. He was somebody who made sure to stay out of trouble. He would offer up to Jack his few, minor indiscretions, but would also feel compelled to add some invented ones that were more serious, knowing that having nothing much to confess would anger his self-appointed surrogate father.

After each 'confession', Jack would say, 'Well, that's very disappointing …', and spank William's bare bottom hard. The headmaster's hand often lingered on the stinging buttocks, William recalls, in what he now terms 'a romantic fondle'.

James Temple, another of my blond, pretty Maidwell contemporaries, struggled academically, and that presented Jack with an Achilles heel. He insisted that James come to his study, late at night, for 'extra lessons'. While James knelt on the pouf with his pyjama bottoms removed, Jack presented him with a series of classroom questions that he'd written out on cards. These were placed on the floor, in front of James's nose, so he could read them out before attempting to answer them.

Jack would spank James slowly and softly at first, before striking harder and harder, till James got the answer right. Then the headmaster would caress James's buttocks and genitals, while the stinging pain subsided, before presenting the next question. And the crescendo of smacks on bare flesh would start again.

Any chink of educational weakness was open to exploitation by Maidwell's predatory headmaster. Perry Pelham, a gentle, quiet boy two years my junior, was good at all subjects except maths. Once, before sitting a maths exam, Jack told Perry, 'To encourage you to do your best today, you should know that you will receive a stroke of my cane for every percentage point that you drop in this paper.' Perry froze. He only got 44 per cent – worse than he would have expected to have achieved normally.

After the disappointing result came in, Jack took Perry to a place where privacy was guaranteed – an area of the school's attics that was out of bounds to boys.

'What is forty-four from one hundred?' he asked.

'Fifty-six, sir?'

'Yes, quite right – fifty-six … But do you really expect my poor old arm to be able to cope with beating you fifty-six times?'

'No, sir,' Perry said, daring to hope.

'So, what is seven into fifty-six?'

A pause.

'Eight, sir?'

'Yes. Correct. So I will give you eight strokes of the cane each night of the coming week.' And he did – up in the attics, for his own private pleasure.

William, James and Perry suffered appallingly in these secret sessions, but there was also a thriving public side to Jack's beatings. Indeed, looking back, it's clear to me now that the purpose

Above, aged four, in September 1968, happily setting out for my first day at Silfield School, with my sister Diana reassuringly by my side. Right, four years later, my sister and nanny Mary Clarke on hand to see me off as I fearfully head for Maidwell Hall as a new boy.

C. SPENCER

My direct ancestor John Spencer (centre) with his brother, Charles, and sister, Diana, painted by Bernard Lens (1682–1740). The brothers were sent to Eton at the age of eight, in the early 1700s, but when they were orphaned their grandmother Sarah, Duchess of Marlborough, had them live under her roof, where they were educated by private tutors.

My great-great-grandfather Frederick Spencer, right, with his brother George and sister Georgiana, by Henry Edridge (1768–1821); the boys were sent to Eton at the ages of ten and eight.

Park House – the place that I have always thought of as 'home', though I only lived there until I was eleven – on the Sandringham Estate in Norfolk.

Me, aged two, with my mother outside Park House.

My mother on a skiing holiday in Switzerland in 1966, with Peter Shand Kydd in the foreground, playing up to my father's camera; my mother and Peter would leave their respective spouses for each other within the year.

My grandparents Jack and Cynthia Spencer photographed by my father in the front courtyard of Althorp, c. 1940.

My grandfather and me, c. 1968.

My father, John Spencer, with his ever-present camera.

Above, my sisters Diana and Sarah, our nicest nanny Sally Percival, my sister Jane, and me, in the grounds of Park House, c. 1969.

Below, a game of chess with my father in my bedroom at Park House, 1970; with Disney stickers on my headboard and a backdrop of the innocent wallpaper that adorned my room from my earliest days till I left for Maidwell.

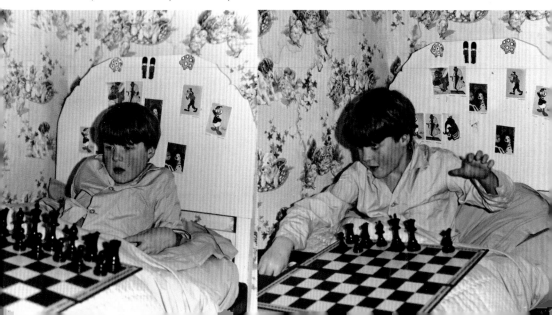

Riding my bay pony, Teddy Tar, on Brancaster Beach, near Park House, c. 1971.

Above and right, with Gitsie, in Park House's garden.

My classmate William Purefoy visiting me at Park House in the summer of 1972, a few weeks before we both first went to Maidwell.

In my Maidwell 'Sunday best' suit.

Maidwell Hall, Northamptonshire.

A portrait of me aged eight, in December 1972, looking extremely happy, a day or two after finishing my first term at Maidwell.

Playing tennis at Park House during my first summer holiday from Maidwell, 1973.

Me enjoying life by the pool at Park House, aged ten.

of Maidwell's strict structure was to provide Jack with a steady stream of boys' buttocks to contemplate and strike. The staff knew that, if they wanted the formidable headmaster's favour, they needed to present him with miscreants.

Robert Lilburne, at Maidwell in Jack's earliest years as headmaster, recalls the austere Oliver Wyatt with some fondness. 'Porch, on the other hand,' he says, 'was an evil sadist with paedo tendencies. He didn't like boys, but he did enjoy hurting them.'

Soon after I arrived at Maidwell, I learned that the school never had a victimless day. After tea, at ten minutes to six, it would be the turn of at least half a dozen of us boys to disappear into the dimly lit corridor that led from the side of the school kitchen to the private wing, where the Porches had their set of rooms.

As soon as you took your first steps down the corridor, your nostrils would recoil at the smell of the place – of pungent wax, oozing out of the dark wall-panelling, and up from the polished wooden floor. Eyes also struggled to adapt, for the few lights were spread apart and dim. You'd shuffle down this gloomiest of passageways, too apprehensive to talk, and stop just short of the Porches' entrance hall. Once here, only whispers were allowed, to add to the drama of the ritual.

Maidwell's deputy head boy would be on hand to hear why you were present, and he placed you in a line, on the left side of the corridor, to await your turn with Jack. While you stood outside the study, you could just make out the outline of words being exchanged within, but the sound of Jack's blows punched through the closed door, echoing round the hall in a terrible warning of what you were about to suffer. Stomachs gurgled, throats dried and buttocks tightened, as terror intensified along the line of small children awaiting the headmaster's cruel attention.

One of my friends was so distressed by the wait outside Jack's study, and by the sounds he heard coming from within it, that he lost control of both bladder and stomach. On hearing of this, Jack burst out of the door.

'What's going on?' he demanded.

'I've spilt something, sir,' the ten-year-old replied.

'Wet yourself, rather! You grubby little boy!' Jack fumed, before furiously sending him back up the corridor to get himself clean.

But someone still had to suffer: a friend of mine who'd only been present as a witness to a transgression was beaten in place of the one who had fouled his clothes. This innocent told me recently: 'That was my "Eureka moment" – I realised, This is all wrong. This shouldn't be happening.'

When your time finally came, you were ushered forward by the deputy head boy. As you shuffled into the gloomy study, your eyes acclimatised to find Jack seated, devoid of compassion, ready to dispense physical pain, the quiet blaze in his eyes betraying his inner gratification.

Jack stared intently, his right knee held tight in interlocking hands, as you stood before him, maintaining the stiff upper lip expected of you. He listened with evident disappointment as your misdemeanour was read out, then issued a short denunciation of your conduct, before flicking a slipper from foot to hand and beckoning you towards him.

He was expert at the next part. He pulled you down so your stomach pivoted on his scrawny knees, before flicking up the vent of your jacket so he could take unobstructed aim at your bottom. The strikes were delivered swiftly and sharply, with the full force of his sinewy arm, before he pushed you away disgustedly. You made for the study door while your head swam with shock and pain, biting your lip and blinking hard.

The head boy witnessed these nightly beatings while standing in the shadows behind the headmaster, his job to record on the school list who had been beaten, for what, on which day, and how many times. One of these head boys, Isaac Ewer, recently told me this list acted as a reminder of where to look for fresh victims: 'I'm sure Jack could look down the list and see, for instance, that Spencer hadn't been beaten for a while – so it was time to change that.'

If the schoolboy offence reached beyond the bounds of the headmaster's slipper, and demanded the Flick or the Swish, the head boy would be told to leave the room. Jack would command the pupil to drop his trousers and underpants, and kneel on his pouf, before administering the strokes in private.

A Maidwell friend of mine, who died a few years ago, spoke of how, during such a caning in the study, Jack reached down with his hand to cup the boy's scrotum. He used his grip on this sensitive part to move my friend round on the pouf. This gave him an angle from which to cane his buttocks with greater force.

Another former pupil told me how he turned his head while being caned and caught sight of a large bulge in the front of Jack's cavalry twills. The headmaster slapped this boy's face hard and shouted, 'How dare you turn round? Look to the front!' before completing the thrashing with added gusto.

One of my Maidwell classmates was summoned to the study alongside a pupil who had cut a sapling in the school grounds. The other boy dared to answer back, and my friend remembers thinking, 'Oh my God ...', as Jack exploded: 'He caned [the other boy] in front of me. It was so hard.'

He then turned to my friend and whipped his buttocks so severely that, when the blood dried, the cotton of his underpants became enmeshed in his torn flesh. My friend was unable to separate his clothing from his cuts that night, till the matron soaked him in the bath and the underwear came free from his wounds.

The Flick received regular airings. At the end of each week every boy in the school received grades for his work. There were seven subjects, which the school listed in order of importance: Latin first, then maths, French, English, history, geography and Scripture. Your form teacher would give you a grade for each.

'Weekly Marks' was supposed to reflect how much a pupil had tried, rather than indicate his academic prowess: 3 was for excellent effort, 2 for hard work, 1 was satisfactory, 0 was not, while a minus reflected 'little or no effort'. Anyone who got an aggregate of less than 7 could expect a rendezvous with the Flick.

It became obvious that, for their supposed lack of classroom effort, Jack was caning the same seven or eight boys every week – some of them were genuinely struggling with their studies, while the others were pretty, athletic and able. We knew this posse as the Saturday Morning Club. No matter how hard these pupils tried, they received Jack's cane weekly. One of them still remembers the pattern of these encounters: 'Jack shouted and then beat me.' Sometimes he'd position the last blow so it crossed the preceding, parallel ones, for added pain.

'I remember one boy suffering this fate,' my contemporary Thomas Scot says. 'And several of us asked, fascinated and appalled, to see the welts. There was a horrified silence when we saw the bloody result of Jack Porch's work; I can picture the scene even now.'

My ability to avoid livid stripes on my buttocks was noted by Jack: 'Charles has had the sense to remain out of trouble this term,' he once reported to my parents. It had been a particular effort because my dormitory prefect had been Edmund Ludlow. He enjoyed special favour with Jack because of his ability to sniff out boys who'd broken the rules and then serve them up to the headmaster for beatings.

My heart had sunk when I found out I was in Ludlow's dormitory. I knew from those who'd been under him the previous term that they'd been beaten on 'every day but two', as one of them remembers still. This wasn't because they'd been caught in the act of talking after lights out, but because Ludlow had quizzed them each morning: had they transgressed the no-speaking rule? The guilty boys, brought up on a code of total honesty, admitted that they had.

Before lights out on the first evening of that term, I shared with my roommates what I'd discovered about Ludlow's methods. I reckoned that the only way to avoid getting into trouble for talking after lights out was not to talk. Everyone agreed. We lay there silently, every night that term, till sleep claimed us.

This wasn't at all what Ludlow wanted, as he needed culprits to hand over to remain so high in Jack's good books. Each morning he would interrogate us: 'Right – which of you spoke after lights out last night? Come on – I want all the names.' But every time we looked squarely back at his darting, suspicious eyes and gave our solemn word that we had stayed silent in the dark. Ludlow tipped from fury to anguished disbelief as the term progressed. He once screamed in frustration: 'You're either the biggest load of *liars* there's ever been or the biggest load of *goody-goodies!*'

But we persisted. Breaking the link between this enabling prefect and the headmaster's painful slipper made the monotony of our nightly silence worthwhile. In a place where we had next to no power, Ludlow's utter consternation was rich reward.

The headmaster's wife was another purveyor of boys to beat. This proved Mrs Porch's only engagement with Maidwell's pupils: she didn't teach at the school and never joined us in the dining room, but chose to live a quiet, separate life. The most common adjective my contemporaries have for her is 'ghostlike'. We'd heard a rumour that her father had been gassed in the First World War, and we took this to somehow explain her detachment. (More recently, I heard from one of Maidwell's teachers that Mrs Porch had been dependent on Valium in the years I attended the school.)

Mrs Porch enjoyed working in her rose garden, a small square near her family's quarters that was enclosed by a finely clipped yew hedge. She wore short rubber boots that peeped out from under long skirts in the winter, while secateurs and a basket were constantly to hand in the summer. The flowers that she cut were reserved for the Porches' private wing, where they stood out in the general gloom.

When three boys joined in a game that involved jumping across one of her precious rose beds, some of their leaps accidentally fell short. A rigorous investigation was held into the tell-tale heel marks left behind in the perfectly tilled soil, with pupils' shoes examined for clues. The culprits were summoned to Jack's study for individual canings of a particular severity.

It was not, I think, the nature of the crime that caused such a punishment. Rather, it was the headmaster's way of showing that any transgression that affected his wife would be dealt with especially harshly: however eerie her presence, she was still the queen consort of Maidwell, by dint of being married to its undisputed king.

Jack didn't just rely on others sending him boys to beat. He also hunted for prey himself.

Maidwell's dormitory occupants were divided into early beds, semi-beds, semi-demi-beds and late beds, according to when exactly, between 7.30 and 9 p.m., they had lights out. He'd come around the most senior dormitories in friendly guise every evening, spending a few minutes in each. We played cards with him – *vingt-et-un* (or pontoon) usually, or a hand of bridge occasionally. He took part to win, but he was at his most relaxed with us at these times. One of my friends once said that during these evening visits, 'We were like the sons he never had.'

But on these dormitory tours, his worst tendencies surfaced. 'He slyly encouraged us to cheat [at cards],' Robert Lilburne remembers, 'and when he caught us would pull us over his knee and spank us using just two fingers of his right hand. I remember only too well deciding not to cheat after twice experiencing his cock digging into my tummy.'

Jack invented a game called 'toe beetles', and his fingers were those 'beetles', probing and tickling our toes, before moving up our legs to our torsos as we screeched with laughter. He would go 'Ha-ha-ha – toe beetles! Toe beetles! Coming to get you! Toe beetles!' in a maniacal voice that, then, we found funny.

We were thrilled to have a playful moment with someone we were, for the most part, terrified of. Even when his bony fingers dug in quite deep, we would whoop with enjoyment and beg him to carry on. We craved the attention of this most powerful of men, however it came.

After lights out, Jack engaged in nocturnal patrols, when he reverted to his most overtly threatening form. Nobody could hear him pad along the corridors in his soft, evening slippers. He cruised like a submarine, his jutting-out ears scanning for illicit whispers. If on the way to or from the bathroom a boy spotted Jack wandering the corridors, he'd speed back to his dormitory and hiss, '*Cave!*' – Latin for 'Beware!' – and nobody dared speak again till the morning. But it was impossible to escape such a committed predator for long.

One night, boys in my dormitory were whispering about nothing much when Daniel Blagrave suddenly chimed in with 'Do you know what peasants are called in South America?' None of us had a clue. 'Peons!' he said, with an emphasis on the first syllable that sparked loud laughter: any phrase with 'pee' or 'wee' in it would have set us off for, however rarefied our family backgrounds might have been, we were, in the end, just ten-year-old boys.

The handle on the dormitory door slowly turned. Terror. It was Jack.

We lay still, hoping to pass for sleeping innocents. Jack put the light on. 'Who was talking?' he asked, his low voice choking with excitement, as he sat down on the nearest bed. Four hands went up, including mine. He beckoned us towards him as he flicked a slipper into his right hand.

One by one, we were upended on his knee and given swingeing blows to the buttocks before being pushed away. I'd been beaten with a slipper several times by him already by now, during his post-tea rituals, but that had been through my trousers and pants. Pyjama bottoms presented no protection, and the pain was shocking in its intensity. One who was beaten with me that night recalls, 'I simply could not believe how much his slipper hurt on this occasion. No mercy whatsoever – for the crime of talking.'

We each sped back to our beds, trying to put on a brave face while our buttocks burned and our eyes smarted. We lay there in silence, piecing together the path that had taken us so quickly from schoolboy laughter to alarm to dizzying pain. Jack left us in the dormitory in shock and resumed his patrol of the corridors, looking for more victims.

Rather than be embarrassed at the amount of physical punishment he meted out, Jack seemed to revel in it. He called his beatings 'whacking', and thought it was something that could be joked about. When teaching us the different cases of Latin nouns such as nominative, vocative and genitive, he renamed the accusative the 'whackusative'. He illustrated each of these words with the pin figure of a boy. The pin boy illustrating the whack-usative was bent over, arms down, bottom pointing upwards. His head was thrown back with sketched lines emanating from his mouth, showing that he was wailing in pain. It was one of the ways in which Jack normalised his way of doing things – his sadism.

I like to think Jack had some scruples about such abuse, and I suspect it lay behind one of his classroom eccentricities. The school sold us fountain pens, which we chewed on hard, so they were often reduced to gnawed stumps. Jack viewed our pens suspiciously, insisting that we leave them on our desks before approaching him in class. If anyone forgot and approached him with pen in hand – perhaps when having a piece of work marked – he'd call out 'No – no – remember St Cassian!' and send them back to their desk with a violent wave of his arm.

St Cassian was, we learned, a fourth-century Christian school-master. Condemned to death for his faith by the ancient Romans, he was handed over to his pupils. They got their revenge for Cassian's years of cruelty to them by stabbing him to death with their pens. If Jack feared meeting the same fate, perhaps, deep down, he knew his conduct was monstrous.

Yet Jack's power and cruelty extended well beyond his licence to inflict physical pain. I wrote home, my first term: 'It's dreadful tidying out are [sic] lockers because there [sic] so untidy.'

Each boy had his own locker, for storing his few personal belongings – letters from home, toys and 'tuck' (or sweets) – but they weren't as secure as their name suggested, as Jack had forbidden locks.

Several times a term, before we came down for breakfast, Jack would undertake a surprise 'locker inspection'. You first learned that yours had failed this test when you saw your private possessions scattered on the floor. Jack hooked his arm round in an arc, then scooped up everything, no matter how fragile, so it tumbled out in a clattering heap. Boys whose lockers had been emptied like this had to put back their possessions tidily while the rest of us ate breakfast.

Jack seemed to prefer it when his acts of humiliation had an audience.

A junior boy on a table far from the headmaster's, but in his eyeline, had the lunchtime task of watching out for a wave from Jack. This signified that the boy must press a buzzer that sounded in the kitchens so the staff there knew it was time to clear the first course plates.

One lunch this boy failed to spot Jack's wave, so he made it more extravagant. But the boy, engrossed in conversation with his friends, continued to miss his cue. Jack now threw both his arms out wide and flailed like a shipwrecked mariner trying to get the attention of a passing vessel. Still no eye contact was made, so Jack got up and stood on his chair, continuing his waving in an even more absurdly overblown way; his fingers were almost brushing the ceiling. The rest of the school laughed dutifully at Jack's antics, and the boy whose attention had been so innocently distracted was made to feel idiotic. 'Will you please pay attention!' Jack shouted across the room, as the boy lunged at the buzzer, crimson with embarrassment. Meanwhile the headmaster regained his seat, while revelling in the mocking laughter that his unkindness had stoked and unleashed.

Punishment at Maidwell often had shame at its core. In the dining room there was a small sideboard called the 'Pig's Table'. A member of staff could send any boy there whose table manners fell short. He would have to take his food and glass with him, and complete his meal, standing there, while facing the wall in disgrace.

I was sent there once, when I was ten, by Mr Green, a student teacher a decade my senior, who had chunky glasses and pimples. His fringe was so uneven that we pupils felt sure that he must cut his own hair. We enjoyed teasing him gently – we believed, imperceptibly – but at lunch one day I overstepped the mark.

One of the serving ladies plonked a glass bowl of wobbly green blancmange in front of Mr Green, so he could dish it out for us all with a large spoon. Its vivid colour was disturbingly bright. We hadn't seen this pudding before.

'It looks weird,' said a friend.

There was a brief silence, then I chipped in with: 'It looks like you, sir.'

This was meant to be a play on his being Mr Green and the pudding also being that colour, but I understood at once that I'd missed the comedic bullseye by a distance.

Mr Green looked at me in stunned amazement, then, as the boys around us erupted in delighted laughter, he curled his lip. As he pointed to Maidwell's version of the stocks, he shouted, 'Spencer – take yourself to the Pig's Table! Now!'

I recognised that punishment for my clumsy outburst was inevitable and deserved. It was a weak joke that had morphed into a strong insult. But being sent to the Pig's Table was, I protested, an inappropriate punishment. 'I shouldn't have to go there, sir,' I countered, desperately. 'It's where boys go if they eat disgustingly!'

But Mr Green had the obstinacy of a weak man, determined to stand by a decision made.

'I said, Spencer – go to the Pig's Table!'

My cheeks flushed puce with embarrassment as I took myself to this place of public degradation, a bowl of green blancmange in one hand and my water glass in the other.

The Pig's Table stood behind Jack's right shoulder. He liked to insult any boy sent there from where he sat, encouraging the senior boys around him to laugh at his cutting comments as they reached the ears of the shamed boy, who wasn't allowed to reply.

I died a thousand deaths that lunchtime, while so exposed. The severity of Mr Green's punishment for a silly joke was symptomatic of the casual abuse that I experienced at Maidwell, but I was never cheeky with him again. I had to conclude that, sadly, there were no weak links in the teaching staff. It took me very many years to understand that this was not by chance. Rather, Jack had taken great care to ensure that this was how it would be.

5

At Arm's Length

Unlimited power in the hands of limited people always leads to cruelty.

– Aleksandr Solzhenitsyn

To keep his abusive system intact, Jack relied on concealment, collusion and cunning. He had no governance to worry about – no outside inspections, as would be compulsory today – and the school's governors seemed to pay little attention to their duties. Besides, they'd all been pupils at Maidwell under the exacting and eccentric Oliver Wyatt, so were used to the peculiarities of their Alma Mater. They probably felt their seat at the board of a seemingly prestigious institution to be an honour rather than a responsibility.

In any case, those selected as governors had little time to devote to their obligations to the school, as they had much to be getting on with in their professional lives. One was a prominent Conservative Member of Parliament, while another spent much time at sea: a naval surgeon, he served as the Queen's physician on long voyages on the *Royal Yacht Britannia*. Such busy men were unlikely to worry about what was going on at a prep school.

Meanwhile Jack ensured that the governors' board meetings took place far from Maidwell, so they couldn't have direct contact with the boys. Once a year he would change out of his cavalry twills and sports jacket and don a suit, before driving off for a half day with the governors in London.

The headmaster also kept parents away from Maidwell, as much as he could. They weren't allowed in the place, except on those days when they had to be there, either depositing their sons at the school or collecting them from it. Family members were forbidden from stopping by, even if they happened to be passing, unless it was while briefly dropping off a birthday cake. Even then, the parents weren't allowed inside the school buildings. These restrictions were presented as being in the boys' best interests, to avoid their being distracted – a nonsensical reason for denying children contact with their family, but one common to prep schools at the time.

An older friend of mine, educated in the sixties at a boarding establishment much like Maidwell, remembers being forced to join other boys in a joyless afternoon walk in the grounds, super-vised by a master feared for his bullying. 'At that moment,' my friend recalls, 'a car swung into the drive and out stepped a glam-orous American lady, mother of one of our contemporaries. As his parents lived abroad, he never went out on exeats.* His mother stepped up to the master and said she would like to take her son

* A set weekend out, such as Maidwell's leave-out.

out for the afternoon, only to be told this was not possible as this wasn't an exeat Sunday. With that she simply slapped him across his face (I shall never forget the sound), took her son with her and neither of them were ever seen again.'

Jack could be fierce with those Maidwell parents who threatened to enter his school or change his rigid arrangements. In November 1973, my mother learned I was to read one of the lessons in the school carol service. She wrote to Jack to say she would like to attend and to spend time with me in the school afterwards.

'The Carol Service will almost certainly be on Monday 10 December at about 4 p.m.,' he replied, affecting vagueness about an occasion long since secured in the school's schedule of events. 'From my end the main points are that this is a Service, not a school show; if parents or anyone else wants to join us, that's fine, but it is on those terms. Hence there will probably be a chance for a word with Charles immediately after, but with all my staff working flat out at that point, I cannot let people into the school, nor will I agree to special arrangements … The administrative complications would be considerable, and since most children have a natural aptitude for blackmail, we should very soon have more visitors than the church will hold.'

While Jack showed a general disregard for Maidwell mothers, he reserved a particular contempt for those who were (like my mother) divorced. He had no time at all for my mother, partly because he seemed keen to ingratiate himself with my father. But Jack must have appreciated that she was a particularly defiant and determined character, so he added extra ballast to the obstructive wall that he now built between her and a visit to Maidwell: 'I am trying to make it all plain, without being unfriendly,' he continued, untruthfully. 'The people who do niggle me are those who expect all our arrangements to be altered to suit them ... So, in the belief that you are the sort of person who would rather just be told straight out what the situation is, I have done so.' Jack's rudeness worked: my mother chose not to sacrifice half a day driving to and from Maidwell, if she was only going to spend a moment with me. All she had hoped for was a little time with her son, but the headmaster probably viewed such irregular intrusions as a risky prospect that was best avoided.

It was easy for Jack to keep his boys away from the world beyond Maidwell's walls. Since we had no access to phones, our only communication with home was by letter. Each morning we would pace impatiently round a pop-up table outside the dining room, waiting for Granny Ford to lay out our mail.

We were, in turn, made to write a letter home each Sunday morning, before church. The supervising master would jot a few bland headlines on the blackboard, as suggestions of what we might include. These mainly involved achievements by the stars of the school's sports teams – feats that can only have been of interest to the families of the boys concerned. But it was innocuous content that kept us from bothering our parents with the depth of our homesickness, or any problematic revelations about life at Maidwell.

It was compulsory to write more than a single side. 'Getting over the page' was easy for some boys, who dashed off their news with enviable speed. Most, though, stared out of the window, hoping for inspiration. My early letters home frequently record having just seen a grey squirrel climbing a tree.

My father had taught me a general kicking-off point for personal letters: 'I hope you are well, and having nice weather?' It was typically English in its restraint – a gentle opening, with a wry, sympathetic nod to the nation's disheartening climate.

I'd deploy this insipid introduction, if really pushed. When my letter was done, I'd hold it up high for the master on duty to view, spinning it round in my fingers so he could see that I had achieved the required length. Only one or two of the masters on duty would read our correspondence through, so most weeks it departed Maidwell uncensored.

My letters home show inner turmoil politely presented. Those that I wrote to my mother betray a desperate wish to please her and a deep confusion at having been sent away. I was, I can see now, pathetically grateful for any maternal attention that she paid me. My first letter home opens with, 'I hope you are well. Thank you very much for your letters. It was very kind [of you] to send them.' Later that first term, when still consumed by homesickness, I wrote to thank her for making the effort to take me out for a weekend's leave-out – from the school where she'd agreed to have me transported. Because I felt so bereft, it seemed a great kindness for her to take the time to see me when she'd clearly decided she had much to get on with, without me.

I finished this letter with 'Sorry for my bad writing.' I completed another with 'I am sorry it is not very long, this letter.' A third from those same early days as a boarder concluded with 'Sorry about my spelling and writing because I know it's awful.'

As an eight-year-old I felt that I had been sent away from home because I had somehow fallen short as a son. The last thing I wanted to do, in such a bewildered state, was make the situation worse by in any way being difficult, or questioning, since that might bring about even harsher rejection. Best to apologise.

These fears in my first year at Maidwell reached a climax on Sunday 20 May, 1973 – my ninth birthday. All pupils had an hour's lie-in on Sunday mornings, but I woke up at my usual time. As I lay there, it slowly dawned on me that this would be the first occasion on which I'd celebrate my birthday while away from my parents. And then I remembered how, a year before, I'd been playing football on the lawn of Park House with my Silfield friends, before a swim, then birthday tea in our dining room – 'Happy Birthday' being sung by family, and friends of several years' standing, as my cake was carried in by my smiling nanny, Mary.

Now I found myself confined to a brusque establishment whose residents I'd known for only eight months. I felt utterly alone on this day in the year that previously I'd placed in a dead heat for excitement with Christmas.

My unhappiness that morning deepened as I lay there in enforced silence. I thought about how my mother liked to say how 'sweet' I was – warmly to my face, and proudly to others. And then I suddenly had a ghastly thought: by turning nine, I must surely be exiting that phase when a boy can be considered sweet and be entering a no man's land between childhood and teenage years, where sweetness surely had no place. If I was no longer sweet, I asked myself, my heart beating faster, how could my mother still love me?

I concluded that, clearly, she could not; and then I started crying quietly, so those in the surrounding beds couldn't hear me. As ever, at Maidwell, raw grief had to be hidden. It was essential that others knew nothing of my distress, for 'blubbing' was unacceptable – even on a birthday. Great fat tears of devastation poured down my cheeks, before plopping onto my pillow. Soon after this, I started to make myself vomit during the nights.

Granny Ford had come into Pink during my first ever evening at the school, to check that we had washed and said our prayers. She had pointed out chipped, white metal chamber pots under some of the beds. 'You'll find these in each of the dormitories,' she said. 'You're only to use them in an emergency – if you need to be sick in the night and know for sure that you can't make it to the lavatories in time.'

In my terror at maternal rejection, I found these pots useful for the first time. After lights out, I waited till the rest of the dormitory fell asleep, then silently lifted the pot out from under my bed and placed it between my thighs. I hunched over the pot and opened my mouth wide, sticking the first two fingers of my right hand down my throat till I found the point at the back that made me gag, retch and throw up.

My induced vomiting was rarely productive – normally I'd look down through glistening eyes to find a thin swill of gastric juices, sloshing around a couple of mouthfuls of that evening's supper. In the morning I'd show my feeble offering to Granny Ford. She and her team were accustomed to dealing with boys' vomit when it appeared unexpectedly, in torrents, through stomach bugs and the like. If it hit the floor, they'd attack the worst of it with a mop and bucket, before dousing the remainder with piles of cedar wood sawdust. This soaked up the moisture while diffusing an unforgettable, muscular aroma – of cigar box, mothballs and forest resin – that wrestled with the stench of vomit before smothering it.

But when I appeared with my lightly splattered pot, Granny Ford would look at it and at me contemptuously, judge that I seemed well enough in myself – no fever; pink of cheek – and then say, wearily, 'Wash it out thoroughly, Spencer. Then put it back where it came from.' This interaction recurred dozens of times over the following years.

It's obvious to me now – but wasn't then – that my making myself sick was a desperate attempt to get somebody adult to show me warmth and sympathy, and to give me some care and attention. It was an emotional cry for help and an effort to exert an element of control over a life that was so out of my control. But I was incapable of understanding or communicating such complicated thoughts, when aged nine.

I see in a letter from that summer term of 1973 that I told my mother about my vomiting: 'I have been sick for a week every night,' I wrote. But this medical snippet was embedded in a long paragraph in which I said how nice some of the new boys were, and boasted of minor feats on the cricket field, so it must have slipped past my mother, unnoticed.

And trying to attract kindness from the tough-as-nails Granny Ford was taking optimism to new and unrealistic heights. The senior matron saw me as a tiresome hypochondriac who was repeatedly wasting her time. She never showed an iota of concern for my physical or emotional wellbeing, and even if she had been concerned, she hadn't the training or the inclination to help. The dispensary, where she treated our aches and ailments, betrayed the minuteness of her medical knowledge. It contained tubs of 'chap cream' that we slapped onto our upper thighs, where our sports shorts chafed, a liquorice gel or iodine for mouth ulcers, and a seemingly endless supply of bandages and plasters. Granny Ford's was a limited arsenal.

The older brother of one of my Maidwell colleagues remembers a medical crisis at the school, in the late sixties, which Granny Ford tackled with her customary crassness. A boy had been found to have dysentery, and Granny Ford was told by Jack that the condition was contagious. 'She had everyone shit into a pot – one by one – in pots placed at the top of the main staircase,' he noted. 'A sample was taken from each. The stench was terrible.' In his mid-sixties, he remembers the school as having been 'Threatening. Bullying. Controlling. Sinister', but this episode of mass, public defecation summed up the bizarre nature of the place more succinctly. 'Crapping in unison – only Maidwell could do this,' he said, with grim resignation.

Granny Ford reacted to any outbreaks in the school with a similar, blunderbuss approach. Aged eleven, in January 1976, I wrote in my diary: 'I was deliced [*sic*]. It didn't work very well because I found three [lice] in the afternoon and one in the evening …'

Unsurprisingly, in a school that lacked medical know-how, and any semblance of pastoral care, its senior matron had no idea how to spot the signs of emotional trauma in children, let alone how to address them. This may explain why Granny Ford was so triumphant when she saw an opportunity to get me back for my many appearances before her with reeking pot in hand.

On a weekday in the winter of 1973, Princess Anne was due to marry, and the school was set to join in the national holiday decreed for the wedding day of Queen Elizabeth's only daughter. That morning I presented my pathetic offering to Granny Ford, and her eyes sparked as brightly as on my first day at the school, when she'd selected the thuggish Corbet to shepherd me through my first few days. 'Well, Spencer, if you're so very unwell, you really must rest – you must take it easy. I insist! It's the right thing to do.' Overruling my protests, she sent me to my dormitory for the entire day – not visiting once – as everyone else enjoyed their day off downstairs. It was the only occasion, out of the many when I showed her my pot, that she sent me to bed.

Doubtless Granny Ford believed this the ideal punishment for what she saw as my tiresome behaviour. But shoving my fingers down my throat remained my night-time default whenever I was consumed by loneliness or unhappiness at Maidwell, which was often.

Not once during my five years at the school do I remember Granny Ford looking at me with kindness, a smile or a glimmer of compassion. My contemporary Cornelius Holland was one of the many others to receive the same harsh dealings from her. 'She was tough as old boots,' he recalls. 'I left the rind from my bacon on the side of my plate once, and Granny Ford ordered me to eat it. I told her, "I will – but it will make me sick." She told me to get on with it. So I managed to eat it and was, as I had warned her, promptly sick.'

Granny Ford will always remain in my memory not only as a person of deep unpleasantness, but also as one forever twinned with the act of vomiting.

When homesickness gripped me during the daytime, I would head off on my own, into the quiet beauty of Maidwell's grounds. My favourite spot for solitude was a thickly wooded clump at one end of Mrs Porch's rose garden. There I'd wish away the next years of my life, longing to be eighteen, so I could have my ten-year boarding school sentence behind me.

Once, on a slow Sunday afternoon, I was pining for home with particular longing. I took myself to the low, dry-stacked wall near the school's main entrance and sat there hugging my knees tight as I watched cars driving freely by, out in the real world. As I fantasised about liberation from the school, and being allowed back with my family, an approaching car caught my eye. Its sleek contours seemed familiar enough to demand closer attention. I read its registration number, and with a jolt I recognised that it was my father's Jaguar. As it passed, I saw him in profile at the steering wheel, looking straight ahead with a distracted smile. I gasped as my heart did a flip. It all happened so fast that I hadn't time to wave or shout before he was gone.

I thought about this incident a lot afterwards. There couldn't have been a more forceful reminder of the gulf between our lives than this: while I was a child confined to a place I didn't want to be – administered by bullies and misfits – he was an adult, free to breeze by, having (as he later confirmed) enjoyed a good lunch with friends nearby. It seemed impossible that, while I was feeling so low and lonely, the lives of those I loved were simply carrying on as normal, outside Maidwell's walls. I felt angry at the unfairness of it all, and I was puzzled why my father hadn't even glanced at the school where he'd sent me. If he had, he would have seen me as I was – lonely, miserable and longing for home – and not how the headmaster so often chose to present me, as a happy little boarder.

As part of his total control of Maidwell, Jack broke the chain between our parents and his teaching staff. Instead of including individual, handwritten accounts from each master or mistress in pupils' termly reports, as is generally the way, he had the staff write their thoughts on every boy's progress in a large book, which he kept tight possession of.

Jack would draw from these pages to compose a letter to each pair of parents, without mentioning any of their son's teachers by name. He therefore ensured that he was the sole conduit of information between Maidwell's front line and home: no parent could start an independent conversation, behind his back, with anyone else working at the school.

Jack's reports were brilliantly crafted, in letters laced with diverting humour of a darkness that would be unacceptable today. Boys were rarely praised, except in a backhanded way – if someone passed an exam, they weren't commended for the achievement, but were sarcastically congratulated for having 'defeated the examiner'. A plump friend of mine was an expert swimmer, but

Jack chose to focus on his bulk. 'At least,' the headmaster conceded, to the boy's mother and father, 'his blubber makes him buoyant in the swimming pool.' It was adult-to-adult, nudge-and-a-wink stuff, designed as cover for a man who needed to keep his secrets under wraps. The parents lapped it up, as he surely calculated that they would. They must have assumed that someone with such a mischievous sense of humour must be popular with his pupils. But the effects of his constant mockery could be deeply scarring.

One of my contemporaries, Robert Tichborne – who had spurned his teddy bear, rather than have it serve as a nightly reminder of the home he so missed – decided to keep himself as busy as he could at Maidwell, so he would have less time to be consumed by his misery at long weeks away from home. But Jack chose not to see Robert's multiple efforts to succeed: 'Instead, he labelled me as "enthusiastic, but thick" – his reports to my parents were always very bitchy,' Robert recalls. 'In place of encouragement, there were sneers and slights. After a term in which he had given his all in the Maidwell rugby team, Jack wrote in Robert's report: 'He thinks he is running much faster than he is.' Jack insisted that all Robert's efforts were wasted; it would be as well to accept his mediocrity.

Such negativity was damaging to the self-worth of a boy who hated his school yet was still doing his best to succeed there. 'What was written was at loggerheads with how I saw myself,' Robert concludes. The headmaster's barbs went so deep that their tips remain embedded within him today, half a century on.

*　　*　　*

Despite his alpha status in the pack, Jack had an uncomfortable relationship with his teaching staff. One of his junior masters recently told me how the headmaster would appear in their common room for a daily cup of coffee. This was always an awkward occasion. 'He wasn't easy,' the former master says. 'He would finish his coffee. Then there would be silence. Then he would walk out, without saying a word.'

In spite of his gracelessness, Jack had a solid grip on his staff because he alone selected them. One of those who taught me at Maidwell explained how he'd been recruited. He'd seen an advert for a vacancy at the school, had applied and was invited to come along for assessment. He was surprised to find that there was no sit-down interview and no request for references. Instead, he was taken by Jack on a stroll round the school's lake. He remembers that the headmaster kept the talk general: he wanted to establish what sort of person he was contemplating welcoming into his strange little world. Soon after his visit, the prospective master received a letter of acceptance from Jack. 'I hope and believe you will be happy here,' he wrote. 'The drift of your questions persuades me that that will be the case.' Jack had decided that this impressionable young man would fit into Maidwell, without causing any trouble.

Meanwhile the headmaster had also established another important fact: that this highly intelligent candidate promised to be an efficient classroom teacher. This was essential for, if Jack was to continue in office without interference from embarrassed governors or disappointed parents, he had to succeed at the school's primary purpose: getting Maidwell boys to pass Common

Entrance, the exam that gained pupils access into some of the best senior private schools in the land. Pupils' acceptance into Eton, Winchester, Harrow, Rugby and Stowe was trumpeted to the parents in the school's annual magazine.

If he feared that a pupil might fall at this crucial final hurdle, Jack placed him on what he termed 'The Danger List'. While on this, any boy was on notice for his place at Maidwell, and was forced to take mock entrance examinations every Wednesday and Saturday afternoon, until he consistently achieved the required pass mark.

If a pupil on 'The Danger List' proved incapable of improvement, he would be moved on from the school with barely a whisper, so as to avoid embarrassment. One of my Maidwell contemporaries, whose parent was a cousin of Queen Elizabeth, is listed in the school's records as having left the school to go 'to a tutorial establishment', without further detail. Jack had decided he was likely to flunk Common Entrance, so he had to go.

The school also shed those with learning difficulties before they could sit this exam, since it made no provision for such students: they were lumped in with the academically weak. Jack was such a ruthless guardian of Maidwell's exam record that I don't recall anyone failing Common Entrance in the five years that I was there.

I remember, when I was perhaps eleven, seeing a friend being driven away, with no notice and without the opportunity of saying goodbye. He sat with sad, stiff-backed dignity in the back of a dark car. One moment he was a popular and important figure in our schoolboy community. The next, he was being quietly moved along because his many qualities didn't include an aptitude for exams. He and I have never seen each other since.

This friend's abrupt loss – as startling as the departure of any of my Park House nannies – made Maidwell feel even more dangerous and unpredictable. The way this place worked seemed to be as mysterious as it was destabilising. This was somewhere that took you away from those you loved; once transplanted, you formed friendships with others despatched to the same unnatural setting; but then, terrifyingly, the small world you had carved out for yourself – to cope, and maybe prosper – could be crushed to pieces without thought or warning.

All you could do, when hope and happiness were in short supply, was haul yourself up and face the demands of yet another Maidwell day.

6

A Day in the Life

Unhappiness in a child accumulates because he sees no
end to the dark tunnel. The thirteen weeks of a term
might as well be thirteen years.

– Graham Greene

Maidwell's strict daily routine kept us busy and submissive. In that way, it somewhat resembled a military camp. The first sound you heard each morning wasn't a bugled reveille, but the clattering percussion of Granny Ford's hard high heels on the linoleum that covered the floors between the dormitory doors. She walked at a fair clip for an elderly lady, the cold clackety-clack of her lively gait signalling her confidence as the supremo of the school's upstairs. She'd fling open the door of each dormitory in turn, calling out 'Wakey, wakey! Rise and shine!' as she marched over to the windows, parting the thin curtains on their metal runners with a rasping whoosh.

We'd roll out of bed, put on our slippers and run towards the washroom, undoing all the buttons on our pyjama tops so we could arrive at the bank of basins stripped to the waist. Granny Ford insisted on this toplessness: 'Otherwise you'll spill water or drop toothpaste down your pyjamas, and *I'll* be the one forced to deal with *that*!' she'd say, her right foot tapping up and down in anger at even the thought of such effrontery. We brushed our teeth and prised the sleepy dust from our eyes as we wiped our faces with our flannels.

Down the centre of the washroom ran a spine of antiquated metal piping, bristling with hooks. I liked to see this as the excavated backbone of some gigantic, battling dinosaur, but its function was less dramatic than its form, for it was here that we hung the towels we'd brought from home. I'd picked mine with my nanny, Mary, during her last weeks at Park House, and was soon embarrassed by the childishness of its design: it had swan patterns on it, while most boys had opted for a plain primary colour.

Clean, we returned to our dormitories to get dressed, make our beds and brush our hair, before drifting down to the half-landing of the main staircase. Here we mingled with friends and maybe played a game of jacks on the low windowsill, while avoiding eye contact with the bullies, before Granny Ford signalled it was time for breakfast by beating a dappled, brass dinner gong with a mallet whose head was wrapped in the casing of a spent tennis ball.

The first strike of the gong sounded the charge that saw us hurry down the stairs to our designated places at one of the eight tables in the dining room. The central one was by far the largest, all but cutting the room in two. Half of this senior table was for the twelve school prefects, who sat in order of seniority, the head boy and his deputy opposite one another at the top.

If it wasn't a porridge day, we'd get breakfast cereal (generally unsweetened, with Sugar Puffs a rare treat), which would have been poured into our bowls the night before. Once, a friend cried out in horror as the milk that he was pouring flushed a spider out from its overnight resting place under his corn flakes.

There would also be a plated, cooked offering each day: a sausage or a fried egg, or perhaps a slice of fatty bacon rising up from a sea of tangy tinned tomatoes. On each of our side plates sat a rectangle of butter, the size of a boy's thumb. Halved slices of white bread were piled on a communal plate in the middle of the table, with pots of marmalade to hand.

On Sundays – different from all the other days because of its absence of classes and its compulsory church service – breakfast was also distinct: a boiled egg one week and a slice of ham the next. When the ham was on offer, so was a gooey English mustard served in dimpled glass pots with old bone spoons. To fledgling taste buds, it seemed strong enough to stun a horse.

As I had learned my first morning at Maidwell, you had to finish everything on your plate: it didn't matter how long that took, or whether it was breakfast, lunch or tea – you just had to do it. When you were done, you tilted your bowl or plate at the officiating matron, to show there was no food left on it, while calling out 'Please!' If she nodded, you added your empty plate to the pile at the centre of your table.

The dirty crockery and cutlery would be whisked away by the serving staff – May, middle-aged and frizzy-haired, with a livid skin graft on her face, and a pair of tall, giggly twin sisters in their late teens, who had long, curly black hair. These ladies acted as the conduits between the dining room and the kitchen, which was presided over by Annie, who had been cook since the 1930s, when Wyatt first made Maidwell a boarding school. Annie's equally long-serving husband, Frank, silent but smiley, mowed the lawns, tended the boilers and mended our shoes.

Our contact with the outside world, through the media, was carefully curated. Two copies of the *Daily* and *Sunday Telegraph* were delivered to the school library, for us boys to share, alongside upmarket magazines – *Country Life*, *The Field* and the *Illustrated London News* – familiar to many of us from home. If an article particularly appealed to a boy, he was permitted to circle it in pencil, write his name alongside, and later cut it out – a practice particularly popular with the half-dozen children in the school who fanatically followed horseracing.

Each morning, a senior boy would spend breakfast hunched over the school's radio, like a signaller operating deep behind enemy lines. The device was set at its lowest volume, waiting for the top of the hour, when the boy on duty would sit back and twist the volume to high, in time for us all to hear the sharp *pip-pip-pip* that marked the start of the BBC's eight o'clock news.

The whole school had to stop eating and listen to the bulletin in silence. Throughout my five years at Maidwell, there seemed to be an almost daily tally of killings in Northern Ireland, while the overseas headlines majored on American dismay, then disgust, at the faltering war in Vietnam, as well as the slow-motion falls of President Nixon and the Shah of Iran. The latter led to the arrival at Maidwell of two well-heeled boy refugees who were quickly accepted, despite initial surprise at their clothing. They were clad in the boating blazers and camel-coloured, flared slacks that their mother judged to be the school garb of young English gentlemen.

After breakfast we had to go to the bathroom. Granny Ford made the junior boys form a line along the wall outside the loo next to her dispensary. She asked each on exiting: 'Did you go – *properly?*', and if your answer was 'Yes, Please', she pencilled a tick against your name in her small notebook. Repeated failure to deliver resulted in a course of laxatives.

Indeed, Granny Ford seemed endlessly obsessed with our bowels. 'All that shitting,' a classmate recalls. 'We were lined up and given pills until we went.' She liked us to swallow these without water, to save on washing up. She also frequently turned to her giant bottles of syrup of figs and of Milk of Magnesia in her tireless crusade against childhood constipation.

Meanwhile the senior four years of the school processed to 'the bogs', a cavernous double-cube of a room with bare brickwork, situated off a dog-leg corridor between the masters' common room and the boys' changing rooms. You entered the swing doors of this most functional of spaces, to find the urinal facing you across the room. This was wide enough for six boys to use at a time and had no barriers to protect you from another's unintended spray or prying eyes. The bogs had a high ceiling, under which hovered a fug of low smells.

To the right were a half-dozen wooden, light-grey booths, for defecation. You stood in line against the wall till the door of one of these opened and the prefect on duty ushered the next boy in to do his business. Inside, there was a hook for our jackets, but no lock on the door. There was also – unusually for such a place – no graffiti. 'Those who scrawl graffiti are invariably feeble failures,' Jack once decreed, before evening prayers. 'They make a mess on walls to feel better about themselves, and about their inadequacies. I absolutely will not have any such unacceptable nonsense at Maidwell.' There was enough menace in this proclamation to keep the school's walls graffiti-free.

If the supervising prefect felt that a loo's occupant was taking too long with their bodily functions, he'd raise one of his feet and push it, aloft, through the open space under the door, while asking, 'In?' The boy within was obliged to say his name out loud for all to hear, before the prefect made it clear that more urgency and effort were required from the booth's occupant.

After the bogs, we'd go outside. In the winter, we were often perishingly cold, shivering in our inadequate outdoor clothing and needing to keep moving for warmth. If you wanted a companion to walk with you, the Maidwell custom was to ask, 'Would you like to "go round" with me?' In a world where family were exiled to a parallel world, this formal invitation to spend time together had real meaning. It was a sign of friendship desired, and a validation of trust earned. Here lifelong attachments could be formed and strengthened. The two of you might amble round the lake or into the Wilderness, chatting. Alternatively, you could kick a ball about or perhaps throw a frisbee, or fly a model plane. On weekdays this gentle free time was ended by sharp blasts of a whistle. It was time for 'drill'.

Drill was the most militaristic part of the Maidwell day, a fifteen-minute exercise session during which the school was divided into six columns – a dozen pupils in each, the ganglier twelve- and thirteen-year-olds at the front, tapering down to the tiny seven- and eight-year-olds at the back. All faced the front of the school, while a single master in charge kept an eye on every one of the pupils at once, as he paced across the front of each column, checking we were all joining in.

He shouted out the exercises: stretching our hands to the sky, touching our toes in a repetitive bob, flinging our arms out wide for chest expansion, running on the spot, and energetic star jumps. Anyone who dared to ridicule drill, or tackled it half-heartedly, would be called out to the front for an earbashing, before being made to sprint round the entire school – sometimes twice – before rejoining their column, breathless and chastened. Sometimes Jack would appear during drill, in camp commandant mode, hands behind his back and look on as we exercised. He had a beady eye and wore an expression of aloof sourness that seemed to dare us to do something wrong so he could punish us.

Drill was meant to wake us up – 'put some oxygen in yer brains', as the master in charge would say – before lessons began. However, I suspect it was also a way of instilling parade ground discipline into us all, five times a week. The favourite barked order was: 'Squad – attention!' before 'Stand at ease!' At this, seventy-odd boys would launch their right feet outwards in unison, so they landed as one in an almighty crunch in the gravel. This was the sound of institutional conformity.

After drill, it was time to head back inside for the first lesson. We each had our own allotted classroom and class teacher, although other members of staff came by to lead lessons where their specialist knowledge might help. There were also weekly classroom incursions that we dreaded.

The roots of these went back to Tuesday lunchtimes, when Jack sat scouring the dining room for anyone whose hair was touching his shirt collar. He'd scribble their name down, in pencil, on one of the scraps of paper he always had to hand, and this list would be collected by the barber when he arrived at Maidwell on Wednesday mornings.

Part of my end-of-school-holiday ritual, along with a visit to the dentist, would be a descent into the basement of Harrods, for a haircut. I despaired when the hair on either side of my head was hacked too far back, as my chubby cheeks would then appear even plumper. My hair has always been quick to grow back so, as the term progressed, I knew the day had to be approaching when there would be a knock on my classroom door and a freshly cropped boy would enter, saying, 'Sir, can Spencer please go for a haircut now?' I'd trudge up the stairs to the washroom, where the barber would beckon me to climb onto his tall stool. His radio would be playing *The Jimmy Young Programme*, a middle of the road BBC radio show that seemed to have 'Tie a Yellow Ribbon Round the Ole Oak Tree' and the Carpenters on a loop.

Since we weren't there as customers, who might need to be charmed or to offer a view on how the cut was progressing, the barber didn't talk, smile or use a mirror. He just cut away, so chunks of hair rolled to the floor before he applied a vibrating electric razor that slid high up your neck with greedy, chattering teeth. It was now your turn to summon the barber's next victim, and boys would collapse in giggles at the sight of you, freshly and mercilessly shorn, as you entered their classroom.

The rest of the academic day was less disruptive. It consisted of three lessons in the first part of the morning, followed by a thirty-minute break, at the end of which 'grog' would be served. Grog was a hearty snack – of bread and jam, or cold leftovers from the previous evening's supper – laid out by the service hatch to the dining room, alongside giant metallic jugs, containing orange squash in the summer and hot chocolate in the winter.

In our tiny Maidwell world, where obedience was all, a 'grog orderly' was appointed to oversee the food's fair distribution. He ensured that nobody helped themselves to seconds until everyone had had their first turn at the table. The grog orderly was an eleven-year-old, with twenty prefects and sub-prefects senior to him in the school list. But during his ten minutes on duty, the grog orderly outranked all the other pupils, including the head boy.

After grog it was back to the classroom, and a further two lessons before heading to the washrooms to get ourselves clean for lunch. We used coal tar soap whose harsh smell stayed on the hands for hours, and pumice stones to attack the stubborn ink stains on our fingers, before brushing our hair in front of a communal mirror.

In the passage outside, with the school boiler hissing to our right, we lined up in front of a prefect for inspection. We approached this senior boy, one by one, with our hands outstretched as if bearing an invisible tray. He'd look down at them, tell you to turn them over, then he'd look up at your hair. I can still remember the three words he'd utter to those who met his standards: 'Over ... Yes ... Yes.' If there was still ink on your hands or your hair was untidy, you were sent back to try again.

This was all done against the clock. While we washed, brushed and submitted to inspection, the head boy stood on the side of the foot baths next to the showers, counting slowly down from ten to let us know how long we had to be clear of the washrooms. Over perhaps three or four minutes he would shout out: 'Ten ... nine ... eight ... seven ... six ... five ... four ... three ... two ... one...', and then not 'zero' but the idiosyncratic Maidwell culmination of '... going ... going ... gone ... now!' Any boy not fully out of the washroom by 'now!' would be held by a prefect, who put a cross against his name on the school list before releasing him. Too many crosses in a term saw you being sent to Jack for a beating.

Lunch was the best of the meals, presumably because it was the only one where the teaching staff ate with us. We knew, from playing sports against other private schools in the area, that we had the best food around, thanks to Annie and her careful management of the kitchen budget. The finest of the dishes were familiar to us, from home.

For Sunday lunch we had 'roast' – beef, pork or lamb, with roasted potatoes, gravy and a vegetable. Leftover meat from Sunday lunch reappeared in different forms over the following few lunches: on Mondays it was 'cold roast', with the same type of meat resurfacing in rissole form on Tuesdays, and then as shepherd's or cottage pie on Wednesdays. On Thursdays or Saturdays, it might be warm Scotch eggs with baked beans, or another British evergreen, toad in the hole, or perhaps deep-fried Spam fritters. Friday lunch was always fish – either plaice (which swam in thick grease), or fish pie, served rather dry, in square pastry parcels.

The only lunch that caused general alarm was liver, served in a thick, sharp gravy. We were given this once or twice a term. Occasionally a boy would slice open his liver to reveal a thick tube running through it. That, and the occasional appearance of the bitter root crop swede as the vegetable of the day, made for a long lunch, as boys really struggled to finish what was on their plates.

Puddings were generally heavy on the carbohydrates. Rice pudding with a crisp brown skin was more popular than its poor relation, semolina, despite the latter being served with a vivid dollop of strawberry jam. Spotted dick, a dried fruit and suet staple of the British Empire, always provoked schoolboy smirks at the table because of its name, though it was generally consumed with gusto. Arctic roll – vanilla ice cream swathed in a tight wrapping of jam-laced sponge – was also a crowd-pleaser, as was chocolate sponge pudding, because of the chocolate custard that accompanied it. Trifle lightly sweetened our summers.

After lunch we were obliged to read, under supervision, in classrooms, while we digested the solid fare. Many boys brought a book or two from home, and we could help ourselves to a book at a time from the well-stocked school library that stood opposite the dining room. The works of Willard Price were particularly popular. His heroes, Hal and Roger – improbably young zoologists – took time off school to travel widely and collect rare animals. Their adventures – to the South Sea, along the Amazon or on safari – allowed us to imagine a world far removed from the rigid confines of a traditional boarding school in the English Midlands.

During the period of reading, we were allowed to eat tuck. Twice a week Granny Ford would man the tuck shop, unlocking a cupboard at the back of fourth form and laying out the contents on a table before her. A boy would sit at a nearby desk and act as her scribe, recording each boy's purchases in a textbook. Our tuck allowance was up to seven pence on a Sunday and eight pence on a Wednesday. This expense would be deducted from the £3 of pocket money we brought to school at the start of each term.

There were tall, clear plastic jars containing Bonbons and Fruit Salads, and Black Jacks (whose liquorice stained the tongue). You could buy four of any of these for a penny, or indulge in pricier options, of which the most decadent was the Golden Cup, a bar of chocolate-coated caramel that set you back three pence. Tuck became the bartering currency of Maidwell, like cigarettes in a prison. Tuck went missing from our unlockable lockers, but being discovered to be a 'tuck thief' guaranteed universal condemnation, as well as a caning from Jack.

Once a term, Jack would appear during 'reading' and tap you on the shoulder, before beckoning you to follow him. You'd walk, silently, down the dread corridor to 'the wing', and into Jack's study. I found this 'term talk' a gloomy affair, Jack asking general questions and zeroing in on any failings in work, sports or conduct noted by his staff. He demanded justification or a promise to do better. I don't recall him smiling or offering any encouragement during these uncomfortable termly encounters, and I couldn't wait for them to end. Then I'd exit the sinister study, relieved that there'd be no recurrence of this unsettling encounter for four months or so.

One appointment with Jack had to be contended with weekly, though.

Every Sunday morning, before church, he compelled us to learn by heart a passage from the Bible or Common Prayer Book and recite it in front of him, with the rest of the school in attendance. Whether the Creed or the Beatitudes, or a catechism, I found memorising these texts extremely difficult. Jack would sit at his desk in the school's central classroom, then call us forward in pairs, so we could declaim alternate verses as he sat there, eyes drilling into us, irritably correcting small errors. If someone lost his way, or the tiny mistakes mounted up, Jack would wave his arm dismissively and bawl at the flustered child: 'Oh do learn it, you blithering idiot! Why *do* you waste my time? Next!' And the boy would retreat to his desk to study the words some more, before joining the back of the line for a further opportunity at passing this ordeal, made so much harder by the curled lip of the irascible headmaster.

Compulsory organised 'games' took place on most afternoons. There was one, main team sport per term: football in the spring, cricket in the summer, while rugby was contested in the Michaelmas mud. The best players in each discipline competed on a pitch called 'first game', while the standard deteriorated through second and third games, down to the juniors battling it out in merry confusion on 'fourth game'. The masters rarely seemed engaged in these encounters, except when taking charge of first game, having accepted that ours was a school where we were very likely to be defeated when playing against any other, since we had so few pupils.

There were also homegrown Maidwell sports, played when the playing fields were waterlogged by rainfall or frozen. 'Scaramouche' and 'Subs & Cruisers' both had few rules but they each required a lot of running round the school grounds, so were useful for getting small boys to expend excess energy in quick time.

If a child was under the weather, or recovering from an injury, he would be declared 'off games'. Unless seriously unwell – when he would either be confined to the dormitory called 'sick bay', or be sent home – he would be given 'front gate-back gate', an obligatory blast of fresh air, during which he had to walk – at a decent pace, and a set number of times – the third of a mile between the school's main gateway and its service entrance. There was always a suspicion among the staff that boys enjoyed faking illness to get off games, so front gate-back gate delivered the mind-numbing payback foisted on supposed hypochondriacs and malingerers.

One term, when several members of the grounds staff were absent ill, Jack made the boys who'd been declared sick work in the gardens in their place. He reported to the parents how 'Those boys "off games" have been acquiring a deep respect for those who regularly toil about the grounds; instruction in estate work is yet another Extra for which no charge is made.' This was the same 'nudge-nudge, wink-wink' humour that he deployed when writing his sly termly reports. It was all part of the smokescreen he blew around Maidwell to keep its worst side hidden from view, and to make it look like a fun place that he administered with a smile, rather than with the cold, intimidating stare that I will always remember him by.

On Thursday and Sunday afternoons there were no organised sports. Instead, we had 'muck-about', when we were left to our own devices in the school grounds, while a single member of staff patrolled on foot. This was often the happiest of times, when pupils' friendships were strengthened, and the tight control of the school was relaxed for a few hours.

During muck-about boys wore hardwearing denim boiler suits over their sports clothes, to minimise the need for expensive laundry as we ventured out into Maidwell's sweeping grounds.

The youngest boys might spend muck-about playing with their toy boats and model soldiers in Dinky Farm, a muddy offshoot of the ornamental lake. Part of Dinky Farm was composed of a viscous grey clay that sucked greedily at your wellington boots. When you managed to pull your foot free, the morass belched out a foul-breathed protest of methane and sulphur.

During September and October, the first months of the school year, many of us would spend this free time conker-fighting. A giant horse chestnut tree stood at the top of the lawn, on the edge of the Wilderness, and we were allowed to throw sticks up into it, to dislodge the conkers. These we drilled through, threaded with string, then brought for fierce competition in a makeshift amphitheatre in a cut-through bounded by the main school and the concrete steps leading up to Miss Best-Shaw's form.

In the small corner of the grounds that bordered the village churchyard, boys might spend their muck-about afternoons tending their individual garden – tiny patches a few feet square where they grew fruits and vegetables, which they were allowed to eat with their friends during the school's teatime. Boys able to grow strawberries found that their summertime popularity bloomed.

We could be inventive with our fun. At the height of summer, over four days, break and muck-about were given over to the 'Maidwell Grand National'. For this we gathered the grass cuttings left by the school's giant gang mowers and piled them into half a dozen 'fences' that were to be jumped over in a succession of hurdling sprints. At the end of the fourth day, the gardeners retrieved the grass and added it to the mulch that fed what remained of Oliver Wyatt's famed flowerbeds.

The Maidwell Grand National was unsupervised by masters. Perhaps that's why so many of my contemporaries still remember it with such affection: it was our creation, entirely free from the stern control the school usually exerted, so we cherished it.

After muck-about or organised games, we shed all our clothes in the changing room and walked naked to a pair of foot baths where we sponged the mud off our legs in some nine inches of muddy, tepid water. We weren't allowed to progress to the showers till our bodies had been inspected by the staff member on shower duty. It was noticeable that the same two masters seemed almost to take it in turns to be on shower duty – a voluntary responsibility, which they chose to sign up for repeatedly.

We had to stand up on the duckboards on the sides of the foot baths and shout out 'Sir!' to attract this man's attention. He would look up and indicate with his twirling index finger that we must spin round, in front of him and the rest of the school, as he ensured there wasn't a splat of mud hiding on any part of our naked form.

Dressing by my number '64' peg one day, after showering, I heard the blood-curdling scream of a friend who'd caught the loose fold below the shaft of his penis in his zip. We stood around him, at a distance, in open-mouthed horror, not knowing what to do to end his torment. The master on shower duty hurried over, pushed through us, then grabbed the zip and yanked it down hard, freeing the trapped skin. The boy stopped screaming and began to sob deeply. He was now in shock, rather than agony. When the master wandered off, silently, it struck me that he had failed to offer a single word of comfort to a boy in such distress. But the compassion that we'd have naturally received at home was never part of Maidwell's make-up.

After showering we dressed and returned to the main part of the school where, every afternoon, we took part in 'tidy up'. During this ten-minute period overseen by the prefects, every boy had to walk round all the classrooms, eyes down, searching for any rubbish on the floor – staples, hole punches and sweet wrappers. We picked it all up and disposed of it, in a communal activity that was doubtless good for boys from privileged homes. It also spared Jack the cost of employing more cleaning staff.

There were no lessons on Wednesday or Saturday afternoons, when organised team sport was king. On Mondays, Tuesdays, Thursdays and Fridays, there would be two more lessons after games, followed by tea. This, the last meal of the day, would be a simple supper such as macaroni cheese, a triangle of cheddar with a sprig of cress, or a slice of Spam with cloying Russian salad, along with an apple, banana or orange.

The sole recognition of a boy's birthday would be his birthday cake, sent or dropped off by parents, and presented at tea. Biscuit cake was by a distance the favourite flavour, while offering up bland vanilla sponge was seen as an embarrassing faux pas. Granny Ford would stand back to allow you to blow out the candles in front of all the other boys, before she cut the cake into seventy-five small squares, which she placed on two plates. The highest honour you could give to another – one that marked him out as your best friend – was to ask him to help dispense your cake to the rest of the school.

After tea there was 'ragging' (which I will explain later), followed by supervised 'prep' (homework), which concluded the long school day.

Christianity, in its Anglican form, was ever-present at Maidwell. Five nights a week, in the later evening, we had prayers, with a hymn, the music played by one of the many boy pianists: this was a school with eight upright pianos, squeezed into corners of the larger classrooms, into stairwells and vestibules barely big enough to accommodate a piano and stool. We'd rehearse the coming week's hymns in advance. They were drawn from a repetitive roster: the dirge-like 'Immortal, Invisible, God Only Wise'; the moderately upbeat 'Let Us with a Gladsome Mind, Praise the Lord for He is Kind'; with 'Guide Me, O Thou Great Redeemer' one of the few rousing (and therefore popular) numbers allowed us. After the Lord's Prayer, we went upstairs to prepare for another night of dormitory life.

Maidwell's upper floors continued the fetish for hierarchy that shored up the school's daytime. When dormitories weren't given the names of colours, they were known by the part of the hall that they occupied. The majority of new boys started in Pink, as I did, before progressing to Tower when a new intake arrived in the school. In time they moved on to Gold. The eight-, nine- or ten-year-old occupants of the latter two vied for superiority, shouting time-honoured slogans at one another: 'Tower has power!' or 'Gold is bold!' While their qualities seemed open to question, they could both agree on one thing: 'Pink stink!' they would tell the new boys, with finality.

The new boys didn't query this verdict, because everyone around them reinforced the truth that they were non-entities, at the base of the school's sharp-edged social pyramid. 'You're a "squit" when you're a new boy,' a nine-year-old helpfully explained to me on arrival, 'but in your second term you will become a "squirt".' This sounded like a promotion so minimal that it hardly seemed worth looking forward to. But life after that did get better.

While loading my things into my locker on the first day of my third term at Maidwell, a sporty boy a year older than me passed by and said, 'Hello, Spencer!' in a cheery voice. It was the first time he'd ever spoken to me, and I realised I was now no longer a 'squit' or a 'squirt', but an accepted ingredient in the school mix.

However far you progressed up the pecking order, standards of personal hygiene remained pretty grim. In the dormitories, Granny Ford taught us how to strip down our beds, the pupils working in pairs to fold bottom sheets neatly for their weekly wash. We then transferred what had been our top sheets onto the mattress: we therefore slept with that sheet for two weeks.

Each boy was limited to three baths a week, taken on alternate nights. There were no baths on Sundays. Granny Ford supervised bath time with her customary brusqueness, her junior matron in attendance. The ladies were fully in charge, running the taps so that the four bathtubs each contained a few inches of water – enough for washing but not for wallowing.

They took a hands-on approach during the weekly hair wash, to see the job was done correctly. They poured the school shampoo – a pungent, dark-green, anti-dandruff concoction – onto our wet hair and scrubbed it hard into our scalps. We'd then lie back in the bath, holding our flannels tight over our eyes, while Granny Ford or matron rinsed it out, with soapy water scooped up from the bath in enamel kidney bowls. Granny Ford taught us to dry our hair by holding an end of our towel in each hand, placing it on our heads, then counting as we went back and forth, left-right, fifty times each way.

Our clothes were washed even less frequently than we were. We wore our sports jacket and corduroy trousers unchanged for half of each term. Our shirt, underpants and pyjamas were switched just once a week. We had to wear our socks for three or four days at a time. On Sundays and Wednesdays, large plastic containers would be placed outside the washroom for us to lob the dirty ones into. Our handkerchiefs were rarely checked for cleanliness and were known with schoolboy humour – and total accuracy – as 'snot rags'.

There were specific cleanliness issues in the mornings for boys who'd wet their beds. This had been a concern at the school since its inception. Edmund Harvey, an eighty-year-old friend of mine, arrived at Maidwell halfway through the founding headmaster Oliver Wyatt's reign, in the late 1940s. Edmund had turned seven the week before his first night at the school. 'It was a little too young to board, when one only saw our parents twice a term', as he recently told me, with dry understatement.

While Edmund navigated the challenges of being sent away from home as a small child, one of his Maidwell contemporaries – a young lord – was so traumatised by separation from home that he frequently wet his bed. Edmund, three and a half years this boy's senior, would quietly help him to deal with his sodden sheets in the mornings.

Mr Wyatt had no sympathy for any 'bedwetters' among his pupils; he was convinced they could stop what he considered to be their 'dirty habit' if only they had the determination to do so. He viewed bedwetting as shameful and babyish and would have had no time for Edmund's kindness to a traumatised younger boy.*

One of the assistant matrons who was at Maidwell at the same time as me, confirmed recently what I had long suspected: that there was a shockingly high incidence of bedwetting in our school. It's recognised now that emotional and psychological stress can

---

* Years later, the aristocrat invited Edmund to be his daughter's godfather. 'He told me at the christening,' Edmund informed me, 'how very much my kindness back then had meant to him. "Stalwart friendship at a truly vulnerable time", he called it. I was most touched.'

cause children to start wetting their bed again, after outgrowing that phase.

Not long ago Cornelius Holland, one of my older Maidwell contemporaries, shared with me how awful his nights had been, after his arrival at the school, aged seven. 'I was a shuddering wreck, but had nobody to discuss it with,' he recalled, more than half a century later. He began to wet his bed. When this was reported to his parents, they never spoke to him about it, but contracted a bedwetting expert in London who came to Maidwell in a futile attempt to teach him how to stop soiling his sheets.

Granny Ford showed her customary ignorance with those who wet their beds, seeing them as wilful perpetrators of a grubby misdemeanour rather than as victims of trauma. She made them strip their sheets and carry them publicly through the first-floor corridors, to where the laundry was collected. She gave them plastic under-sheets to protect their mattresses, but she did so without compassion for the boys with this humiliating affliction. It was simply viewed as a filthy habit that was embarrassingly babyish. In her view it needed to be eradicated, and what better way to achieve that end than through shame?

Aged eleven, Gregory Clement – humiliated daily for bedwetting, beaten by Jack many times a term and known for his incendiary temper – wrote a fantastical piece in the school magazine which would have revealed his inner turmoil to a more alert audience. In his published essay, Gregory wrote about finding himself imprisoned in a 'forbidding, hostile and totally merciless' state, on an island where he is often punished for no good reason. 'I was marooned,' he wrote. 'Marooned on that accursed island for

God knows how long … I had done no crime, why had this happened to me? … I was only sure of one thing – I was alone. It almost drove me mad. I roamed the island like some wild animal. In one of my more violent moods, I tripped and fell into a rushing torrent. I screamed and shrieked as the waters carried me away to complete and utter oblivion.'

But Gregory's profound unhappiness went unrecognised at Maidwell. His blazing temper and his repeated bedwetting were seen as freakish and unforgivable, and Jack caned him many times each term. When I met up with Gregory recently, he described Jack as 'an outlier' when it came to brutal behaviour among dangerous headmasters. 'There was a certain ritual about the beatings that I find disturbing,' he said.

'But the most disturbing thing about Jack was his farewell to me. He said, "Clement, with you I've failed. I've spent five years trying to break you, but I never succeeded. And now you leave …" I mean, how fucking odd to think that, let alone say it! He beat the crap out of me for five years, out of some need to dominate me. It's beyond belief.'

Incredulity and pained outrage pulsed from this man, who some view as a bit of an oddball loner now, not knowing what he was subjected to during five formative years by a sadistic pervert – one whose crimes were never challenged, even by those adults who witnessed them from up close.

Some of these were even in on the game.

7

Willing Henchmen

All through my school life I was appalled by the fact
that masters and senior boys were allowed quite
literally to wound other boys, and sometimes very
severely.

– Roald Dahl

To keep the more outrageous goings-on at Maidwell secret,
Jack needed his staff to be either enablers, allies or mutes.

Granny Ford knew the humdrum part of her matron's role
consisted of keeping our clothes and bowels in order. But she
valued the special status the headmaster afforded her as reward
for her constant trawl for wrongdoers. 'I have eyes in the back of
my head!' she'd claim, menacingly, when on the scent of a possible
offender. And her default, having finally caught a boy misbehaving, was to shriek, in a rising crescendo of fury, 'Right, you can go
right down to Mr Porch!' She knew that her sentence guaranteed a

caning for the boy, and another spoonful of gratitude for her from the headmaster.

Jack's chief henchman among the teachers was a flawed man with an impeccable pedigree. The Honourable Henry Cornwallis Maude, Maidwell's third most senior master, came from a family that made such a mark as politicians in eighteenth-century Ireland that they were, in time, welcomed into the aristocracy. The Maudes' generations of imperial service led to blood sacrifices around the world: one young ancestor was slain in the Boer War, in South Africa, while another fell in the First World War, in Flanders.

Mr Maude's noble lineage was reassuring to Maidwell's parents. When they came to collect their sons from the school at the end of term, Maude would become a big presence in the front courtyard, mingling with the influx of adults as if he were the life and soul of the most civilised of cocktail parties. His eyes were lively and engaged, and his easy charm whispered soothingly to the parents: 'I know I'm only a schoolmaster, but, of course, I am also one of you. Maidwell is a privileged habitat in which your sons and I equally belong …'

But, as with Jack, when the parents had gone, Mr Maude was quite different. The sophistication and polish disappeared into the magic hat from which they had briefly been pulled, to be replaced with a chilling menace that had long been his hallmark. 'Maude was unpleasant and smarmy, a bully and a sadist,' a Maidwell pupil seven years my senior recalls.

Maude had a powder-keg temper. He went from quiet intimidation to thunderous aggression with astonishing speed and frequency. When he entered his classroom, or hove into view in the grounds, a whiff of imminent danger fell into step with his heavy tread. Most of us boys were so scared of this towering ogre – he was well over six feet tall – that it was as if we dare not give him a nickname: he was only ever 'Maude'.

Maude was in his forties yet had the unathletic legs of an older man. These limbs moved stiffly beneath a pronounced pot belly that was generally swathed in a burgundy V-neck sweater. His face – long and pale, and etched with broken capillaries – was generally set hard, below slicked-down, greying hair that he grew long around the sides so it could be deployed as a comb-over, camouflaging his large bald patch.

Maude's head and throat were excessively punctuated by a pair of prominent outcrops: a Roman nose that stood sentinel above an angry mouth, while an especially active and pronounced Adam's apple churned in his neck, bouncing up and down in shrill outrage during the countless occasions when he was enraged.

I had been terrified at joining Jack's sixth form, given the head-master's air of cold intimidation. Luckily I had only spent two terms in his class, and passed through fifth form in a term, but now, aged nine, fully aware of Maude's ferocious temper, I dreaded entering the fourth form, for this was his domain. His classroom occupied a central room in the school that, when you passed it, invariably echoed to his deep voice booming in anger – some poor boy was being torn apart, while his classmates cringed in fear. The two terms that I spent in Maude's form were the most terrifying of my time at school, for I felt defenceless in the face of perpetual and grave danger.

Although his verbal violence was despicable, Maude's physical abuse was horrific. His stock in trade was to throw chalk and board markers at us during lessons. More seriously, he also cuffed us hard about the head with an open hand and yanked us by the ear as he twisted it round, enjoying the screams of agonised protest. Maude was like a vicious child while causing us pain, sticking his tongue out of the side of his mouth in concentration as he set about his task. When in this mode, he was dangerously out of control: he wanted to hit and he wanted to hurt, and he wasn't going to stop till he'd achieved those twin aims.

'He was really the teacher I feared most,' Thomas Scot recalls, as he thinks back to a Latin test. 'The classroom was silent but for the squeaking leather shoes of Maude as he prowled around over the wooden floorboards, peering over our shoulders to see what we were writing, and eventually he stopped behind me. I tried to move so he couldn't read my answers, but he wasn't having any of it, and he thumped me on my head from behind. I literally saw stars as he hit me; the pain was stunning, and I fell unconscious onto my desk.'

Maude sent another friend of mine, John Okey, spinning into the corner of the class after a flurry of flying fists. He then advanced to finish the job, a lumbering middle-aged man closing in on a wisp of a ten-year-old. As Okey cringed in terror on the floor, his arms covering his face, Maude seized the boy's desk and hurled it over on its side, so it spewed its contents across the middle of the classroom. The rest of us watched, terrified at what our classmate might next be subjected to, conscious that we couldn't help at all.

But luckily, for the time being, Maude's rage was spent, and he stomped back to his desk, washing his hands of the assault.

'Pick your things off the floor!' he barked at Okey.

The boy slowly found his feet, pulled his desk back up and retrieved his things while blinking back tears of fear, pain and humiliation.

Maude liked to march around his classroom with a long window pole slung over his shoulder, like a seventeenth-century pikeman. He would, from time to time, hit us with this weapon – 'on the head and shoulders,' Perry Pelham remembers. 'He once knocked out John Bradshaw with that thing' – a criminal assault that had been hushed up at the time. It is impossible that other members of staff were unaware of Maude's attacks, since the sound of them reverberated round the small school, yet these adults did nothing to protect us.

Maude's main subject was Latin, but he took a dim view of the Romans. He told us that it was no great surprise that their empire had imploded, 'because they spent all their time getting massages – and *that* will turn your muscles to mush,' he said, with the air of one who had studied both muscular and moral degeneration in some depth.

With even greater disgust, Maude told us about the Romans' love of the vomitorium – a room to which they'd retreat, on overeating, to make themselves sick before returning to the dining table for a fresh intake of food. 'Disgusting!' he would cry, in rejection of such un-English ways.

Maude believed in inflicting shame, as well as pain. Once he gave us a slide show, in the shadow of the school's main staircase.

Up popped images from classical art, including the famous bronze of David by Donatello, the graceful hero standing naked apart from his hat and his boots, a large sword dangling from his hand. 'This,' Maude said, as we studied the epitome of youthful male beauty, 'could be any of you in this classroom today.' He paused. 'Other than you, of course,' he added, pointing to a severely over-weight boy. Maude laughed loudly, as the boy's face flushed at the insult and humiliation.

Outside of his classroom, Maude carved out roles for himself, the most prestigious of which was master in charge of swimming. He oversaw the boys' tests, to see how far they could progress through the ranks of learner, swimmer, expert and waterman. Privileges were attached to each grade, with experts and water-men allowed an extra swim on Sunday evenings in the summer and to use the wooden punt tethered in a boathouse on the lake. The watermen, comprising only a handful of senior boys, were taken by Maude for a secret naked swim on Sunday mornings, before chapel, usually in the pool, but occasionally in the lake. At the time we thought this a privilege. Now I see it was a perversion reserved for those twelve- and thirteen-year-olds who were the school's best swimmers and generally of a lither, more coltish build than the younger boys.

When we prepubescents peeled off our underpants, Maude would join in, his member springing up expectantly. I remember wondering if all men had penises so big and bouncy. I had no idea that there was a sexual undertone to this most clandestine of forays, after which Maude would make us dry our hair completely, so nobody would know we'd been in the water with him.

One of my closest friends swears that Maude once told him that he wasn't allowed into the lake except via what that master termed 'the human slide'. This was Maude, naked, leaning against a tree, with an erection. 'I had to go over his huge bush and hard member,' my friend recalls, in understanding now that he was then the victim of sexual assault.

Anthony Stapley – the school's only day boy, who lived in Maidwell village – was another subjected to the worst of Maude. On a summer's afternoon five years before I joined the school, Maude insisted that Anthony must immediately do his 'length' – the initial test of swimming pool competence. Anthony reminded Maude that he couldn't swim, but the master angrily overruled him.

'I entered the pool and started my attempt to swim to the end,' Anthony recounts. 'About halfway, I tried to swim to the side but was pushed away by Maude using the pole with a loop on the end, ironically to support a learning swimmer. Each time I continued, then tried to get to the side he repeated the procedure, with me then trying to grab the pole but to no avail, it being whisked away as I tried to get hold of it, culminating in me sinking to the bottom of the pool. I remember it vividly up until the sinking bit.' The drowning boy had lost consciousness.

Maude jumped in, pulled Anthony, limp, to the side of the pool and gave his victim emergency mouth-to-mouth resuscitation, before carrying him back to the school for further medical care. Anthony remembers that Maude 'scared himself that day as I was lying at the bottom of the pool, gone, with plenty of witnesses'.

Jack seems to have accepted whatever tale Maude concocted about the incident, for there was apparently no retribution for his half-drowning the boy.

'On arriving at each swimming session thereafter I hid under the benches and when found, claimed to have a sore throat, feeling ill,' says Anthony. 'Each time Maude sent me to see Matron and I was allowed not to swim. After six sessions I was sent to see a specialist doctor who decided I needed my tonsils and adenoids removed. What a dilemma …! I knew there was nothing wrong with me but kept it to myself, as you do. I duly had the op, magically survived and by the time I had recuperated summer term was over – so no more swimming sessions.' Terrified by his near-death experience at Maidwell, Anthony only learned to swim in his forties.

Maude added to his poolside fun when establishing the Maidwell Photographic Society in 1973, my first full year at the school. His camera would provide much of the imagery for the school magazine, which he would illustrate with pictures of his favourite boys and their artwork. But he seemed to particularly enjoy taking photographs when in charge of swimming, and while some of the other watermen remember him photographing them when they were naked, these images were presumably for his own use, since they were clearly not fit for publication.

Maude had favourites, who were invariably drawn from the cheekiest and most athletic boys. 'You needed to be pretty,' observes one of them now. A master who was a Maidwell colleague of Maude's remembers him contemplating what weekly mark to give the best-looking boy in the school. 'He's looking lovely and brown, after his time abroad,' Maude mulled, out loud, to his colleagues in the common room. 'So he can have a "three".' This was the highest available grade, reserved for pupils who had worked hardest – not on their suntan, but in class.

On Sundays, Maude would often invite his favourites to his home in the nearby village of Draughton. There they would make alcoholic cider, or elderberry wine, which they were encouraged to sample. Mrs Maude was in evidence during these Sunday visits and her kindness made her popular with the boys. The continued expansion of her family was celebrated, with Jack awarding the entire school a half-day's holiday each time a new little Maude was born.

When this fearsome teacher shared in class one day that he and his wife were expecting their fourth child, Gregory Clement – who tended to lack a filter – shouted out, with a broad grin, 'Goodness, sir, you really do like sex, don't you!' On another occasion Maude was swimming slowly on his back in the school pool, in trunks tight enough to reveal their contents in vivid silhouette. 'Crikey, sir, you really do have big 'uns!' Gregory exclaimed, with good humour and bad judgement. On both occasions Maude flew into a rage that saw Gregory being sent to the headmaster on the spot, for severe canings.

Maude had a dog, named Sam – a whippet that trotted jauntily by his master's side. The one time that I witnessed Maude sad and confused was after Sam's sudden death. 'He always liked to chew things,' Maude told my class the next day, his voice flat with shock. 'But last night he bit into the cable at the back of the fridge … He electrocuted himself.' The teacher was utterly bewildered by the loss, just as we were bemused that this cruellest of men possessed the capacity for love and grief.

Even if you weren't much of a swimmer, and spent only a brief spell in his fourth form, it was impossible to avoid Maude's casual cruelty. Thomas Scot fell hard during a game of tag during our second year at Maidwell. 'I cried and was distressed,' he recalls. 'But Mr Maude, who was in charge of the game, told me I was being a big baby.' Still in obvious pain four days later, Thomas was taken for an X-ray that revealed a broken collarbone. 'When I returned to the school later that day with a clear diagnosis,' he says, 'Mr Maude came up to me and laughed: "I knew you'd broken it!" I knew his nature by then, of course, but I was nonetheless dumbstruck by this callousness. What sort of man would say such a thing to a nine-year-old boy, and *why* would he say it?'

Maude was the most frequent volunteer as master on duty when we boys showered after sports. Lolling against the wall, he would suddenly lurch forward and grab any boy whom he judged to be misbehaving, holding him tight by the arm or wrist, and smacking him hard and repeatedly on his bare buttocks. The naked child squirmed, twisted and turned in a futile attempt to avoid the rain of blows from this determined brute with an exceptionally long reach.

I was one of Maude's watermen – not because I was pretty (for, being ginger-haired and chubby, I wasn't), but because I could swim strongly, thanks to good coaching in the pool back home at Park House. I was therefore among those who secretly went skinny-dipping with him on Sunday mornings, but beyond that he never showed me the slightest kindness, during my five years at

Maidwell, and my main memory of him involves an unprovoked attack.

One summer afternoon, when I was probably ten or eleven, he caught me alone in the boys' boot room* after a cricket match. Without word or warning, he sat down on the bench next to me, roughly hauled me forward by the neck of my shirt and threw me over his knees. He then beat me hard, several times, with one of my cricket boots, its metal spikes puncturing the skin on my bottom in a dozen places.

He had no reason to do this, since I'd done nothing wrong, neither did he have a right to do so, since the headmaster jealously guarded his monopoly on corporal punishment, but Maude knew I'd never dare to report him for his violence, even though it left me in tears of pain and shocked outrage.

It was never said, but we all sensed that Jack was in awe of this disgraceful man who, ironically, carried the hereditary title of 'The Honourable' before his name. Such vestiges of the aristocracy were catnip to the deeply snobbish headmaster: once he announced to the school that a wheelchair-bound duke was coming to Maidwell later that day, as a prospective parent, and Jack's excitement at the ducal visit caught in his throat. But I also think that Jack and Maude recognised in each other a kindred spirit, both being subject to shadowy tendencies that needed to be shielded from the light of the world. At Maidwell their sadism found the perfect secluded habitat in which to thrive – just as the

---

* This was between the boiler room and the changing room, and was where we kept our wellington boots, and footwear for rugby, cricket and football.

poisonous dog's mercury flourished, under the tall trees of the Wilderness, at the rear of the school's imposing grounds.

Adult anger seemed to burn like an eternal flame at Maidwell. Its source could be found in the elegantly proportioned masters' common room, a handsome panelled cube that had been the smoking room when Maidwell was a private mansion. Pupils were never welcome in this sanctuary for the teaching staff. If you had to see a master there on an urgent matter, you knocked at its door with trepidation. A voice – it always seemed to be Maude's – would bark, 'Come in!' in a tone that was more challenge than welcome.

One summer term, I took to borrowing a piece of cricket kit that was kept in the common room. On perhaps my tenth consecutive day of coming to ask for the equipment, Maude drawled to his colleagues, in my full hearing, 'How very dull it is to see Spencer in here yet again.'

His was the dominant personality in the common room. Colleagues were frequently reminded of his private, family wealth, as he liked to phone his London stockbroker in front of them to discuss his investments. Among a staff that drank a lot, he led the charge to the village pub. He'd head to the Stag's Head during weekday mornings, if he had a lesson-free hour to fill, encouraging colleagues to join him.

It was noticeable how differently the masters behaved when in their common room haven. They smiled, and they talked to one another in lighter, warmer voices than those they deployed with us. Theirs was the camaraderie of officers in a mess, thankfully removed from the tedious, distasteful presence of other ranks.

Another of Jack's common room henchmen was Thomas Goffe. Like Maude, he was a seething human cauldron; but Goffe's temperature was kept dangerously high by a different flame: his visceral loathing of social superiority. Since many of Maidwell's pupils were the offspring of aristocrats, landowners, and of England's great banking, brewing and manufacturing dynasties, his normal setting was boiling point.

It's a mystery why 'Goffie' chose to work in such a bastion of privilege. Perhaps it was an act of self-flagellation. Or maybe he wanted to hold sway over the defenceless sons of those absurdly rich adults who turned his stomach. It could be that his reason was more run-of-the-mill, and he simply needed a job that was reasonably well paid, with plenty of holiday time, while living in a beautiful part of England. But whether masochism, opportunism or realism brought Goffie to the school, it was unfortunate for the pupils.

Jack must have known that Goffie's class hatred made him a dangerous pick as an educator of well-to-do boys, far removed from the protection of their parents. I suspect that the headmaster accepted this fiery radical into his ranks because he hoped that such an obviously angry man would subscribe to the harshness that he had set as Maidwell's perpetual refrain. And, in this, Jack proved correct.

In the classroom, Goffie looked at us with brooding contempt, his jaw jutting forward, daring us to upset him. He would move his seat from out behind his desk, so he could stretch his thick-thighed legs into the no man's land that lay between master and pupils, claiming it all for himself.

Goffie's hulking presence was intimidating. Cornelius Holland recalls thinking of him as 'a thug'. Goffie was six foot tall, with the earliest signs of middle-aged spread challenging the lower buttons on his slim-cut white shirts. He liked to lean back in his chair while laying his palms flat over his burgeoning stomach, his fingers tightly intertwined. In this semi-supine state, with his knees locked tight, he would continually roll his heels left and right, so his broad feet dipped from one side to the other with the sluggishness of a waning metronome.

Goffie's square head was planted atop a thick neck. His features were flat, cast across a pasty face that was rolled out like dough around small, tight, joyless eyes and thin, pale lips. Dark-haired, he started out at the school smooth-faced except for a pair of rectangular seventies sideburns. Later he grew a beard that had a surprising touch of ginger to it. His arms were hairy enough to all but block out the skin beneath. His bright, brassy watch glinted from deep within this thick undergrowth.

When giving a pupil a dressing down, Goffie curled his lip and meted out harsh, adult contempt to small, vulnerable boys. If, during these moments of channelled aggression, Goffie called his victim 'me little cock robin', all those listening knew for certain that things were going to get very bad, very fast.

When he wasn't intimidating us, Goffie loved to talk about a previous job, when he'd been a dustman. Towards the end of this nostalgic ramble, he invariably held up a memento of that demanding, physical time: a little finger that he'd broken on his rounds, which had set crooked. The pain of the break had been passing, but his pride at this injury was perpetual. It set him dramatically apart from the cosseted boys that he found in his care. It was almost as if, to him, the twisted digit was a battered hammer and sickle that countered the ostentatious coats of arms of his most privileged pupils.

Goffie liked to weave his political theories into our classroom work. He warned us that when we reached adulthood, because of our pampered backgrounds and privileged education, we had a duty to only accept elite employment. To take lesser jobs, he said, would be akin to stealing another man's livelihood. If we sank to that, it'd be like taking food out of a poorer family's mouths.

At a time when Britain's inflation rate was particularly high, Goffie complained to us that many people were overpaid, adding that he'd be prepared to accept a lower salary, 'provided those who think themselves somehow above me suffer too'. These were complex points for boys so far from working age to understand.

More baffling still was a proposition that he put to my class when I was perhaps ten years old. 'If I gave you this choice,' he asked us, 'which option would you choose? *Either* you could die *or* your life could be spared but your mothers and fathers would have to die instead ... Go on, which would you choose?'

While this is clearly a bizarre topic to pose to children, it was a particularly callous one to present to youngsters whose daily wish was to be reunited with their absent parents. But now it's clear to me that there was cruelty behind Goffie's question: he wanted to shake our fragile worlds.

Seeing the shock and astonishment on our faces, Goffie warmed to his theme: 'In fact, let me put it this way: what if the choice was for you to lose your life or for your mothers, fathers and all your brothers and sisters and your grandparents to lose theirs instead?'

We looked at each other incredulously. It took time to formulate our answers, but as they started to flow it was immediately clear that we were unanimous: we would all prefer to die than survive in a state of the most appalling grief. As one boy said: 'Sir, if we chose to save ourselves, what would be the point of our lives without our families anyway?'

But Goffie would have none of it, waving away our opinions as the sentimental twaddle likely to emanate from half-formed minds: 'When it came to it – I mean, when the moment of your death actually arrived – you would choose to live, and let all the others die. Trust me.' We dared to titter in disbelief at how wrong we felt him to be, but we didn't dare to laugh at Goffie. Indeed, I only remember two occasions when anyone was brave enough to do that.

The first happened one lunchtime in the school dining room. A pea rolled off Goffie's fork and lodged firmly in the outer tendrils of his thick beard. Vividly green, and moving up and down as he chewed, it was impossible to miss. Excited whispers rippled round the dining room, and when Goffie looked up from his plate he was taken aback to see dozens of boys fixated by something about his person that he gathered was below his eyeline but which he could neither see nor feel. It was making the schoolboys collapse into giggles. And for a few moments this frightening, humourless bully knew what it was like to be judged ludicrous and to be mocked.

He barked furiously at the boys on his table, demanding they tell him what on earth was going on, and one of them bent forward to let Goffie know in a whisper what was causing the hilarity. He prodded his beard with stubby fingers till he located the offending pea and plucked it out. The rest of the school accepted that the show was over and returned to their normal chatter, but the boys on Goffie's table felt the blast of his fury for, in his view, having exposed him to general ridicule.

The second occasion on which Goffie was the butt of laughter was, I'm pleased to say, my fault. He had a particular dislike of me, which perhaps stemmed from my family's local prominence. Whatever his reason, he was a terrifying menace during my time at Maidwell, so I count this occasion as one of the high points of my early life. It was my sole moment of one-upmanship, against a powerful and relentless adversary.

I was one of the pupils who Goffie would physically hurt. He lashed out at me during class time, thumping me across the head with his wide, hairy hands so that I reeled with a dizziness and throbbing pain that I'd not known since the wall- and head-bashings that Nanny Forster had meted out at Park House. He wore a chunky, gold-coloured signet ring, and on several occasions he caught me with this during his thunderous slaps, intentionally rolling his hand over at the last second so the ring's front would cut open my scalp.

He got away with this because, back then, I had a thick mat of red hair, and the trickles of my blood would congeal into the roots before drying there, invisibly. One of my classmates, Daniel Blagrave, wrote to me recently, 'I remember clearly the vile Goffe hitting you and drawing blood. It was physical abuse pure and simple.'

At the time I calculated that, Goffie being in his mid-thirties, he was twenty-five or so years older than me. I knew that I had no hope in a contest with someone more than twice my size, but I was comforted by a promise that I made to myself: when I got to be in my mid-thirties, I would seek out this thug and dish out suitable revenge at a time when my tormentor's strength must have waned.

Goffie was in charge of the school's football team, but that was my weakest sport, so I never entered his orbit on the playing field. However, we were destined to be repeatedly thrown together in the classroom: he was the master in charge of history, my favourite subject. Yet our common love of the past failed to bring us together, except in jolting duels.

Goffie liked to teach in a structured, linear way, which was effective in its prime task of getting Maidwell boys to pass exams that gave access to their parents' choice of senior school. But this spoon-feeding of information left little latitude for, or appreciation of, pupils who had a love of the subject that extended beyond the rigid syllabus.

I devoured history books from the school library, and my parents sent me others on all aspects of military history. Jack wrote to my parents at the end of one term, when I was eleven: '[Charles's] own private reading continues to be wide ...', before he noted, '[but] things have not gone as well as they should in his history lessons; I rather suspect, perhaps wrongly, some element of personal conflict [with his teacher].'

The headmaster knew of the tensions between Goffie and me but, to the best of my knowledge, chose never to address them in person. Perhaps he thought it risky to take to task a tricky master, whose silence about Maidwell's dirty secrets he greatly appreciated. It was certainly safer for him not to upset such a volatile figure as Goffie. In any case I was left to defend myself against a formidable, adult bully, without help from above.

One term we'd been studying early eighteenth-century English history. During this course, Goffie took us through the Battle of Blenheim, a crucial but little-taught engagement in which John Churchill, 1st Duke of Marlborough, defeated the supposedly invincible forces of France's Louis XIV. By chance, I had been given a book on that battle by my father, because we had a family connection to the victor. My father was so amused by my fascination with the engagement that he took a photograph, which I still have, of me reading this book while on a family holiday in Paris, the Sun King's capital.

In a written test a few days later, Goffie set as one of his questions: 'Put down as many generals who fought in the Battle of Blenheim as you can, apart from the Duke of Marlborough.' He was seeing if we could remember the names of the French and of the Austrian commanders, both of which he'd mentioned to us earlier in the week. Unbeknown to Goffie, I'd recently studied Blenheim's battle plan in great detail and had found myself intrigued by the exotic names of many of the leading players from that fateful summer's day in 1704.

At the end of the test, Goffie told us to swap papers with the pupil sitting nearest to us. I exchanged mine with Richard Ingoldsby, and when we got to the answers to his question about Blenheim's generals, Goffie said, 'Marshal Tallard of France and Prince Eugene of Savoy.'

'Sir?' said Ingoldsby, holding up his hand. 'Spencer has put down twenty-four generals' names for this one!'

Goffie looked at me as though I was either a lunatic or a fantasist. Sensing that my humiliation was guaranteed either way, he smiled a thin smile and lay back in his chair, hands on stomach, and said, 'Read 'em out!' So Ingoldsby did: 'Eugene, Tallard, Marsin, the Elector of Bavaria', and so on, through my list, till ending with 'Churchill'.

'Aha! *No marks*, Spencer!' Goffie shouted, triumphantly. 'I said, "*apart from* John Churchill, Duke of Marlborough" and you've put down Churchill. You should listen to the question, next time, me little cock robin!'

'But, sir,' I replied, 'I haven't included the Duke of Marlborough. The Churchill I'm referring to is General Charles Churchill, Marlborough's brother ...'

Goffie looked at me incredulously. He blinked and gulped hard, before slowly flushing with rage and embarrassment. The whole class whooped with delight at the spectacle of a brutish master being publicly humiliated by the boy he particularly picked on.

Of course, Goffie's nastiness towards me increased after that, but it was worth it. At Maidwell, we pupils were always outgunned by the most malicious members of staff; but I've always been grateful to the Battle of Blenheim for giving me one rippling broadside of success that I could treasure forever.

Mine proved a small victory in a losing campaign – after that day, when I looked up in class, I often found Goffie staring at me with cold fury – but it kept my morale high. I view this as a token win against one of Maidwell's most frightening teachers.

But what were these men thinking, when exerting all their adult power against defenceless prepubescents? And surely it shouldn't have been up to mere boys to stand up to men as obviously wicked as Goffie, Maude and Jack?

8

Potential Saviours

The truth of the matter is that you always know the
right thing to do. The hard part is doing it.

– General Norman Schwarzkopf

The only way in which such an alarming trio as the
headmaster, his aristocratic sidekick and the thuggish history
teacher could have been neutralised would have been if
another adult at Maidwell had stood up to them and acted as
whistle-blower.

There was never any hope that the deputy headmaster, John
Learmont, could have made such a brave stand. His senior position gave him an unobstructed view of the rottenness that ran
through Maidwell's core, but he was a weak-willed man who was
unlikely to have ever addressed it. I suspect that's why Jack chose
him as his second-in-command.

We called Learmont 'Leo', but he had none of the lion-like
qualities that his nickname suggested. Rather, he seemed

consumed with disappointment and resentment. Leo was a strange-looking man. The top of his head was a bald, pink dome that flaked under the summer sun, while lower-down white curls abounded, looping like the piping on an improbably ornate wedding cake. He had the tonsure of a monk, but the demeanour of a man who had yet to find his vocation.

It's hard for a small boy to judge a man's size, but I reckon Leo must have been six feet tall and weighed around seventeen stone. He carried his mass cautiously, on rigid legs that ended in buffed, laced brown leather shoes of great robustness. They had hobnails in their soles, which made an important noise when he walked on hard surfaces.

The headmaster gave his deputy demeaning duties. At the summer sports day, when all the parents descended on the school, he was deployed as the scribe, noting down the result in every heat of each competition. This prevented his interacting with the adult visitors.

In the winter, when the lake froze, Jack would ask him to use his bulk for the good of the school. 'The heaviest master called Mr Learmont is going to walk on the lake to see if the ice is thick enough for us to skate,' I wrote to my mother excitedly in December 1973, after two days' snow.

To counter such humiliations, Leo tried to impress the pupils. While we abandoned swimming in the unheated pool in October, when its temperature dipped below forty-eight degrees, Leo would make great play of taking his daily dip for a further month. He liked to boast that there was no need for towels, except for a quick final rub, since you could brush most of the water off you with the flat palms of your hands – a trick he said he'd learned when serving in the Navy.

Leo was proud to identify as a Yorkshireman, subscribing to the cliché that Englishmen from that northern county are no-nonsense, tough and to the point. He told us often of his allegiance to Leeds United, in those days one of the more successful football teams, again from Yorkshire. Equally, he enjoyed declaiming music hall acts from decades past in his native county's distinctive brogue.

I suspect all this relentless Yorkshireness was his way of distancing himself from what he saw as the softness of this pampered, southern school, where he served without distinction. It is his tragedy that he never understood just how distinguished he would have been if only he'd chosen to call time on the abuses all around him.

One of my Maidwell friends asked me recently, 'Why didn't Leo do something to help us? He was the deputy, and it was down to him to report what was going on.' But Leo wasn't made of the right stuff.

As was normal with such a small teaching staff, Leo's responsibilities were many and varied. He was in charge of French, of the school rugby team, of the choir and of teaching the violin. French was one of my better subjects, I was in the rugby team and in the choir, and I scratched away at the violin, so our paths crossed frequently. What I saw was an uninspiring man, so disappointed in his own limitations that he raged impotently at the world.

An older classmate remembers the deputy headmaster as being 'In the same bracket as Porch: serious and slightly scary. Nobody ever fucked about in his classes.' When Leo appeared on the rugby field in shorts so tight around the crotch that another of my classmates recalls them as 'grotesque', we whispered about them rather than openly mock them.

Leo played the piano fluently and led the school's weekly hymn practice. But if we failed to hit the right notes, he would quickly become furious. His face flushed, and his eyes and lips constricted, while his stout hands thumped the piano keys with a force that betrayed his tightly wound inner workings. At such moments the nastiness that infused many of Maidwell's masters broke the surface.

Leo never threatened us with physical violence, but I don't remember him once being kind, and he could be curiously sharp, while his quick temper made him prey to misjudgements.

One winter's morning, when walking with friends in Maidwell's front courtyard, I started blowing on my hands and said I'd be back soon, as I wanted to nip back into the school to get my gloves.

A younger boy, George Monck, mentioned that he was heading back to get his own gloves and said he'd pick up mine at the same time. I told him there was no need, but he kindly insisted and I thanked him. I'd have done the same for him, but he got his offer in first.

A couple of minutes later, Leo appeared, bristling with anger, Monck scurrying to keep up by his side. 'Who do you think you are, you insignificant worm?' Leo bellowed at me. 'How dare you send another boy to get your things for you?'

'But I didn't, sir,' I said, and explained what had happened.

'Spencer's right, sir,' confirmed Monck, leaving Leo stumped, the victim of his own biting prejudice against a pupil with a particularly privileged background. He harrumphed and chose to stomp off, rather than apologise.

Such an unfocused, self-regarding figure was never going to have the resolve or spine to confront Jack. But others, of lesser status in the school, were braver. In my second year at Maidwell, while in Jack's sixth form, I was taught maths by a warm, middle-aged teacher who possessed a kind, quiet charm. Miss Vecqueray would dip in and out of the school in a small car – she insisted on living at home so she could care for her ailing parents. During her workday at Maidwell, she would leave her adoring dog, Andy, in her car, his ears pricked on alert watch for his mistress's return.

Miss Vecqueray was a gifted teacher. She kicked off her lessons with quickfire rounds of mental arithmetic, the benefit of which remains with me still. She also inspired us in ways that the more traditional staff must have scorned.

Pupils were forbidden to use the school's front door, except on the first and last days of term when our trunks were being shepherded in or out. But Miss Vecqueray would lead us through them, into the front courtyard, before sending us in various directions to work out mathematical angles in a living, open setting, rather than merely on paper, at our desks. Meanwhile in the science lab, she had us scrambling round on our knees, counting square floor tiles to help our calculations, making her subject into an enjoyable game instead of a dull discipline.

Occasionally, she would take some of us in her car, which one of my contemporaries describes as 'an hour of kindness in a very brutal existence'. She was used to helping others locked up against their will, spending some of her spare time educating inmates in a nearby prison.

Miss Vecqueray cared about our living conditions at the school and would complain to the headmaster about how unnecessarily chilly the place was in winter. During his visits to the masters' common room, she'd ask him to turn on the heating, while rubbing her hands on a teapot to emphasise how cold it was.

One term in 1974, Miss Vecqueray failed to reappear in the classroom. Nobody explained why. We had last seen her looking frailer than normal and using a cane. Eventually we heard rumours that she had contracted cancer. After her diagnosis, she took a cruise that was paid for by grateful Maidwell parents. She returned, was admitted to hospital and soon died. When she did, we pupils lost a rare ally in the common room – one who challenged the norms.

At the start of my third year, Michael Barker arrived as her replacement. He was six foot four, square-shouldered, with dark, wavy auburn hair and a turned-up nose. He'd been something of a sporting hero when a pupil at Wellingborough, a senior boarding school near Maidwell, and we boys thought it glamorous that he spent his Saturdays as a linesman in professional football matches around England.

To me Mr Barker was, by a huge distance, the nicest master in the school. He seemed to like us boys and got to know our personalities. In an institution that was paring away at our individuality and self-worth, this was immensely appealing. He made us value ourselves and, bored by the humdrum, he added humour to his classroom, livening up his questions by using names ridiculous enough to make children chortle: once, when we had to work out a ship's velocity, he called the vessel 'the Saucy Sal'. Such gentle silliness livened up maths considerably: we giggled, before settling down to our set questions with purpose, eager to impress this teacher who was, happily, so different from the others.

Mr Barker didn't just change my outlook to maths, he also changed my name. He said I didn't suit the formality of being called 'Charles' and declared he would instead call me 'Matt'. The quirkiness of this appealed to me, and I went along with it.

In conversations after lessons, I confided in Mr Barker how much I hated being away from home. 'I'd rather go to a state school than continue as a boarder here,' I said. 'At state schools they go home at the end of each day …'

Mr Barker smiled: he had taught in a deprived area of England and told of the incest some of his pupils had suffered there, as well as other hard to imagine terrors. 'No, Matt,' he said, 'you're too precious a flower to ever be allowed to go to state school.' He saw how crushing I found his conclusion: 'We're just going to get you through this, and you'll be fine,' he added, and I believed him. I don't recall a similar moment of thoughtful encouragement from any of the rest of the staff during my entire time at Maidwell.

It'd be wrong to paint Mr Barker as a saint. This extremely powerfully built man's temper could be terrifying. His face turned puce, while his voice boomed. But he was never physically threatening, and the flashes of wrath soon burned themselves out.

I feel that Mr Barker had a clear view of how cruel several of his colleagues were. I would catch him looking at the worst of them out of the corner of his eye with evident disgust. But given his junior status in the staff, he knew he was not in a position to do much about it.

David Johnson – in his late fifties and early sixties when we overlapped at Maidwell – was the oldest master there. He had been a lawyer, but found the grind of that profession unfulfilling, and so turned to teaching. While proud of one of his brothers-in-law for winning the Nobel Prize for Physiology, Mr Johnson had limited academic ambitions.

He seemed content to remain a mid-ranking all-rounder in Maidwell's teaching hierarchy, despite his age and intelligence. 'The higher the monkey climbs the tree,' he'd tell his colleagues in the common room, 'the harder he falls on his arse!' So he busied himself at the school, while averting his eyes from the crimes around him.

Mr Johnson had a striking physical presence. He was of medium height, but his plumpness made him appear shorter. Livid rosacea cast across his face in a flush that extended down into the creases of his jowls, lending him the hue of an angry turkey cock. His fine head of thick silver hair – slicked back in a scentless sheen – was of a generous length that never seemed to vary. He would comb this mane with slow, exaggerated strokes while staring intently into one of the many mirrors dotted around the school. His comb was always to hand, in his jacket's top outer pocket, behind a white handkerchief whose triangular top pointed rigidly skyward.

Mr Johnson's clothes were hardy perennials. His sports jacket had dark panels with rust-coloured checks, while his shirts (cotton in summer, woollen in the cooler months) were white, etched with the thinnest of coloured lines. He favoured sweaters in warm tones – burgundy or butterscotch – and they had an exaggerated V-neck that plunged to the point where his belly started to billow out. His ties were navy blue or darker, and his trousers had turn-ups, under which flopped the laces of his sand-coloured hush puppies. He trod softly in these, his toes pointing outwards more than most, but his bulk meant you could always hear him coming – rubber soles kissing the wooden floorboards with a bouncy, swishing squelch.

We called this man with dark-brown eyes, sprouting eyebrows and thick-framed spectacles 'Johnno', and we did so with some affection. He engaged with us in light conversation and used our nicknames when doing so. He had a sense of humour that he shared as generously with us boys as he did the sweets that always rustled in a paper bag in his pocket. We couldn't help but feel his warmth.

For those of us desperately missing our pets at home – my letters to my mother often led with 'How are all the animals?' – we loved hearing Johnno talk about his cat, Mugwump. We never met Mugwump, since the Johnsons lived in a cottage in the village that was out of bounds, but we warmed to tales of this cat's boundless gluttony and laziness – delicious snippets of domestic life that briefly transported us far from our regimented existence. From the few interactions we had with Mrs Johnson, when she popped by to drop off something for her husband, we knew she was quietly kind. I liked to imagine that Mugwump had a pretty fun life, his food bowl chock-full of treats.

I see now that Johnno had the wisdom and the wherewithal that might have enabled him to blow the whistle on those corrupting forces who ruled Maidwell. To his credit, he subverted Jack's ability to cane boys when they fell short in their weekly marks by making sure that he was the last of the masters to write down his grades. Two of those in the Saturday Morning Club have told me, separately, that a 2 for good effort from Johnno saved them from dipping below the minimum allowed aggregate of 7, thus sparing their buttocks from the viciousness of the Flick – for that week, at least.

But Johnno was in awe of Jack – an awe that I believe was shot through with fear and sycophancy. When composing the lyrics for one of the school's annual in-house musicals, Johnno concluded the main song with a climactic salute to the man he hailed as 'Jack – that great master of Maidwell'. And while in the principal's presence, Johnno would wear a weak, obsequious grin, from which his eyes remained disconnected, while he pulsed mild panic.

Johnno knew about the cruelty, and he had a trained legal mind that surely could have framed a coherent report of the grave transgressions he had witnessed. But for all his charm, Johnno was unable to rise to the challenge. Worse, he even aped some of the abuses; for, disappointingly, he had a nasty side. Once this flowered, there could be no possibility of his doing the right thing for us boys.

At his worst, Johnno could change from cheery friendliness to shouty fury in a second. Oblivious to his own hefty girth – or perhaps because of it – he liked to address any overweight pupil as 'little fat boy'. One of his regular victims was the Honourable Thomas Grey, a lord's son who (despite his larger size) was one of the school's leading athletes. One day in class, Johnno called Grey 'little fat boy', and Grey had had enough. To our incredulous delight, he replied 'Yes, little fat man?'

Johnno went berserk, spewing molten rage, his face transforming from its customary red into a rich crimson. As he began to calm down a little, he formulated a sentence suitable to the slight: 'You will go *right now* and report yourself to the headmaster *on the spot!*' Grey stood up, shocked and crestfallen, exited the classroom door and took himself down the ominous corridor at the end of which stood the headmaster's study door. After knocking, he was summoned in, and found Jack at his desk. Grey had to explain to him why Mr Johnson had sent him there.

It would have been pointless trying to put things into context by explaining Johnson's taunts. Such a defence would have been deemed impertinent and deserving of an even harsher reckoning.

There could be no forgiveness for a boy who not only had answered back, but had insulted the elder of the common room. Jack told Grey to pull down his trousers and underpants, and to assume a kneeling position on the pouf, where he was caned six times with the Flick. If Grey learned any sort of lesson from this episode, Johnno failed to. He continued to deploy his 'little fat boy' gibe liberally.

Like Jack, Johnno presented as a pious Christian. He spent his afternoon off each week mowing the grass in Maidwell's churchyard, next to the school. His religious beliefs strayed into the classroom. In the school's gym one day, Cornelius Holland spread his arms out and laced them through the climbing bars behind him, before jokingly proclaiming, 'Look! I'm Jesus on the Cross!'

'Blasphemy!' screamed Johnno, in a tone that touched falsetto, and sent Holland to Jack for an immediate thrashing.

These spectaculars aside, Johnno's day-to-day unpleasantness involved pelting boys with blackboard chalk. If he spotted a pupil failing to pay full attention to his lesson, he would strike him as hard as he could with these multi-coloured missiles – his right arm going back slowly to full slingshot position, then whipping forward at maximum velocity. When Johnno hit a boy, he congratulated himself loudly on his marksmanship – 'Good shot, sir!' While he once hit one of my friends on his eye socket, it's amazing that, to the best of my knowledge, he never caught anyone flush on the eyeball.

Meanwhile Johnno was the martinet who led the school's daily drill, where he maintained parade ground discipline. What an odd sight we must have made – seventy-five boys bobbing and weaving, in all weather, while being shouted at by an overweight man, well beyond his prime.

PE was another of Johnno's incongruous offerings. Tucked away near the back gate, the school gym was little more than a tall, unheated barn, with stark lighting and basic equipment: climbing bars running up the main wall; a vaulting horse, draped in battered brown suede; while worn, brushed leather medicine balls lay largely unused in a corner. Four thick ropes, the colour of tobacco-stained fingers, flopped down from the gym's ceiling.

Perhaps one reason for Johnno's move from practising law to teaching boys at this prestigious boarding school could be found in his marked snobbery. He must have studied the boys' backgrounds in some depth for, at the end of our weekly gym sessions, he would order us all to stand at ease in front of him, waiting to be individually dismissed by his cryptic utterances.

When he said, 'My family owns half of Yorkshire', Richard Ingoldsby would run off to shower and change. Likewise, 'We live in a castle in Cornwall' would see Cornelius Holland start to head back to the main school.

Yet Johnno's own background remained a mystery to us. He liked to drop hints about a somewhat puzzling military past – one that, given his age, must have encompassed the Second World War.

One of his thumbnails was crushed and corrugated: it had turned the colour of dried mustard. Someone was brave enough in class one day to ask him what had happened to it.

'I caught it in the breech of a cannon.'

'In the Artillery, sir? What rank were you?' the boy pressed.

'I just couldn't say,' he replied, with a modest smile. 'It was all so long ago.'

We shouted out our guesses, and his hints left us with the strong impression that he had ranked somewhere between a captain and a colonel.

'A major, then, sir?'

He smiled enigmatically, without clarification. It was all rather odd. The suspicion has always remained with me that, if he ever had served as an officer, it was probably as a junior one.

It was easy to set Johnno off on a red herring, where he would talk at length about a topic that we had slipped into the class conversation. As he warmed to his theme, we could put our pens down, relax and silently congratulate ourselves on having got him off track. Once he spent an entire class talking about appendicitis and what he believed caused it – 'If you swallow twenty-nine pips from a tomato, one of these could end up in your appendix.' This deeply unscientific analysis was welcome, when we should have been discussing, say, the monks of Anglo-Saxon England.

During one lesson he set the scenario of us pupils being soldiers in Northern Ireland, conducting a house-to-house search for terrorists. 'You walk into someone's kitchen, and there's a bottle of whisky on the table ...' John Okey butted in mischievously, 'Oh goody – I'd help myself to that!' We laughed, but Johnno paused. He smiled victoriously and said in a still voice, 'And then, Okey, you'd be dead. The whisky bottle has been boobytrapped by the IRA. Boom!' He threw his arms out wide, a massive grin on his face.

Johnno led musical appreciation, a Wednesday evening fixture when we read at our desks while he played us records from his collection. He favoured old-fashioned humour, particularly the nineteenth-century comic operas of Gilbert and Sullivan, as well as the ditties of Flanders and Swann, a pair of Oxford graduates popular in the 1950s and 1960s. The material harked back to Britain's imperial era, when humour and racism were allowed to overlap. Johnno's favourite song of theirs was about the ghastliness of foreigners, with the refrain: 'The English, the English, the English are best, I wouldn't give tuppence for all of the rest ...'

His love of music saw him write the school concerts, composing fresh lyrics for established tunes. In one I played a fourteenth-century English king, Edward III, while my stage queen was my first Maidwell friend. 'The boy who stole the show,' recorded the school's review, 'was undoubtedly William Purefoy, portraying Queen Philippa with considerable verve and nerve.'

In another of Johnno's productions, I was an investigative journalist. On Radio Luxembourg in the mid-twentieth century, there was a regular musical interlude promoting Ovaltine, a malty, bedtime brew. It started:

We are the Ovaltineys, little girls and boys
Make your requests, we'll not refuse you
We are here to amuse you ...

Johnno borrowed the lilting, playful music from the commercial, while changing the words to:

We are the boys of Maidwell, happy little boys
Now our concert is before you
We do hope it will not bore you ...

These words are revealing of the culture that Johnno, for all his laughter, knew to prevail in the school. To claim that we were 'happy little boys' misrepresented the truth. Many of us were miserable.

We had the adaptability of youth, though, and the instinct to make the best out of a bad thing, which often involved the forging of good friendships. We were not 'happy', but coping.

And why should we worry that our best efforts to entertain would somehow 'bore' our audience? It reminds me of that ugly Victorian line that 'children should be seen and not heard': a dictum that anticipates children being incapable of saying anything of interest to an adult.

But the lyrics that Johnson composed that have remained uppermost in my memory, more than four decades on, are these:

> At ten to six, it doesn't take two ticks to get covered in
>   perspiration;
> I like a rag, a good old Maidwell rag –
> Give me some blood on the floor.

In an unguarded moment, Johnno – good old, jolly old Johnno – unwittingly delivered up the key that unlocks a door to some of Maidwell's more telling peculiarities.

9

Blood on the Floor

Macho does not prove mucho.

– Zsa Zsa Gabor

The 'ragging' referred to in Johnno's song comprised a daily ten-minute period of physical aggression when Maidwell's pupils were made to burn off energy and settle scores in a lightly supervised free-for-all. Each evening the school's handsome central hallway became a wrestling ring, with no pupil excused the melee.

The tradition of ragging had been established during Oliver Wyatt's headmastership. One evening during the Second World War, Wyatt's boys ragged so fiercely that they tore down blackout blinds – required on windows to deny German bombers tell-tale flickers of light from the ground. This prompted an angry visit from the police. But ragging survived this interest from the law, and flourished. By the time I arrived at Maidwell, it had long been the fulcrum of the school's evening schedule.

Tea ended at ten to six. While those due to be beaten by Jack exited left out of the dining room – faces tense and pale, stomachs churning – the rest of the boys turned right, bellies full, ready to do battle with one another. They peeled off their jackets and draped them over the main staircase's banister, creating a lumpy mound of green and brown tweed. Adversaries were selected, and ragging began.

It was fighting at its clumsiest, involving one-on-one grappling, with opponents pushed, tripped or hurled to the floor, where violent tussles continued. A junior master would be notionally on duty, occasionally casting an unconcerned eye over the jumble of thrashing bodies.

Ragging's few rules had been passed down by previous genera-tions of pupils, with basic fair play in mind: scratching, biting, kicking and half Nelsons were forbidden, while judo throws and punching an opponent's torso were allowed. The greatest no-no was hitting someone below the belt – in the 'grollies', as we called testicles. Equally, any call for air had to be honoured instantly.

Ragging was rough enough to make tears inevitable. Some boys wouldn't know their own strength, and the disparity in weight between the slightest and the largest could be considerable. At the same time, the school's bullies found their worst instincts vali-dated and encouraged by this daily brawl.

Heads would bump together, or they might be shoved hard into the unforgiving wooden floor that contained an endless stock of splinters. I recorded in my diary how, one evening, a boy's lip struck the floor so hard that it erupted in a bloody explosion. The first time that one of my friends ever saw stars was during ragging, after hitting his head against the iron, Victorian radiator that stood against one of the hall's walls. His temple missed its sturdy, barrel-shaped tap by a couple of inches.

We ragged, and ragged hard, until the master on duty jangled the school handbell at six o'clock, signalling an immediate end to hostilities. We put our jackets back on, straightened our ties and made for our classrooms. As we rubbed fresh bruises and allowed our panting to subside, our minds moved quickly on to the evening prep that was our last academic work of the day.

Ragging was also allowed any time we were outdoors, in the grounds. In an old-fashioned school like Maidwell, in the mid-1970s, such fighting was seen as a healthy activity for small boys: it wasn't so much permitted as encouraged – an outlet for aggression that was the core strand in the surprisingly hardy regime that thrived beneath the school's veneer of gentlemanly civility.

Maidwell even fostered a form of knife culture, with every boy expected to have his own sheath knife, and often a penknife as well. The sheath knife dangled from your hip throughout the day – being taken off only when playing sports, when ragging or when entering your dormitory.

The way in which we all carried these weapons remains, to me, one of the more puzzling aspects of my Maidwell years. At the time, boys might have taken small penknives as useful tools on camping trips. But how could anyone have thought that seven- to thirteen-year-olds having six-inch blades to hand was a good idea? Such knives have been illegal in Britain since the 1980s, even for an adult. Yet ours were such an accepted part of the school that Jack bought us a sharpening stone, with oil, so we could keep our blades keen at all times.

Our knives were cherished and admired. My first sheath knife was given to me by my father after a trip to Norway: it had naive engravings on its antler handle. By the time I was twelve, I possessed half a dozen. The one I prized most was a commando dagger with a blade nearly seven inches long. Jack once borrowed it during a classroom science experiment, to stir some crystals in a giant test tube. But even that weapon, with a wartime provenance, couldn't compare to Nicholas Love's favourite blade.

Love, three years above me, was famed for two things. First, he was the 'School Molecatcher', charged with despatching moles before they threw up mounds of earth on Maidwell's precious lawns: his spring traps were often successful, and he skinned his many victims, before pinning their pelts to blood-flecked wooden boards for tanning.

Love was also known throughout the school for his enviable collection of knives, of which his perfectly weighted Bowie knife was king.

There was a soft-skinned redwood tree in the grounds, within sight of the headmaster's wing, into which we were allowed to hurl our knives. This was where Love perfected his throwing technique and accuracy. We would watch as his Bowie knife seemed always to go into the bark tip first, and he could nominate precisely where it was going to pierce. At Maidwell, such a talent inspired awe.

Sometimes we would run at this redwood and see how far up it we could scramble before reaching as high as we could and plunging our blade in. We'd also play games of 'dare' with our knives, standing with our legs wide apart, taking it in turns to pitch our blades into the ground between each other's feet. I find it astonishing that nobody received a serious puncture wound during my five years at Maidwell. While enraged, some boys would threaten others with their weapons, but none ever saw this through.

A similarly lax approach to the boys' safety prevailed when it came to Maidwell's many great trees. We were encouraged, no matter our age, to climb up any of them, provided we didn't go higher than fifteen feet from the ground. In such an extensive area, it was impossible for the single staff member on duty to supervise us effectively, and boys could often be seen at giddying heights, waving from the tops of full-grown oaks or elms. There was also a Maidwell tradition called 'tree-jumping' – a test of courage during which boys launched themselves from the mid-height branch of one tree onto the springy lower boughs of its neighbour.

Another surprisingly rough element of genteel Maidwell Hall could be found in its gang warfare. Two gangs held sway when I arrived there: the Harrison gang, led by one of the school's two most frightening bullies, and the Broughton gang.

Andrew Broughton, the second gang's leader, was tough as teak, having leadership and courage in his DNA: in the 1930s, his grandfather had taken command of a doomed military position facing huge numbers of enemy tribesmen in a forlorn outpost of the British Empire. He fell with his men and was posthumously awarded the Victoria Cross, the senior British medal for gallantry. As impressive to us as this ancestral honour was Andrew's unbroken ranking as Maidwell's conker-fighting champion.

The rival gangs were allowed to build camps around the grounds. These were intricate affairs, with screens of bamboo as well as branch beams that had been hacked down with the boys' sheath knives. The bullying gang leader Harrison had a secret machete, which made short work of Maidwell's undergrowth. We borrowed the school's spades to dig out defensive trenches, and underground chambers served as headquarters.

The most ambitious camp in my time was dug out of the thick clay between some evergreens at the school's southern boundary. It boasted particularly well laid out defences, and its field of vision left attackers nowhere to hide. Throughout an entire term, the two gangs ran at each other hard, punching and kicking as each fought to command this finest of forts.

Ragging, having knives and building camps were all aspects of the school that we took for granted and enjoyed at the time. Such activities harked back, I can see now, to an age when it was considered crucial to toughen up boys, if you wanted an officer class. Napoleon's vanquisher the Duke of Wellington is famously meant to have said that he won the Battle of Waterloo 'on the playing fields of Eton'. By this he meant that his high-born officers had learned to take stiff punishment during rough play as boys, and so prepared themselves for the physical demands of battlefield combat.

The Maidwell I attended still subscribed to Wellington's ideal, and it helped to form military leaders of note. The most aggressive outdoor tussle I had when at Maidwell occurred with a boy two years my senior, who knocked me down, pinned my arms with his knees and pummelled my chest until a master pulled him away. My assailant would go on to command the SAS.

Maidwell's role in providing officers for the armed services was referenced in three black-framed charts in the school's second form. These showed, respectively, the insignia for officers in the Army, Navy and Air Force. I can still name the Army and Navy ones in order of seniority now, thanks to seeing them so often as a schoolboy. A gentle form of brainwashing left its mark. It was of a kind that had underpinned an empire.

Reverence for British military tradition was strongly encouraged by my paternal grandfather, who had valued his time as a cavalry officer during the First World War and hoped a military career lay ahead of me.

My grandfather's was the only family visit I received during my time at Maidwell. He was a stubborn character, used to getting his way, and he would have given short shrift to any objections that Jack might have had to his dropping by on my eleventh birthday, in May, 1975. The meeting wasn't allowed inside the school itself, but in the grounds, so I awaited him on that part of the front drive that led to the playing fields. At the wheel of his Rolls-Royce was Hutchings, a peak-hatted charmer of a chauffeur, with the wiriness and alertness of a greyhound.

My grandfather was round-shouldered and slow-moving by then, his belly popping out under high-waisted trousers. He passed me a bundle wrapped in brown paper and string. Inside were four books of military history, one of them a history of his regiment, the Life Guards. I thanked him for the gift and for visiting, and kissed him goodbye, noting the citrus waft of his hair oil as he bent down before settling back into his sumptuous back seat. Mr Hutchings gave me a wink before starting the car back to Althorp.

Less than two weeks later, while playing with friends in the school courtyard, I had that fluttering sensation of others' eyes being on me. I turned to see Jack and Leo, headmaster and deputy head, standing stock still, staring at me. Their faces were hard and cold. Out of some sixth sense, I thought to myself, Oh – Grandfather has died!

Taking me to his study, Jack confirmed my intuition: 'I have some very sad news, I am afraid – your father called this morning to say your grandfather passed away last night.'

This death of the head of the family meant that my father was now the owner of the ancestral property, Althorp, and we would be moving there, severing our links to Park House. Being sent to Maidwell had turned my life on its head. Now, having just turned eleven, I would be leaving my home behind forever. I pleaded with my father for us to remain at Park House, but since he'd waited more than fifty years to inherit, he was deaf to persuasion.

We were transplanted from our warm Norfolk home to the formidable Northamptonshire mansion within weeks of my grandfather's death. My sisters and I were assigned a tiny room each, in the attics. Several times a night I would awake to the slow plod of the nightwatchman, on his perpetual patrol for fire or burglars, the beam of his torch catching under the base of my door. Meanwhile making friends locally proved difficult. Living at Maidwell for two-thirds of the year, and staying with my mother for half of the remainder, there was little time to build relationships with anyone other than the staff. At the same time, there was the difficulty of being the boy from the Big House, when it came to making new friends, with awkwardness on both sides.

My father's girlfriend, Raine Dartmouth, was frequently at Althorp, and she had an aversion to pets. My pony, Teddy Tar, was loaned to a riding stable, and I never saw him again. While my dog Gitsie made the move to Althorp, in my frequent absence she soon became the shadow of Maudie Pendrey – the head house-keeper, who was married to the butler.

A Norfolk farmer's daughter, Mrs Pendrey particularly enjoyed the winters, for then she would indulge in what she called her 'sport' – binding up the bottoms of her trousers with twine and descending into Althorp's outhouses to attack rats with a metal poker. And, whatever the season, the sociable Mrs P. was open to a bottle or two of Pils lager. When she swore blind that she had talked to the ghost of my grandfather in the library, soon after his death, we supposed that it was beer that had acted as medium. A lover of life, Mrs P.'s raucous laughter made the ninety-roomed mansion, standing alone in the middle of a 550-acre park, a little less chill for its new young inhabitants.

On my grandfather's death, I received one of my family's hered-itary titles, Lord Althorp. Although I wasn't the only boy with a title in the school, this change in my name led to a noticeable shift in attitude towards me by some of Maidwell's staff.

Johnno took the most umbrage. In an otherwise positive head-master's report, he served up a damning verdict, which Jack wove into my next school report: 'Perhaps it was natural that a change of name and all that goes with it should go to his head a bit,' the letter said of me. 'We have been tolerant; he has had his fun. That is enough of it, and we want no more.' To Johnno, the most snobbish of all the masters, a nominal change of status that was a curiosity to me seems to have grated with him.

This resentment spread through the common room. One afternoon the next winter, with Maidwell's sports fields frozen, the school was sent on what I see I told my diary was 'a shattering cross country run'. I was walking off a stitch during this ordeal when I suddenly felt a sharp sting in the back of my thighs that made me cry out in shock. One of the masters had run quietly up behind me, and whipped me hard across the back of my thighs with the lanyard of his sports whistle. He then jeered, 'Get a move on, my lord!' as he powered on past me. I dropped my hand to find he'd left me with livid, open welts that burned despite the extreme cold of the day.

It was the sort of casual nastiness that could thrive unchecked in an institution whose principal enjoyed inflicting pain. His cruel example encouraged others to join in the fray – even the boys.

10

Bullying

At eight years old, you were suddenly taken out of this
warm nest and flung into a world of force and fraud
and secrecy, like a goldfish into a tank full of pike.
Against no matter what degree of bullying, you had no
redress.

– George Orwell

The basic decency and compassion that Miss Lowe had
instilled at Silfield in my earliest schooldays ran counter to the
callousness of Jack's cold command. We could, of course, be
unpleasant to one another at my primary school but, at Maidwell,
institutional bullying bloomed unchecked.

Name-calling was the school's everyday mode of oppression.
Jack had a quiverful of insults that he enjoyed unleashing at us,
some so obscure and outdated that I've never heard them
since: 'scapegrace', for example – an early nineteenth-century
term for a badly behaved child. And woe betide any pupil who

dared to whistle: 'Oh do shut up!' he'd snap. 'You're not the butcher's boy!'

Having identified a body of students who were getting the same things wrong, again and again – work, behaviour or both – Jack termed them 'palookas', an archaic word for clumsy idiots. He was so gratified by the general bemusement at this insult that he composed *A Palooka's Guide*, which he circulated in the school. It was, essentially, a manual on how to be less irritating.

Jack's favourite adjectives for his pupils were 'tiresome' and 'clueless', always spat out in exhausted irritation – as if his life would be so very much easier, if we boys could only be bothered to think and act with a modicum of care. He seemed to view himself as a patient mentor, put upon by endlessly disappointing acolytes.

Other frequent forms of address for his charges were 'nincompoop', 'half-wit', 'cretin' or 'you great booby'. Jack dished out these slights liberally, in a voice of patience snapped, and disdain earned. Those he deemed unintelligent and the overweight were his favourite targets.

Progress through Maidwell's classes was achieved through academic merit: a studious boy might spend one term in seventh form, two in sixth, one in fifth, two each in fourth, third and second, and then find himself in first form for the remaining five of his fifteen terms at the school.

Equally, a pupil who struggled in the classroom might never reach first form at all. Those in this slower stream found themselves mocked by the headmaster, for being lazy, stupid or both. Jack nicknamed one boy, who particularly struggled with his studies, 'Bird Brain' – and this was how he was thereafter known, to staff and pupils alike.

Jack viewed classroom struggles as shameful failures that deserved a general airing. Exam results would be pinned on the school noticeboard, and each pupil's academic results were circulated to all of Maidwell's parents. They could see where we had placed, individually, in our seven subjects, while a column to the left recorded each boy's age order in the school. This was embarrassing for those who might have slipped a class or two below the rest of their age group.

Echoing Jack's contempt, one term Maude made the three least academic boys in his form sit side by side, in the middle of the classroom. He named this trio 'Dunce Central'. One of the three recently told me how the mockery he received at the school persuaded him to believe he was so hopelessly dim that he might as well give up. 'You were taught to fail at Maidwell,' he concludes now, accepting that his boyhood spirit was flattened by the relentless bombardment received from Maidwell's senior masters.

Jack was also an incorrigible fat-shamer. He addressed the largest boys as 'jelly bellies', while those who were somewhat overweight, he referred to as 'semi-jelly bellies'. He reserved particular scorn for John Danvers, a kind, exceptionally tall boy, who was chubby. Jack called him 'Man Mountain' – a low jab always guaranteed to elicit schoolboy laughter. Whenever Jack stuck him with the barb of this horrible gibe, John would paw at the ground with his right foot, blushing with hurt and embarrassment, his eyes glistening with tears.

Domineering headmasters have long brought cruelty in their wake. The author of *Tom Brown's School Days*, Thomas Hughes, recalled how bullies had thrived under Rugby's all-powerful principal, Dr Thomas Arnold: this breakdown of order left the vulnerable 'without their lawful masters and protectors, and ridden over rough-shod by a set of boys whom they were not bound to obey, and whose only right over them stood in their bodily powers'.

Jack's oppression created a similar power vacuum that Maidwell's bullies happily filled, with the wordless encouragement of some of the staff. They used the nastier boys as disruptors and agitators, and some seemed to enjoy the ensuing blood sport.

Children picking on other children is part of life. But school bullying can, I'd argue, be harder for the victim who is a boarder, given there's no escape to the haven of home at night – sometimes for weeks on end. And it is made that much worse when there is no authority to call upon for protection.

My contemporary John Downes was selected as quarry by the bullies because he was, thanks to extraordinary intelligence, clearly 'different': John spouted his many original thoughts in something of a verbal torrent. Some of the nastier boys marked out his eccentricity as an intriguing vulnerability. John sent heart-rending letters home, detailing his ill-treatment at their hands, but his loving parents were hoodwinked by Jack's amusing end-of-term reports into thinking their son's accounts had to be the wild exaggerations of an overactive mind. For the rest of his too brief life, John looked back at his boarding school days with loathing. 'He was bullied at Maidwell,' his widow confirms, 'and I've always suspected that the teachers endorsed this in a "survival of the fittest" kind of way, allowing the weaker boys to be picked on and not intervening.'

'Weaker boys' came in different forms, but the youngest were always prime prey. From what I came to know of Granny Ford during the subsequent five years, I'm convinced that she chose Miles Corbet as my new boy caretaker deliberately. Corbet's bullying was so notorious that the senior matron must have felt sure that his innate nastiness would break the surface as soon as my father was gone. She was unleashing a sharp-beaked raven at a lost lamb.

Corbet formed, with Tom Harrison, a partnership in terror. Such was their spite that they were feared as much as any of the more malicious masters. All the Old Maidwellians I have spoken to remember this duo with a shudder still. 'Bloody nasty,' says one, while another dubs them 'appalling bullies'. Eventually, given the inevitability of promotion in such a small institution, Harrison and Corbet became prefects, but they failed to rise to their new responsibilities. When one or the other was in charge of 'inspection' – checking our hands were clean and our hair tidy before lunch or tea – they would strike the palms that we had to hold out to them hard, with a cane, while falling about laughing. You couldn't refuse to present yourself to the prefect on duty, so there was no escape. Neither was there anyone to go to for help: Corbet and Harrison were so frightening that no boy senior to them in the school dared to admonish them.

Who knows what loss or injury caused them to be so spiteful? Something they had learned or suffered at home, maybe?

Whatever the reason, they pulsed a tireless malice that was particularly dangerous to the defenceless.

Henry Marten was a gentle, lumbering loner who had chosen refuge in a world of his own construction that was as far removed from Maidwell as he could imagine. He found a safe place in a sort of 'radio-land', where he could indulge his encyclopaedic knowledge of pop music, and adopt a mid-Atlantic accent. Given that his mother was an English aristocrat and his father a retired general, his persona was incongruous, but harmless. Yet it rarely paid to stand out, at Maidwell.

One afternoon during tidy up, Harrison singled out Henry for his special attention. He placed himself in front of Henry, facing him, then mirrored Henry's steps in an awkward, menacing waltz. Henry tried to sidestep his tormentor, but he proved impossible to shake off. Henry knew he couldn't fight back against a stronger, wirier adversary, so he set about the school's afternoon chore with unusual keenness, hoping Harrison would lose interest. But every time Henry scoured the floor for rubbish to pick up, Harrison flicked him hard around the eyes and on his eyelids with a thick elastic garter, while loudly guffawing. Harrison enjoyed his sport uninterrupted, the prefects too scared of him to step in.

I was so upset by Harrison's cruelty that I felt compelled to break the school's sacred code: I went down to Jack's study and told on Harrison, thus becoming a 'sneak' – the lowest form of life for Maidwell boys. Jack listened quietly to what I reported, nodded, then dismissed me. That evening he summoned the bully to a reckoning.

Harrison hunted me down as soon as he was released from the headmaster's study. Dragging me into a corner by my jacket lapels, he demanded: 'Hey, Spencer, did you *dare* tell Jack that I had been picking on Marten?' I looked him in the eyes, where maddened fury swirled. It seemed pointless to delay the certainty of being beaten up.

'Yes.'

The candour of my reply came from a place of weakness – it was a surrender to the inevitable, rather than an act of defiance – but somehow it pulled Harrison up short. 'Oh!' he said, releasing me. He then walked off, dumbstruck. Luckily for me, he never mentioned the episode to anyone, so I avoided the ignominy of being marked down as a sneak. There could have been no coming back from that.

Corbet and Harrison became so out of control that they even dared to take a tilt at a member of the school's staff. Mr Fairfax, the junior master, owned an ageing sports car, a Triumph Stag, his most prized possession. It acted like Cupid's chariot on his dates with a succession of the school's assistant matrons, one of whom he escorted to the opening night of *Jaws*, in nearby Northampton, another of whom he would eventually marry.

One day, while driving alone, Mr Fairfax careered out of control on a bend in the road and his car flipped upside down into a ditch. The mechanics who retrieved it pointed out that the tyres had been slashed. Since the car had been parked at Maidwell before the smash, Mr Fairfax knew those responsible lodged under Jack's roof. The headmaster's investigation led to Corbet and Harrison who broke under rigorous interrogation and admitted that they'd cut the tyres with their sheath knives.

The reckless endangering of a man's life should have resulted, at the very least, in the pair's expulsion, if not criminal proceedings. But Mr Fairfax told me what happened instead. Jack had a quiet chat with him and established that the car had been worth £300. The headmaster then spoke to the bullies' fathers, who agreed to stump up £150 each, after which the matter was hushed up.

Was this, I've often wondered, because one of the culprits had a father who was a powerful figure in the British Establishment, and Jack – a snob to his core – didn't want to upset him? Or was it perhaps because the headmaster was nervous that the boys, if questioned further, might divulge damaging details about his cruelty to their parents, and the world? Either way, there existed a delicate complicity between schools like Maidwell and the families that contracted their sons to their care – an arrangement in which the families, as clients with social muscle, tended to win out when it really mattered.

Name-calling had become so normalised by the headmaster that it blossomed throughout the school. Boys who were slow in thought-processing would be mocked by teachers and pupils for being 'schtum!' – the German word for silent, adapted to denote an unfathomable depth of stupidity. The wielder of this insult would smack the side of his own face hard, indicating that the boy he was taunting required a slap to the head to put his brain into gear.

Equally, when one Maidwell boy wanted to revel in the misfortune of another, he'd push his tongue down between his bottom front teeth and his lower lip, forming a frog-like bulge, while making a sing-song sound of derision. This was how a pupil gloated at another for getting into trouble, or for suffering disappointment. It was schoolboy *schadenfreude*, with an added twist of Maidwell spite.

Physical bullying also coursed through the school. No teachers ever ventured into the bogs, and a prefect oversaw good order there only during the twenty minutes after breakfast. The rest of the time there remained a free-for-all, and you had to keep your wits about you when in this grisly place of ablution.

Some boys snuck up behind you while you were peeing at the urinal, before shoving you with all their might. Caught off guard, you could easily stumble, with your neck snapping back at the force of the push, so you went feet-first into the sluice where urine sloshed and gurgled.

You were similarly vulnerable when seated on the loo. Some boys liked to climb silently onto the loo seat in the adjacent booth, so they could reach across and pull your chain hard, when you were least expecting it. The water below you churned up, splattering your buttocks with whatever swilled in the pan.

The same bullies could also come crashing into your loo with a high kick, since the doors had no lock. They whooped as they pointed in derision at their mortified victim, seated with his trousers round his ankles.

The meaner pupils also enjoyed baiting boys who had short tempers. Robert Tichborne, a senior when I joined Maidwell, remembers how he navigated his way through his five years by learning 'to fight both the fear and the iciness every day'. But his very first day at the school offered a particular challenge, which set the tone for the rest of his time there.

When Robert's parents dropped him at Maidwell as a new boy, it was obvious that his father had physical disabilities. These stemmed from childhood polio. On spotting this, one of the more powerful and popular boys in the school teased Robert by imitating his father's movements. Robert was so livid that he attacked with all the force that he – an eight-year-old – could muster. 'It was homicidal fury,' he says, and it took three members of staff to pull him off.

But this vivid display of temper caught the eyes of the crueller boys. They made a habit of picking on him, hoping to provoke another tantrum for their amusement: in Maidwell terminology, this provocation was 'razzing up'. 'My nightmare place,' says Robert, 'was the Uppers [dormitory]. It was out of the way, so more could be done there with impunity. I was teased a lot. [The Uppers' boys] were in large numbers, and they thought they could get away with it.' And they did, because Maidwell was a place where intimidation flourished, from the headmaster down. 'Bullying was expected to happen,' Robert recalls.

He received the nickname 'Bertie', said in a slow drawl that was meant to denote that Robert was stupid, and it was picked up and casually used by Maidwell's teachers too. Robert hated being mocked, and he loathed the school: 'It was terrible. It was a very dark place.' He was so traumatised by the bullying he suffered there that, when he looks back on his Maidwell years now, he says

Above, with Mr Smith, Park House's stalwart gardener; right, catching a ride on his lawnmower; both c. 1973.

Below, with my eldest sister, Sarah, and my Dutch Barge Dog, Gitsie, on Park House's lawn, c. 1973.

The statue of Mercury on Maidwell's front courtyard, where we had to do 'Drill' each weekday morning.

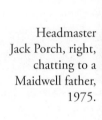

Headmaster Jack Porch, right, chatting to a Maidwell father, 1975.

Porch, right, charming parents on one of their rare forays into the school grounds.

Maidwell boys in boiler suits building a camp at the back of the school in 1975; I am in front, second from left.

Tug of war on Sports Day, 1976; I am third from left, giving it my all.

Below, helping clear up the hurdling fences after Sports Day, 1975.

Busying myself reading in Park House's drawing room – taking my mind off the dread I felt at returning to Maidwell for yet another protracted stint away from home.

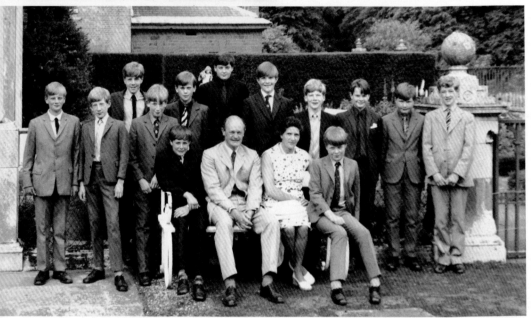

Mr and Mrs Porch and the Maidwell prefects visiting Althorp in the summer of 1975, soon after it became my new home. I am sitting next to Mrs Porch.

In a hotel, during a 1976 visit to Paris with my father and sisters, reading up on the Battle of Blenheim – the eighteenth-century clash that served up my one classroom victory over Goffie.

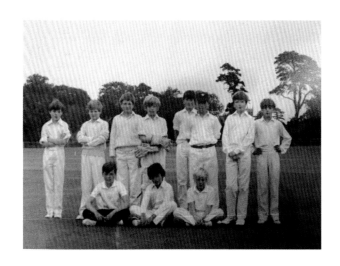

Mid-1970s cricket matches at Park House: top, I am standing fourth from right; bottom, I am standing at the far right.

Maude, right, by his swimming pool; he and Johnno, in glasses to the left, flank a visiting father and his Maidwell old boy son.

Me by the lake at Maidwell, pointing out landmarks to my father.

Getting changed by Maidwell's swimming pool for the final time, on my very last day at the school, in July 1977. Within an hour of this photograph being taken, I was being driven home by my father – sad to be saying goodbye to friends, delighted to have finished at the school.

Maidwell parents and boys gathered for Jack's retirement, at 1978's Sports Day.

Leo and Johnno overseeing Sports Day, 1978.

Jack's farewell speech on signing off from his fifteen-year tenure at Maidwell, witnessed by his wife, Ann, and the school's chairman of governors, 1978. Whether he truly retired, or was forced out, he never again held a similar position of authority.

The charcoal drawing of me at aged eleven by Robert Tollast (1915–2008), soon after 'Please' had come into my life and turned it on its head.

The imposing silhouette of Maidwell.

he sees them only in black and white. Colour was reserved for his memories of time at home.

Gregory North was another with a hot temper, He was so famously explosive that his school nickname was 'Sparky'. We younger boys would watch from afar, too scared of his aggressors to rescue him, as he was subjected to a twentieth-century equivalent of bearbaiting.

Gregory would start by trying to ignore the taunting, before realising that it wasn't going to go away. A sad smile would play on his face, when he recognised what he was in for, and then he'd blink hard, as his emotional control ebbed away, and tears welled up.

When his tormentors ran at him or shoved him, Gregory would lash out at them with flat, flailing, hands: he kept his fingernails long and sharp, for use as defensive weapons. While he often succeeded in drawing blood, the bullies never stopped coming for him. His time at Maidwell must have been nightmarish, and I feel terrible now for not having done more to help him.

With the bullies holding such sway, Maidwell echoed *Lord of the Flies*, William Golding's novel about a group of boys alone on an island, without adults, where order disintegrates catastrophically. 'The world, that understandable and lawful world, was slipping away,' the author noted, as the more toxic boys fanned the anarchy.

Given the everyday nastiness of Jack's Maidwell, and the chaotic undertone that it lent the school, I suppose it was easy for Maleficent to slip in, unseen.

11

Please

Cruelty, like every other vice, requires no motive
outside of itself; it only requires opportunity.

– George Eliot

Despite our privileged backgrounds, we Maidwellians of the
1970s were, of course, no different from most boys our age in
finding the subject of sex endlessly intriguing. Our actual knowledge of this special interest, however, tended to be rudimentary
and confused.

I can't remember the topic, or even the possibility, of homosexuality at the school being addressed by Jack, till my final days at
the school. A Maidwell master from the time, with whom I spoke
a couple of years ago, mentioned an occasion on which two pupils
who were a year older than me were caught 'being silly together',
as he termed it, in the science lab – a setting for experimentation,
but definitely not of the sexual kind (unless you were one of the
school's locusts). The boys were dealt with secretively, and bizarrely

– forced to wear swimming trunks instead of underpants beneath their corduroy trousers, as a daily reminder of their departure from Maidwell's tight moral pathway.

Near the front gate of the school grew a thick shrub spreading low, whose flourishing branches hid a large void within. Various of the more physically mature boys would disappear into this for what the rest of us knew to be secret encounters that somehow involved sex. One of the partakers told me recently that this had been a form of club, operated on an invitation only basis, mainly involving the examining and measuring of penises, where sexual fumbling also occurred.

Again, typical of boys our age, we remained on constant high alert for words that alluded in any way at all to genitals, breasts or bodily functions. In one of the musicals Johnno composed for the school concert – *Space Odyssey 1984: A Space Age Opera* – he gave each of the Russian cosmonauts in his space-race fantasy a name that ended in '-ov' – there was Buzzov, Startov, Putov; but when the fourth one introduced himself on stage as 'Sornov', the schoolboy audience erupted in joy, having effortlessly jumped to the conclusion that this Russian's penis had, somehow, been sawn off.

We had vague ideas as to words that were sexual, but these were random and unstructured notions rather than concrete knowledge. Among the pupils, Gregory Clement shocked and delighted us by composing and sharing a poem that he called 'The Sex Life of a Baked Bean'. It started with the highly original line: 'Screwy, screwy in the corner of the jar ...' before going nowhere much. Meanwhile we giggled at 'Duralex' – the manufacturer's name stamped on the glasses we used in the dining room – because it was close to Durex, the maker of what we only knew as 'rubber johnnies'. It was innocent, silly, age-appropriate stuff.

Being students at a school for boys only, we generally had no notion of female sexuality. Daniel Blagrave had our fullest attention after lights out one night when passing on his father's supposed view of intercourse: 'My dad says that women don't like sex at all – they find it all very uncomfortable and unpleasant. But,' he continued, reassuringly, 'if you're lucky, a woman will let you do "it" to her if she loves you enough to put up with it.' This struck me as a very noble way for a woman to deal with what was clearly a most awkward situation.

Senior boys imparted little that helped their juniors to understand the few complexities of sex that they, in their relative maturity, had mastered. Those who were capable of ejaculation were referred to as being 'potent', and they were proud of their abilities. One of my dormitory prefects brought an empty eardrop bottle to bed one evening, and after a few minutes of rustling sheets insisted on showing us what he'd expressed into the bottle. This proved more a harrowing freak show to us ten-year-olds than an instructive demonstration.

Several of the masters dropped sex into conversation in inappropriate or jarring ways. Johnno had an earthy side and he enjoyed lobbing carnal titbits to us. Among his many reminiscences of his Army days, he told how his soldiers were given bromide in their cauldrons of tea 'to control their libido'. But I doubt any of us had any idea what this magic potion was, or recognised the alien force that it had been sent to curb.

Johnno even found sensual content in the Bible. One of his favourite Old Testament tales was that of King David lusting after Bathsheba, a beauty he spied from his palace as she bathed on the flat roof of her home. Johnno built the scene for us: the stifling heat of the Middle East; the delicious luxury of an open-air wash, in the cool of the evening; a young lady slipping nimbly out of a thin gown; and the all-powerful David transfixed by her naked perfection. Inflamed with desire, the king arranged for Bathsheba's warrior husband to be slain in battle, so he could claim the widow for his bed. Johnno looked misty-eyed at the passion and drama of it all, but this was all quite sophisticated, adult stuff for prepubescent boys to process.

Maude seemed to enjoy introducing us to the long-ago origins of sexual terms: '*Fornix* is the Latin for arch,' he explained, 'therefore "fornication" is basically two bodies, arching together.' He also told us that '*crus*' was the Latin for leg and explained how this gave rise to the expression 'intercrural copulation'. 'This was,' he explained, 'an ancient practice – totally accepted at the time – whereby Roman men could achieve sexual satisfaction with their boy-lovers while avoiding anal penetration.' Both of Maude's revelations were so startling to such an unworldly audience as to sear into the mind.

Jack explained that the word pornography was not, as we might suppose, based on the visual, but rather took its origin from the written word: 'It comes from the Greek – *pornē* and *graphein* – literally, "whores' writing" ...' He shuddered at the ghastliness of such a fine ancient language spawning such a distasteful term and returned to safer topics.

Jack would have struggled to be disgusted by what his pupils considered to be pornography. Some older boys had copies of *Health & Efficiency*, a monthly naturist magazine, which was known as 'the nudist's bible'. It featured a regular-looking naked woman on its cover, with a strategically placed man – also naked, but nothing on show – talking attentively to her in a humdrum setting, such as the kitchen.

I added to the illicit literature of the school by smuggling in a copy of my mother's *Cosmopolitan* magazine. I hid it under a floorboard, held down by a screw that I could undo with my Swiss Army knife. We would retrieve my *Cosmopolitan* after lights out and take turns reading it under bedclothes, by illicit torchlight. The articles made only the vaguest sense to us. We were like Victorian explorers of the Nile basin, armed with scant knowledge of Egyptian hieroglyphics, stumbling across ancient tablets that no man had seen for thousands of years.

One piece from that well-thumbed edition, a journalist's unhappy account of her sexual adventures, had the title: 'How I Lost the Contraceptive War'. It proved a catalogue of burst condoms and other frustrating failures, which culminated in her throwing away a diaphragm whose spermicide felt as if it were on fire, so she could have sex with a Frenchman she'd met in a park. ('J'ai besoin de pipi,' she fibbed, when heading for the bushes to dispose of the device.)

As we got older, certain, more obviously erotic passages in best-sellers held us in thrall. The Second World War books of Sven Hassel received Jack's approval because of their martial theme, but he was unaware that they contained vivid sex scenes. These kept the boys engrossed. And I don't believe that any twelve- or thir-teen-year-old Maidwellian got past the pages in *The Godfather* where Sonny has sex against a wall, during a wedding, with the maid of honour, 'forcing her pelvis higher and higher'. The spine of each copy was broken at that very early point.

At the age of eleven, then, my understanding of sex was pretty normal: relatively innocent, totally unstructured, but beginning to gain some small momentum; I noticed when a model exuded magical femininity from a billboard high on the walls of Liverpool Street Station, where we met my mother after the train ride from Norfolk. And, that same summer, when on a family holiday in Ibiza, I developed a crush on a blonde German barmaid who worked out of a cabana on the beach.

My budding sexuality should have remained curious yet unknowing for a little while longer. Instead, my innocence was taken down a different course, where confusion, shame and self-doubt lurched out from the shadows.

The assistant matron was, by some distance, the most junior member of staff in the front-facing part of the school. The role was filled by a succession of eighteen- to twenty-two-year-old women, from what were considered 'good' families, who would be au fait with the peculiarities of boarding school life.

There must have been eight or ten assistant matrons during my Maidwell years, staying a term or two to plump up their résumés, passing through the school almost silently as they looked ahead to better things. Little was expected of them, and in return they received poor pay and a minimalist bedroom: it had just a bed, a chest of drawers, a rug and a washstand.

One of those who filled this position during my time at Maidwell told me recently how she had been recruited. With a few months to fill before starting at university, she happened to read an advertisement for the vacancy in *The Lady*, a magazine that has sourced and placed domestic staff since the nineteenth century.

She wrote to Maidwell, asking to be a candidate for the post. To her astonishment, she was accepted by return – without having to give an interview or references. She suspects she was the sole applicant. She arrived at Maidwell on the first day of the following term, having never seen the place before and without having been vetted or vouched for. This, despite the position being one of care for young children shorn of parental supervision.

The assistant matron supported Granny Ford, performing administrative work connected to housekeeping, laundry and basic healthcare: sewing pupils' name tapes into their clothes, clipping fingernails and brushing down the boys' Sunday suits after the weekly church service. She was also in sole charge of tea time several times each week.

This junior officer of the school appeared as part of the wider hierarchy only at lunch times, when she sat at the head of one of the smaller dining room tables, presiding over half a dozen ten-year-olds. As with all female members of staff, we had to address her as 'Please'.

While I can't remember most of the other assistant matrons, the one who will remain with me till the day I die first caught my attention when she was involved in something of a Maidwell lunchtime spectacular. George Monck, an eccentric loner, suddenly let rip with an enormous sneeze. Thick elastic bands of green snot shot out of his nostrils, some settling on his top lip, while others curled over his mouth and jiggled off the bottom of his chin. He sat rigid with horror at what had happened, as the boys around him backed their chairs away with loud protests of disgust.

This assistant matron was sitting a couple of places away from the humiliated Monck. She could have curtailed his embarrassment by telling him to get out his handkerchief and mop up the grisly mess. But, instead, she collapsed into heaving laughter, tears rolling down her flushed cheeks, her hand in front of her mouth, incapable of fulfilling her duties as the adult on hand.

At the time I thought how odd it was that this person who was meant to care for us failed to help Monck, a vulnerable boy in distress. Looking back now, nearly five decades on, I see this apparently innocent, unfortunate episode as betraying far more than I appreciated at the time: this young woman of nineteen or twenty was hopelessly immature. On that basis alone, she shouldn't have been in charge of children, reliant on her care.

But this incident is not why I remember this assistant matron. For it turned out that this lady we had to call 'Please' – tall and slender, with brown hair and rosy cheeks on a handsome face – had a defect far more serious than a lack of maturity.

* * *

I've long since given up trying to understand what lay behind her actions. It's beyond my comprehension. Whenever I have tried to make sense of it all, I've found myself drifting dangerously towards attempting to assemble a logical defence for someone I simply don't know. All I can do is to say what happened.

In the middle of term, when another boy was shown the door after repeated academic failure, I was moved up into the school attics to one of the pair of dormitories there called 'the Uppers'. I was the only new addition to the Uppers halfway through that term. Our dormitory was long and thin, divided almost in half by a protruding wall. My bed stood in the section furthest from the doorway, near a window that looked down on the school's front courtyard far below.

I was, by a few months, the youngest there, so when the half a dozen boys already in situ made me feel welcome, I felt pretty grown up. It was considered something of a privilege to be at this remove from the bustle of the main school. In the Uppers, the eleven- and twelve-year-olds could feel the first hint of liberating seniority after years of subjugation. There was no prefect to keep an eye on us, and Jack rarely patrolled up there, since the assistant matron's bedroom was adjacent to both dormitories, and he trusted her to keep everything in order in the Uppers after lights out.

I've always been a light sleeper, a childhood fear of the dark causing me to wake at the slightest noise. At Park House, I always went to bed with a lit candle in my room.

I'd only been in the Uppers for a night or two when I awoke to whispers coming from the other end of the dormitory. I lay still, trying to work out what was going on. I looked at my watch: it was half an hour since lights out.

Then I saw the beam of a small torch and could make out that it was dancing around in the assistant matron's hand. I presumed that she must be doing some form of rounds – maybe checking on our safety. I noted how she tiptoed to the side of each bed in turn, careful not to wake those who were asleep, but pausing and chatting quietly to those who were awake. When she came close to me, I pretended to be sleeping and she moved on.

The next night, the same thing: rustling, secrecy, torchlight, and the whispers of boys and a young woman. I then heard the crunching of food being devoured. We weren't allowed to eat or drink in our dormitories, so I knew that 'Please' must have flouted the rules, bringing forbidden treats in for those boys who were awake.

After several nights of lying still, I decided to get up and walk to where the noises were coming from. The assistant matron appeared startled, and the two or three boys she was sitting with looked at me with wary hostility.

'You mustn't tell anyone about this, Spencer!' one of them challenged.

'Of course I won't!' I said, and joined in the biscuits and grapes that 'Please' had brought in, delighting in the mischief of it all.

It wasn't long before I learned that the assistant matron was dispensing more than sugary snacks.

* * *

Because of my particularly light sleep, I soon established that handing out food after lights out was only the first of two such incursions by 'Please'. She'd return an hour later to see if anyone remained awake.

Seeing my eyes open on one of her later visits, she sat on the side of my bed. She was smiley, kind and chatty. I found it exciting to have such an easy interchange with a member of staff. She was so different from the others, and she seemed to share my dim view of Jack, of Granny Ford and of the grimmer masters, making her own irreverent, comical observations about each. She talked about things that mattered to me. In the hard, male environment of this traditional boys' boarding school, where I missed my mother terribly, this calculated deployment of feminine warmth couldn't fail to entrance, beguile and ensnare me.

Quite soon after hatching what I saw as our thrilling friendship, things changed. During a lull in our conversation one night, 'Please' reached forward, cupped my head and pulled it up from my pillow so our faces met. I was rigid in her arms as she kissed me on the lips. Then I felt her tongue push forward into my mouth. She tasted of peppermints.

'Please' moved her tongue around deep inside my mouth and it dawned on me that I was receiving the sort of kiss that I had only seen on a screen. I started to imitate her tongue's prying with my own clumsy movements.

After what seemed an age we stopped and I drew breath. Then she started again, pulling me to her and French kissing me for minutes at a time. She giggled and smiled in between, as she took a break from her seduction.

This routine continued for months: her furtive night-time visits started with a distribution of food, then a later, quiet return to swoop on her chosen targets, while the other boys were dead to the world. At the time those few of us on 'Please's' seduction list had no idea that we were the victims of sexual abuse: I was unaware that such a crime existed. We knew only that we shared an astonishing secret – one that we only discussed very occasionally, when absolutely alone, and outdoors.

Being mere boys, of course, we soon assumed we were 'in love' with the adult assistant matron, and this led to a sort of a bond, but also to an element of competition that she encouraged and directed. We didn't know this, but we were drowning in an adult sea.

She toyed with us, keeping us tight on the end of her line. I begged her to wake me up, if ever I had gone to sleep before her second nightly visit, and she said she would, but never did. Perhaps she wanted to punish those who were insufficiently committed to her to stay awake till she arrived.

'Please' seemed to have an unofficial hierarchy among her prey: we learned, from our secret conversations, that she chose one of us each term to share her bed and would use him for intercourse.

'What's it like – doing "it"?' I asked one of them.

'You push in with your willy and her flesh sort of pushes you out,' he replied, trying to sound worldly, but using the vocabulary of the child that he was.

What he was describing was, of course, beyond the limits of my understanding. It was utterly intriguing, though, and I'd lie awake wondering if I would be chosen for this mystifying, push-and-pull procedure. When I asked 'Please', she hinted to me that I would be, soon.

Instead, she added me to the second rank of her victims: those she intimately touched. While we kissed, one night, she reached under my bedclothes, trailing her fingers in teasing, looping circles down my stomach until alighting on the little that an eleven-year-old boy can muster.

The first time she touched me there, she placed my hand on her breasts, and I could feel her pounding heart beneath, while I – many months from joining the 'potent' boys in the school – felt fit to combust at the sensual and mental overload.

Soon afterwards she pulled forcefully at my arm and pushed my hand down, under the tight elastic at the top of her underpants. I had no idea what I was meant to do, so started by twirling my finger round her crinkly pubic hair. Eventually, she took me by the wrist and moved my hand for her sake.

She was a master of emotional manipulation as well. We hung out with her in the Music Room – a small space near the Uppers, along from Please's bedroom, which pupils could use in their free time, and which other members of staff seemed never to enter.

She would set the emotional tone of this sanctuary. With a sudden huff or a deliberate turning of her back, she would publicly shun one of those children that she was molesting. The other boys in her thrall would spot this change in her mood and side with her with such open hostility that the one ostracised would feel compelled to leave the Music Room in wounded rejection. He would be readmitted into the circle of sexual secrecy only when 'Please' started smiling at him once more. This woman's control over mesmerised boys was total, for we were starved of feminine warmth, and desperate for her attention and affection.

Please told us that she thought she would have to move on to her next job, in the women's branch of the Royal Navy, earlier than planned. I was so fraught at the prospect of losing her that I started cutting at the inside of my arm with a penknife. If I hurt myself often and painfully enough, I felt sure, then God, Fate, whoever, might have the grace to let her continue at the school – visiting me, combing my hair back from my forehead with her hands before the lingering kisses that lit up my nights.

The possibility of her having to leave Maidwell early was, I now feel sure, just a ruse, to set panic among her emotional dependants, perhaps to make her feel desirable and needed, perhaps to keep us more tightly hooked. But weeks later, when she said that she would, for sure, be staying on till the end of the school year, I ran through the school's hallway, punching the air, and shouting 'She's staying! She's staying!' with the boy sharing her bed that term. We jumped up and down, waving our arms in childish euphoria, unaware that we were, in fact, merely the unwitting victims of a voracious paedophile.

Men who learn what 'Please' did to me tend, at first, to give me a laddish thumbs up: 'Lucky you!' they say. But then I explain that it wasn't at all like that. If I had been in my late teens, cavorting with a female member of staff, it might have been – but I was a child. 'Would you say that if the genders were reversed?' I ask. 'You know, if it was a twenty-year-old man sexually molesting an eleven-year-old girl?'

Then they get it.

The effect of what she did to me was profound and immediate, awaking in me basic desires that had no place in one so young. I'd felt a vagina, when my friends were longing for a first kiss; and I'd been touched sensually, while drinking deep on those long, heady embraces. And it had, to my shame, felt good.

You can't put the genie back in the bottle, as the cliché goes, and this childhood abuse meant that I wanted full sex from a too-early age. The assistant matron had given me a taste, and I wanted the full serving I felt she'd promised me but withheld. I felt a compulsion to lose my virginity as soon as the chance arose.

Late at night, on a trip to Italy with my mother and stepfather, I looked from my bedroom window on to the square below and spied a short-skirted lady standing in a corner under a streetlamp. My stepfather had spotted her when we returned from supper and whispered to my mother, '*Una prostituta*', and she'd nodded. In short order, I padded down the stairs and slipped out of the *pensione* without a word.

'*Quanta costa?*' I asked, using words I'd heard my mother say when opening the bargaining for a handbag earlier in the day.

'*Trenta mille lire,*' she replied.

I opened my wallet, which contained all my pocket money, and unscrunched some notes. I counted out 3,000 lire, thinking that was what she'd set as her price, and offered it to her.

'No! – *TRENTA mille!*' she shouted, insulted at my miscalculation, and I added the outstanding 27,000 lire.

She led me up into a room, which was, like the Uppers, in an attic. As it was about to happen, I said, 'I don't know what to do', and she looked at me blankly, not understanding English.

After a further pause, I let the woman take the lead, silently and firmly. It was a dynamic that felt familiar. There was no joy in the act, no sense of arrival, no coming of age. I believe now that I was simply completing the process set in motion by the assistant matron's perverted attention. Afterwards I felt hollow and cold. I didn't sleep with a woman again for five years, until I was seventeen and my girlfriend eighteen.

I found out when still extremely young that 'Please' had done much the same, at another boarding school, before she started at Maidwell. I met a boy from that other place who indicated that she'd subjected him to the same inappropriate and baffling experiences, and he was still in touch with her. Presumably she'd told him that I'd been on her list, as well, because he confronted me aggressively when we met, acting as if I'd strayed onto his turf. So, the veil that she'd put over her actions was not impenetrable. Perhaps, if Maidwell had maintained a proper system for vetting staff, they would have got wind of her sexual deviance and wouldn't have employed her.

I still have a memento of this sexual trauma. A society portrait painter, Robert Tollast, came to the school in 1976, to capture in pastels some of Maidwell's boys. I sat for this silent artist whose hands swirled furiously over a canvas, and he produced what looks like a simple, formal portrait of a privileged boy, in jacket and tie. But he has captured much more than that, as sensitive artists tend to.

Here I am in my full Maidwell melancholy, staring into the distance, my bright red hair and soft, pink cheeks set off by large, sorrowful blue eyes.

It is a study in sadness – of a boy, lost.

12

My Parents

If I were to give advice, I would say to parents that
they ought to be very careful whom they allow to mix
with their children when young; for much mischief
thence ensues.

– Saint Teresa of Avila, sixteenth-century
Spanish aristocrat, mystic and nun

At the time of this abuse, 'Home' and 'School' remained two
distinct spheres in my life, with negligible overlap. None of my
family knew that this assistant matron so much as existed until
this past year. Indeed, none of them knew anything of Jack and
his appalling rule. It wasn't discussed.

'Why didn't you tell your parents what was going on?' those
who know of some of Maidwell's graver failings ask. It never
occurred to me to do so. Neither did it to any of the many pupils
from the school that I've spoken to.

One friend, dreadfully sexually abused at the school, had
a breakdown at work after a week of escalating trauma. A

professional helped him to establish that this episode had been triggered by his son having turned nine – the age he had been when first molested at Maidwell.

He had never spoken about his suffering at the school, even with his parents. 'I couldn't talk with them about the sexual violence I'd suffered,' he explained. Part of his reticence was born out of good manners: 'I never wanted to confront them over their choice of school for me. They sent me there for the best reasons.' In middle age, after his breakdown, and after his parents' deaths, he enrolled in six weeks of therapy: 'I didn't stop talking – I vomited it out, then felt I had taken the scab off.' It was after this that he reached a calm, if sad, acceptance of what he'd suffered.

When at Maidwell, I was so young as to have no context for my life: I knew no different and had no concept that kind and caring boarding schools might exist. I assumed that the environment in which I was placed was normal.

I also had a childish assumption that my parents – whom I then viewed as all-seeing and all-knowing – wouldn't have dreamed of sending me to live away from home for five years without thinking hard about the options. They told me that they loved me, so surely they'd have researched carefully to find the place where I'd be happiest and could most readily thrive?

Generally, we weren't as close to, or open with, our parents back then as children tend to be today. Isaac Ewer, a few years ahead of me at the school, has as one of his principal memories of his first day at Maidwell astonishment at being driven to the school by his father. It made a lasting impression because, he explained, 'I didn't spend much time with him. Things were very formal between fathers and sons back then.' On that seminal journey they chatted as never before.

Two of my contemporaries had such distant relationships with their respective fathers that they recall having physical contact with them on only one occasion, each. The first received an encouraging handshake when being left on his first day as an eight-year-old new boy. The other had to wait till his fifties, when his elderly father suddenly reached out a hand for comfort, hours before death. I was lucky that my father was more openly loving than many of his contemporaries from the same privileged background. He would kiss me in greeting till the end of my teens.

But my father was forty years older than me, and he was otherwise very conventional. He subscribed to a cliché that he repeated to me several times: 'Schooldays are the happiest days of our lives.'

While he followed my Maidwell career with reserved interest, I never thought to share with him Maude and Goffie's viciousness, or even the general tenor of Jack's misrule. My father occasionally would ask about life at school, but he never focused on specifics. He went through Jack's term reports with me, for a few minutes each school holidays, greatly enjoying their smokescreen humour, while sure to celebrate any positives that they might contain.

I felt it was somehow my duty to pretend that things at Maidwell were all right: to have done otherwise would, I knew, have upset him, especially after he had let slip how expensive the school's fees were. I didn't want to disappoint him, or others who seemed so keen that I enjoy the place.

When Mary Clarke – my last nanny – wrote to me out of the blue, in 1978, to ask how my life was going, I replied with boasts of minor academic and sporting achievements at the school I'd just left. I was fourteen and had neither the tools nor the context to understand, process or explain the dark side of the place where I'd spent the past five years. I didn't even know that physical, emotional or sexual abuse existed as concepts, let alone as crimes.

I came from a background that expected you to 'get on with it' – to stomach a rite of passage that previous generations had endured in their turn, and to do my best to seem to enjoy the experience. My loving, gentle grandmother wrote to my father, after he and my mother dropped my eldest sister at boarding school: 'I thought of you and Frances yesterday, taking Sarah to school for the first time: it is a horrid moment, but I am sure she will love it.' That was all. No dwelling on the family trauma. It was just one of those childhood things – like measles or mumps – that had to be got through, without fuss.

After I visited my grandfather during my first term at Maidwell, he noted with satisfaction in his diary: 'Charles seems to be happy in his new school.' Presumably he asked me how it was going, and I – who had only a distant relationship with this elderly, gruff patriarch – must have put the positive spin on things that I knew was required.

This, when the truth was quite different: throughout my time at Maidwell, I was slave to a dread despair that I've rarely known since. It was unleashed by the unstoppable passing of the hours – even the minutes – before I'd be taken back to the school. This gloom got so bad that in the final days of the holidays I'd regularly consider shooting myself in the foot with one of my father's shot-guns: physical agony seemed preferable to the psychological torture of being sent away to that place again.

Important family landmarks marched alongside the life of the school with a tread so distant that it seemed to fall in another world. On 4 December 1972, for instance, while we tackled Miss Best-Shaw's 'end of term test' for seventh form, my grand-mother died from her brain tumour. I wasn't with my father or siblings when this thunderbolt hit our family, and I was unable to speak to them about it, face to face, for the remainder of that term.

Likewise, on a lighter note, as soon as I got my 1974 diary, I noted that 24 January would be my father's fiftieth birthday. But this landmark fell during term time and was overtaken by a Maidwell headline; for, that day, the junior master, Mr Fairfax, was tackled hard on the football field, fell awkwardly and dislo-cated a leg. Some of his colleagues carried him to the common room on a stretcher, his screams of agony continuing till Maude plied him with numbing alcohol. As usual, Maude overdid things, so that Mr Fairfax was considered too drunk for an anaesthetic when he got to hospital, and the doctor snapped the dislocated limb back into place without sedation. Meanwhile my father saw out his fiftieth with three of his children away at their respective boarding schools.

My father changed while I was at Maidwell. During his mid-forties he'd begun to put on weight quite dramatically. Perhaps he'd turned to comfort eating in the years after my mother left their marriage? To my shame, I began to be embarrassed when he appeared at school. He looked so unhealthy and, after a difficult relationship – correspondence between him and his new girlfriend, Raine, shows they barely navigated their first years together – unhappy. And I hated that he drove my grandfather's Rolls-Royce when collecting me: it struck me as embarrassingly ostentatious. But I see now that he came from an entitled background, where certain things were taken for granted – such as driving the most luxurious make of car. In many ways, this man I loved so much simply wasn't cut out for the modern world.

Once, when I was ten and released from Maidwell on a leave-out weekend, we went to London. After going to the cinema to watch *Murder on the Orient Express*, we returned to his mews house for the night. In the morning, he and I had to confront the fact that he had no idea how to prepare breakfast. He was used to this being done for him, whether at home or when staying with friends. He had brought a refrigerated bag with him from Althorp, packed by the imperturbable butler, Mr Pendrey, which included a single bottle of milk. My father always gulped down glasses of the stuff in the mornings, and I saw that there wouldn't be enough of it for us both to drink, if we were also to pour some on our cereal, so I insisted on a glass of London tap water instead, leaving most of the milk for him. Normally, a parent would have forgone limited resources so their child could be provided for. But my father came from a background where others did things for you, so my small sacrifice went unnoticed.

Apart from fighting with distinction in the last year of the Second World War, my father's life experiences in his teens and twenties – attending Eton, having a ceremonial role in Australia, and serving as a courtier to King George VI and then to Queen Elizabeth II – had prepared him for taking over the estate at Althorp, but not for everyday practicalities. He was an old-fashioned gentleman, trusting and respectful of others, and this rendered him incapable of seeing through Maidwell's deceitful veneer.

This was true of many of the parents. When they came to collect us from the school, we'd rush excitedly out to meet them and be greeted by a bewildering sight. Those masters who'd been routinely unkind to us, with curled lips and tightly wound menace, were transformed. With our parents present, they wore the twinkly smiles of kindly carers. They referred to us lightly by our Christian names. Jack would even laugh.

It was a convincing sham that persuaded those who'd received tearful letters from Maidwell that there was nothing to worry about, after all. Surely there could be no reason for complaint, with these charming masters in charge?

My father was certainly taken in. 'What a nice man that Mr Maude is!' he once said. 'He had such lovely things to say about you!' We headed home, with me silent, unable to vocalise how awful such teachers really were. As for Maude, the only positive thing I could ever recall him saying to me was how lucky I was to have Cupid bow lips, in a way that even then struck me as deeply odd.

My mother never sufficiently engaged with Maidwell to have a chance of sniffing out its rottenness. I think she saw the school as my father's choice, and therefore his responsibility: she only visited it for an hour, a few months before I started there, and was happy to second his proposal. Besides, she had exciting developments in her life to divert her.

A few months after I started at Maidwell, she and my stepfather decided to move from Appleshore, their house in the south of England. Peter wanted to live someplace where he could not only sail, but also farm. While Park House remained 'home' in my mind (and it still does), my mother's relocation intensified the disquiet I suffered as a boarder. It was one more uncontrollable moving part in my small, ever-changing world.

My mother and stepfather's hunt for coastal farmland ended in the purchase of Ardencaple, a 1,000-acre farm on a small island, Seil, off Scotland's west coast. Ardencaple's rugged landscape of tidal coves, lush marshland and majestic hills was a romantic's dream.

My mother was always fun. During the portion of the school holidays that I went to her at Ardencaple, I spent most of my time outdoors: on the sea in spring and summer – mackerel fishing, lobster potting and sailing; and, during the winter, walking its rocky shore with gun in hand, and blind springer spaniel Cara at heel, hoping to bring back a duck for the pot.

In the summer we picnicked with my mother and Peter's friends at the bothy, a restored quarryman's cottage in Ardencaple Bay. The islands unfolded from this point in a bobbing patchwork of green and grey. We navigated the nearer ones on a yacht and reached those of the Outer Hebrides after churning ferry rides.

Ardencaple became a haven I came to crave during long Maidwell terms. I sensed that it was a counterweight to that formal, snobbish, often cruel school. The Scots we encountered couldn't care less about the English class system: they took you as they found you. At Althorp I was 'my lord', even then; at Maidwell

I was known by my new surname, 'Althorp'; but at Ardencaple I was my most authentic self – 'Charles'.

The only problem with my mother's new home was its remoteness. To avoid a ten-hour drive from London, we children boarded 'the sleeper' – the overnight train to Scotland. We'd arrive in Glasgow early the following morning, then take an antiquated train, its windows black with dirt. This rolled slowly to the village of Crianlarich, whose pivotal position in the hills allowed its few inhabitants to call their dot on the map 'the gateway to the Highlands'.

We'd reach Crianlarich at around seven in the morning, to be greeted by my mother. She'd already have had the first of her many daily cigarettes. Because she continued smoking as she drove, a ritual part of the ninety-minute drive to Ardencaple was my vomiting into the high bracken that shrouded the lay-bys.

Later, as a parent, I'd wonder how my mother and stepfather, with seven children boarding at schools in southern England, could select such a faraway spot as their home, however beautiful it was. Meanwhile, each February, they'd venture much further away, to their sheep station in Australia, in order to avoid the grim finale to the British winter.

But wherever she was, my mother proved to be a wonderfully prolific correspondent. Spotting her looping scrawl, in blue felt pen, gave my Maidwell mornings a lift. She put few words on the page – perhaps a couple of irreverent thoughts, ending with 'Much love, Mummy' – but it was cherished contact, while the number of letters I received from her was the envy of many of my fellow boarders. My father wrote less often, and in a more serious, considered tone.

I recently found a Maidwell postcard from each of my parents in a drawer at Althorp. My father sent his – written with his fountain pen, in neat up-and-down script – from Austria. Its image is of three members of Vienna's Spanish Riding School, resplendent on grey mounts. On the back he wrote: 'Good season of opera here & wonderful pictures & palaces to see. Viennese very kind & friendly. Hope your violin is going well. Love, Daddy.' It was earnest, correct and thoughtful: I had no interest in opera or palaces, but he probably felt it his duty to awaken in me an appetite for both; and it was typical of him to encourage my modest musical efforts.

My mother's card, sent during a weekend with Peter in Italy, showed a detail from a painting of a bloody clash between two medieval city-states. 'Don't know who won or took part in this battle,' she wrote. 'Looks like a good punch-up. It's All Saints Day, so fabulous singing in all the churches. Sitting in the sun, drinking wine. Have a good half-term. Love, Mummy.'

While these cards reflect two extremely different characters, and attitudes to life, they also make me appreciate now that one of the great advantages for wealthy parents of packing their children off to boarding school was a licence to indulge themselves. With the childcare contracted out, why not travel to Europe for some fun? The assumption was that someone responsible was looking after the children on their behalf. But at the exact time that my parents were, respectively, in Austria and Italy, I was being sexually abused by the assistant matron.

* * *

Since my mother chose never to attend sports day – which doubled as parents' day – I felt particularly excited when a unique opportunity arose for her to visit me at Maidwell. At the end of 1976's Christmas term, I was chosen to sing the first verse of 'Once in Royal David's City' as soloist in the annual carol service.

When my father learned of this, he contacted my mother to say he'd like to witness my performance. She replied that she wanted to go and, because their relationship was such that they felt unable to be under the same roof together – even that of a church – he conceded.

I was in an agony of nerves in the days leading up to my solo, a hymn book in my hands during breaks and muck-about, as I sang quietly to myself, trying to master the higher notes. I was determined to make my mother proud.

When my moment in the carol service arrived, I did my best, then immediately scanned the congregation to see if my mother had enjoyed it. But I couldn't see her anywhere. Just then, the heavy latch on the church door clacked open, and in she walked. Never able to resist a good time with friends, my mother had driven up to Maidwell from London after a lunch that had gone on later than planned, and so missed my solo.

Jack took me aside after the service, with rare kindness. 'I was so upset that your mother arrived when she did,' he said, 'that I nearly got you to sing your verse again.' I looked down, anxious not to reveal my distress. 'But that wouldn't have been right, of course: we don't do encores in religious services.'

Jack and I both knew that my father wouldn't have missed my solo: I'd played in the Maidwell rugby team throughout that same term, and he had attended every home fixture, always congratulating us at the end of the match, in a season when we won every fixture. If he'd been coming to this carol service, he'd have arrived first to get the best available seat in the church, and he doubtless would have struggled to stop himself from applauding when I finished, however poorly I had sung.

I had been caught up in another family drama at the school a few months earlier, when I had just turned twelve. One evening Jack told me to come to see him after tea, before I headed to carpentry class. When I entered his study, he looked sheepish. 'Your father has asked me to tell you that, erm – well – he is engaged to be married to Lady Dartmouth.' I was stunned. I hadn't taken to Raine Dartmouth at all, when she was my father's girlfriend, and now she was to be my stepmother!

'Hasn't he got the courage to tell me himself?' I asked, in a clear, low voice. My face flushed with shock and anger, as tears pricked my eyes. Jack shifted in his seat. 'Well, I thought you might think something like that. But, of course, these things are very hard for a child to understand. You see, a man has many needs ...' and I drifted away from his words of explanation, feeling let down by my father and desolate at his imminent marriage to someone so horrid. Jack would write to my mother: 'I put to Charles what his father had asked me to put to him, but he can be a very obstinate boy and I did not try to talk him round ...'

I walked to the carpentry workshop by myself that evening, shared the desperate news with my friends, and – incapable of concentration – spent the class practising karate chops on wooden planks. I was in turmoil, far from home, angry and hurt, with no family member to turn to or talk to, when one was urgently needed.

My father encouraged me to replicate his happier experiences at a similar set-up to Maidwell, forty years earlier. With fond memories of having his school friends come to stay at Althorp, he told me to invite boys from Maidwell to Park House for cricket matches during my first summer holidays at my new school.

As he must have anticipated, this greatly boosted my schoolboy popularity. Park House, with its heated swimming pool, tennis court, tree house and acres of garden, was a paradise for small boys, and the annual invitation to my cricket weekend became quite prized. Equally, I began to grasp quite how enormous my privilege was, after seeing it through the eyes of appreciative friends.

Such time at Park House was wonderfully removed from the rigid confines of the school where we boys lived and studied. While my father had planned for my guests to sleep in twos and threes in Park House's bedrooms, he didn't mind when we all converged on one room, dragging blankets, camp beds and mattresses behind us, so we could spend the nights together. We chatted into the small hours, without fear of punishment, creating bonds of friendship far from the reach of Jack, Maude, Goffie or that great enabler, Granny Ford.

My father enjoyed what became an annual invasion – one easily transplanted to Althorp, on my grandfather's death – and got to know my school friends well. But his view of Jack towards the end of my time at Maidwell became more nuanced, and curious. 'It is odd to devote your life to young boys like that,' he said. 'They leave your school when they're just starting to become more interesting.'

This was, I suspect, the nearest that either of my parents came to working out that Jack was a very strange man indeed.

13

Leaver

You may leave school, but it never leaves you.

– Andy Partridge, founder of rock group XTC

Mid-January 1977. The end of the Christmas holidays was upon me, as ever too quickly, and my sense of deep foreboding was tightening its grip. For three days before the start of term, I was felled by migraines.

It was time to forgo the cosy afterglow of family festivities for another stark, protracted blast of boarding school exile. I'd already done my customary, grim arithmetic, and calculated that in this, the penultimate stretch of my fifteen-term sentence, I'd be under Maidwell's roof for eighty-one of the next eighty-eight nights.

My mother dropped me at Euston Station, kissing me goodbye as she wished me luck for the term ahead. She walked quickly away, looking at her watch as she backed out of my world, without so much as a glance behind her. I knew she'd be carrying on her life as she wished, while I'd be contained, yet again, in Jack's rotten realm. Along with the familiar pangs of longing for home, I was now old enough to feel a surge of anger, tinged with jealousy.

A junior master was on hand to escort the posse of glum schoolboys on the train north. When I presented myself to him, his dim flicker of recognition betrayed his lack of enthusiasm for his day's dull duty. He crossed my name off his list, waved me away without a word, and I joined the clutch of other Maidwellians on the platform.

On the train I sat with John and Thomas Waite – quick-witted brothers who were regulars at my annual cricket matches. Some years before, they'd suffered what was to the rest of us unimaginable tragedy: the death of their father.

In our exposed worlds, where parental protection was often absent yet always craved, this was the stuff of nightmares. The Waite boys never talked about it, but we all did, behind their backs – not in gossip but in terror, praying such catastrophe would never befall us. Death, we felt, should only harvest in the fields where our aged grandparents weakly toiled.

The junior master looked resignedly out of the grimy window as we juddered into yet another desolate, provincial station. There were eight stops, each one slowing up the return to Maidwell, so that a journey of just seventy-five miles became a trek lasting an hour and three-quarters.

Familiar knots of anguish tightened in my gut. These were the pulsing spasms of homesickness and dread familiar to generations of Maidwell boys sent up these same railway tracks. Andrew Motion, who boarded at the school in the 1960s, wrote of the rippling grief on just such a start-of-term trip: 'Nobody talked for the second half of the journey,' Motion recalled. 'I saw Lety, who was normally tough, leaning his head against the window and staring at the fields getting dark. He was crying. So was Mackay ... I could hear [Kit] was crying too, even though the wheels underneath us were clanking like a fairground.'

My train pulled into Northampton, a nondescript station then, its customary greyness washed even thinner by the winter gloom. There was a café that seemed always to be closed, the gaudy, rippling lights of a slot machine the only sign of life within.

Our small contingent traipsed behind the bored master to the outside courtyard, lugging our suitcases. There were so few of us that we could squeeze into three taxis. It was pitch black by the time we entered the school's front gate, headlights catching the avenue of trees that marked the start of the drive in a flickering whirl of shadows.

My throat dried as I looked left, across the sweeping lawn, to the imposing, turreted silhouette of the school. It was dotted with thin white light, emanating from the ground-floor classrooms and the dormitories above. We drove into the front courtyard, gravel crackling its lively warning, until the tyres stopped with a crunch that said, in a cold, strong voice: you're back now – and you're here to stay.

After putting my personal things in my locker, I turned to check the noticeboard and found that I was to be a prefect in charge of a dormitory, and that Jack had chosen me as one of the three senior prefects. The one privilege this afforded me was being allowed to watch television for half an hour each evening with him and his wife.

But such notional seniority didn't spare me from the ways of this peculiar school, whose need to punish overrode reason.

Maidwell's twenty senior boys – the prefects and sub-prefects – were allowed to go on afternoon walks in the surrounding countryside, on days when we had no sports fixtures. We had to be accompanied by at least one of our peers, and needed to let the master on duty know the direction in which we were headed.

I struck out on one such walk with John Waite. We'd only gone a hundred yards from the back gate when we arrived at a triangle of grass next to Maidwell's main road. John and I started horsing around, trying to trip one another up, before descending into full ragging mode, grappling on the village green in a competitive tussle.

A few cars went by, the adults inside smiling at the sight of boys being boys. But one of the passing drivers was Leo's wife, Mrs Learmont, who taught art at the school. She stopped, craned her neck to better take in what we were doing, then drove off.

That evening, John and I were summoned to the headmaster's study. We had no idea why.

'What on earth do you think you were both doing – wrestling like that, in a public place?' Jack asked.

'We were just ragging, sir,' I replied, assuming that would be an end of it.

'Well, Mrs Learmont saw you at it, and she was appalled. She says you two were rolling around like – like copulating kittens!'

It was a strange description and begged the question as to how we all looked at ten to six each evening, piling on top of each other in the sanctioned free-for-all of ragging.

As John and I stood before him, so perplexed at the accusation that we could think of nothing to say in our defence, Jack rushed to his guilty verdict: we were banned from going on any further walks outside the school grounds for the remainder of the term. It was a heavy sentence for doing what we were always encouraged to do: rag.

The injustice I felt at this punishment added to my increasing relief, in my final couple of terms, that my time at this place was ending. After some loose ends were tied up, over the coming six months, I could see freedom looming.

An honorary relationship topped and tailed my five years at Maidwell. Among the first things you learned when joining the school was that (other than leave-out or long leave) only a truly exceptional reason would win you an escape from the place.

One of these occasions had arisen during my first term: as one of Queen Elizabeth's thirty godchildren, I was invited to Westminster Abbey for the celebration of the twenty-fifth wedding anniversary of the Queen and Prince Philip. I stood with my father, wearing the grey suit reserved for Maidwell church on Sundays, and I remember the Queen's kind smile as she looked down at me, perhaps the youngest in the congregation, when she passed.

This magnificent service was to prompt my first written journalism: as an eight-year-old struggling to catch the brilliance of the aisle procession, I wrote in the school's annual magazine how 'bishops and archbishops went by, covered in diamonds and rubies'.

The Queen was kind enough to send me a gift each Christmas, and one year I was thrilled to receive from her a radio disguised as a pocket journal. I smuggled this back to Maidwell and listened to Radio Luxembourg at night under my blankets.

I'd decided to be confirmed while at Maidwell because I was terrified that, if I waited until I was a new boy at Eton, Queen Elizabeth might attend the service. I was wary of standing out too much when starting at a new school, and had been told that Windsor Castle to Eton was a short hop. But the monarch's progress from one of the royal palaces to a small church in Northamptonshire was, my mother assured me, out of the question. So, in early March 1977, I was confirmed by the Bishop of Peterborough at Maidwell, with all sides of my jumbled-up family present: my parents (as ever, on non-speaks), my three sisters, my maternal uncle, as well as three of my godparents. It felt extraordinary – even bewildering – to have so many of the figures who peopled my non-Maidwell life at the school.

My nerves about the Common Entrance exam, which I needed to pass to get into Eton, only increased when I learned that I'd have to take some of the exam away from Maidwell.

I was a Page of Honour to the Queen from the beginning of 1977 – one of the four boys who carried the train to the monarch's gown at the State Opening of Parliament each autumn, and at the Knights of the Garter* ceremony, which the Queen hosted in Windsor each June. We were chosen from the sons of the Queen's friends and courtiers, and two of the others were strangers to me,

---

* Members of England's highest order of chivalry.

while the other lived near to Park House and had attended Silfield School with me.

The 1977 Garter ceremony – special because it was taking place in the Queen's Silver Jubilee year – was slated for a day when I would be sitting Common Entrance. Jack liaised with Eton, and it was arranged that I could take the papers at that school, under supervision.

This was never going to suit me: I was a nervous exam-taker, rarely reproducing whatever classroom form I had under pressure. In the end it was arranged that other page boys, not of Common Entrance age, would carry the royal train that day.

I took my Common Entrance papers in the school's science lab, next to Miss Best-Shaw's seventh form where my Maidwell years had begun. I was fiercely concentrating, while perched on one of the stools, when Johnno sidled up next to me, his squeaking hush puppies heralding his approach.

With the flourish of a waiter presenting a prize dish to a discerning diner, he placed a folded copy of the *Daily Telegraph* over my written answers. He pointed at the large photograph at the head of the front page, which I saw was of my eldest sister, Sarah, alongside Prince Charles. Its caption noted something I knew already – that Sarah was the prince's new girlfriend.

Even then, as a thirteen-year-old boy, I thought Johnno's interruption a curiously thoughtless distraction during a crucial moment: these exams would help decide the course of not just my next five years, but my life. Yet Johnno's snobbish delight in the family backgrounds of his pupils was a force he could never hope to master.

Once Common Entrance week was completed, we had the 'leavers' talk' with Jack in the Porches' sitting room. This was a much-anticipated event because of the grown-up themes that we knew would be addressed. He briefed us on the various dangers awaiting us once we'd left what he described, ironically, as 'the safety of Maidwell'.

His first topic was alcohol. 'You really must not feel the need to drink it,' he said. 'I often put ice in ginger ale, and people just assume I've got a glass of whisky.'

Next was sex. He told us not to masturbate: 'Apart from anything else, if you do it frequently you will be absolutely exhausted.' When he turned to intercourse, he said: 'Everyone does it. Even Mrs Porch and I do it.' One of my fellow leavers remembers how I reacted to that particularly startling image. 'Suddenly you couldn't contain yourself anymore,' he says, 'and I thought you were going to explode as you tried in vain not to laugh. It was terribly embarrassing and absolutely delicious at the same time.'

Jack continued with the next chapter of his talk, as I composed myself. It tackled the dangers of promiscuity: 'You see all these films with James Bond hopping into bed with lots of women. Well, they're nonsense. If a man really behaved like that, he would be in a lot of pain from all the diseases he'd pick up. And, frankly, that would serve him right.'

He gave homosexuality equally short shrift. 'At your next school, there will be boys who try to persuade you to have sex with them. You may well find that their main argument will be, "well, everyone else is at it"; but this is simply not true – everyone most certainly isn't – so don't fall for it.'

Jack's introduction to sex was incongruous. He felt he was opening up new horizons for us all, but at least two of us in that room had been deprived of the innocence of childhood at the hands of his assistant matron. He finished the leavers' talk by giving us each a tie, to wear proudly as Old Maidwellians. This was as close to a leaving ceremony as Maidwell came.

The last week or two between the completion of Common Entrance and our exit from Maidwell were taken at a far gentler pace than the preceding five years. The masters were no longer interested in us leavers. We were excused lessons, and allowed to enjoy Maidwell as the beautiful rural setting that it had been before its transformation into a school. We paddled in a stream in the valley that lay towards the village of Draughton, catching sticklebacks in jam jars. Some structure was introduced to our day when we made a short movie with the school's cine-camera. In it we played prisoners of war, making a bid for freedom, and – this time – embarking on a successful run for home.

This was a stint with boys who I knew intimately after five years together, who I assumed would remain in my life forever. But perhaps half of my Maidwell contemporaries I have never seen again.

Sports day was our last time together. It was a hot July afternoon in 1977, and Jack greeted the parents with a large noticeboard by the school's front door. This most monochrome of men used a variety of coloured pens for his various announcements, as if to give the impression that there was a rainbow of delights beneath his grey exterior. In that jokey 'we all know what little boys are like, don't we?!' tone of his end-of-term reports,

Porch finished his written advice to parents with: 'Before driving off please check that you have your boy's TRUNK, NIGHT CASE, WATCH, MONEY & all the junk which he left in his locker until the last minute.'

My father obeyed another of Jack's pointers that day, when placing a card under his car's windscreen wiper. On it was written my school number, '64', my numerical identity in use for the last time so Maidwell's garden staff could load my trunk into the correct vehicle.

The sports began at 2.30 p.m., and were completed an hour later, after which parents were invited to visit the boys' art exhibition – held in Miss Best-Shaw's seventh form, and above the gym – or to go to the pool while the boys swam. My father attended both, chatting to masters and fellow parents, and recording my last Maidwell afternoon with his camera, before moving on to tea with the other adults – an echo of the new boys' tea party five years earlier. I joined the rest of the boys, as we ate at our set places in the dining room, eight of us for the last time.

At 4.25 p.m. we were all able to rejoin our parents by their cars and I set off from Maidwell at the end of a term for the very last time. I looked back across the lawn as the school receded, before disappearing behind the Wilderness's trees. I could scarcely believe that this was it: I was now an old boy of the school. There was a rumbling hum, as we crossed the cattle grid, and then the road. We turned left, for Althorp.

A week later, when I learned that I had been accepted by Eton, I assumed I was free of Maidwell, once and for all. But that wasn't the case at all.

14

Looking Back

The farther backward you can look the farther forward you are likely to see.

– Winston Churchill

For years after I left his charge, when Jack occasionally reappeared in my life, I never thought to hold him to account. I even turned to him for advice during my first weeks at Eton.

I found the scale of my new school daunting. At Maidwell, I'd lived in a walled manor house with seventy-five pupils, while at Eton I was one of 1,300 students, aged thirteen to eighteen, sleeping in boarding houses dotted around a town, constantly moving between far-flung classrooms and sports pitches. The pace of the school was as challenging as its layout, the surprising amount of homework meaning my academic day often started before daybreak and kept me at my bedroom desk late into the night.

Assuming that my former headmaster understood the workings of a school better than anyone, I wrote to him. 'Dear Sir', I began, then asked him how I was to cope, let alone flourish, when permanently tired.

Jack's reply was typically brusque. He began by admonishing me for my letter's salutation: '"Dear Sir" is how you address someone that you do not know. I am not a stranger, or at least I should hope I am not. If you choose to write to me in future, your letter should begin: "Dear Mr Porch …".'

He then ridiculed me for imagining that schools would be designed to suit their new boys. They were rather, he explained, devised to meet the needs of older pupils as they approached important exams: I would be disappointed if I imagined differently.

It was vintage Jack: he was reminding me of the boarding school pecking order, whereby I should accept I was a 'squit' again, while knowing that I would eventually rise to become a 'squirt'. Stung by his lack of compassion, I don't believe I wrote to Jack again during my five remaining years at Eton.

A few months after this exchange of letters, my father told me that Jack was to retire. 'It's very odd,' he said. 'He's not been there *that* long. He's only fifty-one. And there's no word that he's moving on somewhere else. He's surely much too young to retire altogether? Most strange.'

The circumstances of Jack's leaving remain unclear to me. I heard that the parents of one of my contemporaries had been appalled to see the state of their boy's buttocks when he returned home for the holidays. They looked with horror at the scars from a recent thrashing, and they complained loudly to the governors, who then decided to move the headmaster on. But this may be myth.

The school presented his sudden departure as very much Jack's decision: he'd served as headmaster for a little more than fifteen years, they said, and he'd therefore decided it was time to move on. When one of his former masters wrote to say how sorry he was to hear that Jack was going, he replied in typical manner, distracting from the truth with cleverly constructed, amusing words: 'I have no trauma – or should I rather say *traumata*?* – at the prospect of departure.'

There were 110 applicants to fill Jack's shoes, whittled down to the choice of John Paul, a forty-year-old with a suitable résumé: a Cambridge degree, a stint in the Army, a role in the Church and relevant teaching experience. He must have seemed a safe pair of hands.

Leo had assumed that, as Jack's deputy, he'd step up to become headmaster, but he was interviewed for the job and rejected. Perhaps, in the wake of Jack's departure, the board of governors had uncovered the way in which the school was run, and how the boys were treated? If so, it is possible that they felt Leo was too close to Jack to be Maidwell's future. Perhaps they simply accepted that he wasn't headmaster material. Rather than stay on after this slight, Leo moved on, to become deputy head at another boarding school.

In July 1978, exactly a year after I'd left the school, my father took me, and his ever-present camera, to the Maidwell sports day, where Jack's departure was to be observed on a warm, overcast English summer's day. My father photographed me mixing

* The plural of trauma.

243

excitedly with pupils from a year or two below me – boys with whom I'd shared so much, for so long, under Jack's headmastership. I had already begun to understand that the friendships forged at this school were its golden legacy.

Once pupils had concluded the sporting part of the afternoon, they were allowed to join their parents, who'd come in large numbers to say goodbye to the man who'd taken care of their sons, in place of themselves. It was only polite to bid a collective farewell to the man who'd written those end-of-term reports that had made them chortle.

The fathers lounging on the grass that afternoon comprised a thick smattering of upper- and upper-middle-class Englishmen, including various lords, a senior judge and a leading Conservative politician. The older of these men wore three-piece tweed suits, while the younger ones were in jacket and tie.

The mothers donned floral print dresses or long skirts, their hair either long enough to brush the tops of their shoulders or piled up tightly into buns. Those ladies who'd arrived earliest were perched on the few rickety chairs at the top of the grass slope that looked down on proceedings, while the rest were seated on the grass. It was all very understated and English.

Jack and his wife stood together, she in an uncharacteristically soft ivory dress with matching hairband. A suave, dark-haired man I'd never seen before came forward to stand behind a plastic-topped school table. On it, he laid out his prompting notes, as well as a small parcel, clad in cellophane. He introduced himself as the chairman of Maidwell's governors, then went on to salute Jack for his decade and a half of leadership, before thanking Mrs

Porch for what he called, with unconscious irony, 'her constant support'.

As he concluded his remarks, the chairman passed the parcel in front of him to Mrs Porch. She unwrapped it, to find it contained a modest silver vase, the size of a large grapefruit, for displaying her precious, cut roses. I think Jack received a watch.

The headmaster had listened to the speech with a flat smile, his hands behind his back, his feet apart – 'at ease', in military parlance. He then moved forward to offer thanks, and to cede power.

How many adults there that day knew the truth about Jack's Maidwell? How many had no inkling? How many had some idea, but little wish to know more? And how many knew his tastes full well, but chose to do nothing?

Perry Pelham told me recently what he witnessed towards the end of the headmaster's final day. Jack went up to another boy and said to him, within Perry's earshot: 'You haven't seen the last of me, I'm afraid. Your parents have asked me to be your tutor during the coming holidays …'

Maude and Goffie were also nearby and overheard the words. Maude said, 'Well, Jack has kept a little boy to play with, after all!' and the two masters laughed at the ingenuity of their retiring head's perversion.

15

Facing the Past

We just philosophise, complain of boredom, or drink
vodka. It's so clear, you see, that if we're to begin living
in the present, we must first of all redeem our past and
then be done with it forever.

– Anton Chekhov

When I was at one of the lowest points in my life, in my
early forties, Maidwell and Jack came sharply back into focus.
This, after I'd spent many years trying to confine my time at the
harsh school, with its grim-faced headmaster, to the deeper
recesses of my mind.

My second marriage had followed the first into failure, leaving
two more of my offspring as children of divorce. Feeling beaten, I
decided to tackle whatever was attracting partners unsuited to me,
and me to them, so the pattern could end.

I sought professional help, assuming that something fixable was
wrong with me. I hoped that a switch could be flicked, after which
my life choices would improve.

I took myself to a clinic near London and, supposing I'd be staying there for some time, I came with suitcase in hand. As I stepped out of the cab, that 'new boy' dread danced wildly in my belly once more. But I was also excited, confident that – once admitted – I would immediately be placed on the appropriate route to wellness.

After a short, anxious wait, I was beckoned into an office of surprising sumptuousness. With gilt-framed paintings and antique furniture, it felt like the drawing room of a stately home. The master of this grand domain rose to usher me in with courtesy and confidence, then beckoned me to sit down. As he sank back into his leather chair, I saw he was wearing beautiful velvet slippers, adorned with rich gold stitching in sweeping loops.

He asked me why I had come to see him. I set about laying out my past in the way I did when starting with a new therapist. It was all there, I thought – my mother leaving home when I was so young, my parents' bitter divorce, my father's subsequent depression, his marrying a hard-to-like stepmother, repeated family loss, before finishing up with my marriages.

'So,' I said, 'it doesn't sound very good, does it?' I gave a weak smile, hoping we could move swiftly on, to initial diagnosis, without my having to delve any deeper. 'Do I have something wrong with me?' I continued, keen to receive a label from this renowned therapist. In my mind, this badge would be the first step on the path to a conclusive cure.

He came back at me with a flurry of no-nonsense questions, addressing the possibility, frequency and quantity of all manner of thoughts and behaviour. After twenty minutes, his checklists completed, the therapist nodded, then looked up with an air of composed assurance: 'Well, I do have a diagnosis for you, and it is this: you've had what we professionals like to call "a fucked-up childhood" ...'

He moved quickly on: 'You most definitely don't need my services, or those of this place, because your problems aren't those of addiction. What does need addressing is the toxic residue of your distant past.' He promised to come back to me with suggested treatments and, as the startling diagnosis began to sink in, told me I was free to leave.

I found myself setting off into the dark drizzle of an English winter's evening, clasping my unopened suitcase. I walked at a good pace, realising I was going to get soaked, being miles from home in an area with a dearth of public transport.

I had covered just a few hundred paces when my mobile phone rang. It was Rona, a colleague and friend from my decade as a reporter on NBC's *TODAY Show*. She has long had a knack for calling me out of the blue when my life is upside down.

'What are you up to?' she asked. I stopped walking, sheltered under a dripping tree, and told her where I was and what I had just been doing.

'Yes,' Rona agreed, unsurprised. 'The doctor's right. You don't need rehab.' She informed me of a residential course that she had been on, and which she swore by, judging it more effective than years of traditional therapy. She thought it perfect for me, because of its focus on processing childhood trauma, through forgiveness, acceptance and an understanding of how to cope with disruptive patterns of behaviour. 'Leave it to me,' she said. 'I'll get you in on the next programme – I know the directors there.'

A few days later I was enrolled, confronting my past alongside dozens of strangers. Going around the room that first evening, sharing our individual issues candidly with the group, I heard some desperate tales, against which my problems seemed embarrassingly trivial. One man could barely get his words out, being so tormented by his suffering; he could manage little more than wails of pain.

We moved on to private, one-to-one encounters with an assessor. I gave mine the usual download, after which he asked: 'And your ambition for the week ahead is …?'

'I have two,' I replied. 'To stop the endless cycle of poor choices in my romantic life. And to be a father that my children can be proud of.'

The assessor then prodded further, getting me to flesh out my childhood tale. Along the way, I took a slight detour from my well-honed narrative to touch on my time at Maidwell. It was light and cheery, with dark humour sprinkled in as a diversion.

But my skilled inquisitor sensed something. 'Tell me more about this place, Maidwell,' he said. I progressed from a superficial overview of the school to an intimate account of its grimmer secrets. In a whisper, I shared my being sexually abused by an adult at the school. I tried to explain the sense of being powerless in a terrifying setting – one that was patrolled and controlled by a headmaster set on inflicting pain on the boys in his care.

Because of these revelations, my intensive therapy received an extra strand: as well as addressing my childhood dealings with my

parents and stepparents, I would also have to process the legacy
Jack had bequeathed me. He had, I was told, been as key a part of
my life during the early years as my father or mother. 'You see,' the
assessor told me, 'Jack was your surrogate father.'

The programme schedule was already long: after gathering for
breakfast at 7.30 a.m., we worked on ourselves from 8.30 a.m. till
9.30 p.m., with breaks that might be shortened or cancelled altogether as the therapists thought necessary. But my days continued
on, alone, for an hour or two more, since I had Jack to address and
to come to terms with.

I have the paperwork from my time on this course. I see my
childhood's less pleasant nannies appeared in walk-on parts
during my treatment. Addressing them as if in person, I wrote to
Nanny Forster: 'I don't remember you ever smiling, let alone
laughing, nor do I recall you playing with me. I can see your white,
starched uniform, and your whacking me with wooden spoons. I
accepted this as normal, and never complained.

'Your punishment was brutal: banging my head against the wall
… I remember the hard white plastic and concrete [of that wall]
now. [This was a] punishment that resulted in dazed pain, the
impact startling in its intensity, crushing in its deliberate cruelty.'

But my focus was Maidwell, as I began to address its lifelong
impact on me. My first lesson was that children put through such
a protracted trauma, at such an early age, often go on to have
problems with intimacy, which can stem from a terror of abandonment.

Asked, that week, to recall a single childhood event that still
resonated with me above all others, I wrote: 'The headmaster, Jack,

catches me and the others in our dormitory talking after "lights out". He calls us over, and beats us savagely on his lap, repeatedly, with his slipper. He is quick, efficient, and cruel.'

When prompted to capture my feelings at that precise moment of punishment, I noted the 'physical burning' in my buttocks and also the mental message that I took away from the beating: 'He has the power to hurt me.' It was the first time I'd written about Maidwell, and it reconnected me with my utter powerlessness when there.

During that time of intensive therapy, I had to think back to Jack as he was, and in doing so I found myself reaching for adult tools – judgement; context – to make sense of someone who I'd previously reacted to instinctively, as a child. I was no longer a schoolboy, in awe and afraid, but a grown-up. I felt able to hold another to account for their actions, albeit decades later. How would I feel if someone did that to my children? I asked myself, and my horror at this thought released a surge of violent protectiveness.

In time, I allowed that feeling to reach, then envelop, the boy I had been. In middle age I finally recognised the extent of the damage done.

After I had completed the course and begun to drain the abscess that Maidwell had left me with, I was eager to go to see Jack. I was not angry *with* him, so much as curious *about* him: why had this man, who had total control of the place, set Maidwell up to be such a harsh and challenging environment for very young boys to have to navigate and survive? What were his reasons for choosing such an unforgiving tone for the place?

Did he regret it? What would he have done differently? Did he accept that our constant exposure to, and fear of, physical punishment had been both wrong and cruel? Had he perhaps suffered a bleak childhood, which caused him to make us suffer in turn?

Soon after I'd received the counselling that unearthed the impact Maidwell had had on me, I received an invitation to a rare school reunion.

I had no wish to go, but I saw the opportunity to seek answers from those who oversaw the bleakest part of my formative years.

'I was so sorry not to be able to attend the recent reunion,' I wrote, disingenuously, to Maidwell's then headmaster. 'I have so many vivid memories of my Maidwell days (1972–1977),' I continued, with more honesty, 'and, although still in touch with several contemporaries ... it would have been fascinating to reconnect with others.

'I would really like to catch up with some of the staff at Maidwell when I was there, and would be really grateful if your assistant might kindly dig up any information or contact about the following:

'Alec Porch;

'John Learmont;

'Henry Maude;

'I think I heard that David Johnson had died, many years back?

'Thomas Goffe – whose teaching was one of the causes of my going on to read History at Oxford ...

'Of course, I realise that a long time (32 years) has passed since I was at Maidwell, and you may have limited records on which to call. However, any help that you can give will be very gratefully received.'

I never got so much as an acknowledgement to my letter, which seemed odd for a place that prided itself on imparting and exhibiting good manners. I supposed that the school knew about this appalling chapter in its history and wanted the book that contained it to remain firmly shut.

16

A Different Generation

Parents wonder why the streams are bitter, when they themselves have poisoned the fountain.

– John Locke

What, really, was going on, when very wealthy people subcontracted the care of their child to the unpoliced regimes that ruled distant and secretive places? I suspect it was a simple reflex, this decision to perpetuate the method of education that they had experienced themselves: a significant number of parents convinced themselves that they hadn't really suffered, when subjected to similar, a generation earlier. Whatever the cost of repeating the process – both emotionally and financially – it was as well to carry on as before; as expected.

And pretty much every other parent from the same social background was in on this great conspiracy – some secretly devastated, others relieved to be shot of the inconvenience of having their children around the house.

I've spoken to some of the parents of my Maidwell classmates. Several of them still recall term-time letters from their sons, forty to fifty years ago, that contained pleas to be brought home from the school that they loathed, in ink sometimes smudged by their child's tears.

The majority of this dwindling generation admit to feeling guilt at ignoring their children's anguish, while hiding behind two defences: first, that they were only doing the same as everyone else from their social background; and, second, that they thought their sons would become all the stronger, for having survived their ordeal.

We have seen how Maude hit Thomas Scot so hard during a Latin class that he knocked him unconscious. When Thomas came to, he was tearful with shock and gripped by a painful headache. 'This was the part that went into my report,' he recalls. '"Thomas has been crying in class", without reference to the fact that I had been knocked out by the teacher. When my mother read this, she was absolutely furious with me. Why was I crying in class? What was wrong with me? I couldn't tell her the truth … Our parents were complicit.'

Some parents remained oblivious to the details of their children's terrible treatment at Maidwell into old age. A decade ago, when in his mid-fifties, Anthony Stapley told his parents about being half-drowned by Maude in the school's pool: 'My mother … firstly asked me why I didn't tell them about it. I responded that I didn't expect to get any sympathy. After a protracted pause she then said: "Anyway, why couldn't you swim your length by then, at the age of eight?"

'Mainly, I imagine,' he told his mother, drily, 'because I hadn't been taught how to do so down on our farm …'

Anthony's mother had been similarly indifferent when he returned from Maidwell as the victim of more obvious cruelty. 'I received one particular beating where Porch left me in his study while he went to the Wilderness to cut a green bamboo,' Anthony recalls. 'On his return he theatrically shredded the end by whipping the edge of the desk, then I was told to drop my trousers and underpants and was "soundly beaten", about eight strokes. On removal of my underpants that night, and for the next few weeks, at home being the only day boy, I had to prise them from my lacerated, healing buttocks. It is strange to think that I didn't say a word to my parents about any of this, especially as I returned home each night. Equally strange that I must have had blood-encrusted underpants for at least a fortnight, and nothing was said or suspected. My mother must have washed them.' This beating was so vicious that the scars were visible on Anthony's buttocks for four decades.

While some parents chose to ignore the evidence before them, others were delighted to be spared what they saw as the grind of child-rearing. Jack told one of his junior masters that quite a few of those sending their boys to Maidwell 'put their horses first, then their dogs – and, after both, they place their children'. These people found their offspring's need for nurturing a dull distraction from life's enjoyment.

My contemporary Cornelius Holland is adamant that his late parents had huge affection for him, but they were detached, as was common for adults of their background at that time. Instead of wanting to devote themselves to his everyday care, they had what he terms 'a total devotion to their holiday times'.

When Cornelius was a seven-year-old new boy, his parents dropped him at Maidwell in their Rolls-Royce. And that was that. They didn't visit him at the school again or take him out on any of the forty leave-outs or long leaves that punctuated his fifteen Maidwell terms.

They cited as their reason the three hundred miles between their home and the school they'd chosen for him: 'My parents unwittingly connived with the distance, and their inability to be there: Northampton to Cornwall being so far apart was, to them, really good news.' During his five years at Maidwell, he only saw his parents in the school holidays.

Once, Cornelius was overjoyed to learn from Jack that his parents would be taking him out, after all. But when the longed-for day arrived, the parents chose not to come. They sent their chauffeur in their place. He drove Cornelius the two hours to a cinema in London, where they watched a movie together, before the chauffeur drove him straight back to Maidwell.

In the decades between his leaving the school and his parents dying, Cornelius's family didn't discuss his time at Maidwell. 'It wasn't even touched on,' he remembers.

His older brother, who sums up Jack's tenure as 'All extremely sadistic', confirmed to me: 'My parents had nothing to do with the school – including visiting the place.'

Total disengagement with the boarding school child was rare in the 1970s, but in earlier decades it had been more normal; and those living abroad might not have seen them during the holidays, either. English schools advertised this year-round service, calling it 'entire charge'.

How could Maidwell boys succeed in communicating their despair to such disconnected parents? Robert Lilburne, twelve years my senior, decided to run away from the place, when aged eight. 'I did it because I was miserable and yearned for home,' he says. 'I slipped away out of the front gate and walked.' He hitchhiked half of the twenty miles, then walked till just short of home. 'My father in a car appeared coming towards me, leant over, opened the passenger door and told me to get in.' Robert's heart sank as he recognised that he was heading back to Maidwell, while his father remained, he reflects, 'stern and remarkably unquestioning'.

Robert remembers that on his return the headmaster at the time, Oliver Wyatt, came striding out of the school while loudly repeating 'Oh, you twerp!' and 'thwacking his riding cane down the side of his breeches. I got the feeling I was going to be in deep trouble, but my father muttered something to him, and I was sent to the changing rooms and told to go back to class. That was it. Didn't see my parents until end of term and [Wyatt] never said anything else about it.' Nor did Robert's parents.

The Maidwell boys who succeeded in transmitting their despair to their parents did so not with reasoned logic or self-inflicted wounds, but through displays of raw distress. These tended to occur when the return to school tipped over from looming nightmare to present reality. 'I broke down [when] returning to Maidwell from long leave in the winter of 1976,' my contemporary Daniel Blagrave, who was twelve at the time, says. 'I remember clearly my father saying to my mother in the car on the way back that this wasn't normal.' They immediately removed their son from the school and sent him to a gentler place where he was happy, appreciated and successful – he was fortunate that his parents trusted their instincts. Another of my contemporaries at Maidwell was less lucky.

We last met James Temple, his naked buttocks pointing upwards, being spanked and caressed, late at night, in the privacy of Jack's study. He hated Maidwell from the start, long before he was secretly abused. 'I used to cry my eyes out at that school for my first year – I was terrified,' he recalls.

Throughout his career as a boarder, when the last day of the school holidays arrived, he'd run and hide in the fields that abutted his home. When found, he'd be dragged kicking and screaming to his father's car for the drive to Maidwell.

James had an aunt who witnessed one such episode. She was Australian, and fresh to this peculiarly English ritual. Horrified, she berated James's parents for being 'appallingly cruel' in taking an obviously traumatised small boy to a place where he clearly had no wish to be.

James only very recently shared with his mother how unbearable he'd found his time at Maidwell, and the abuse that he'd suffered there. With her permission, I sent this aristocratic lady in her eighties questions about her intentions fifty years ago, through James, and in his voice.

Some of her replies echo those of any mother, traumatised at leaving their son by himself at school; but others show her particular pain on realising that her worst fears about Maidwell were exceeded.

Q. What sort of place did you think you were sending me to?
A. A small home-from-home school, with beautiful grounds, full of people with the same backgrounds. And it was fairly customary that you went to the same schools your parents or family went to. So I sent you to Maidwell like [your uncles].

Q. What did you think and feel when I used to cry, and hid to avoid going back to school?
A. I would cry inside every time. I would be full of anxiety and dread at the end of holidays or half-terms. I could never take you back to school as I would have been in floods of tears, so I got your aunt to travel with you and your father. It was agony watching you cry and be taken from me, knowing you didn't want to leave, but I had to be brave and not show too much emotion. I used to feel sad for days afterwards, and always wondered how you were. I wanted to call the school and find out, but that just wasn't the done thing.

Q. What did you think of my letters?
A. Your letters just filled me with sadness. It was agony reading your words and seeing your tear stains on the letters. I found it so hard to read them as it left me so worried as to whether we were doing the right thing, sending you away. I was always told that 'This is character-building stuff', and that you will pull through and be a better person for it. I still have

your letters, and to this day reading them would be too
upsetting.

Q. What did you think of Mr and Mrs Porch?
A. Rather strange and unapproachable. I have always been a
little shy and I found the Porches rather intimidating and
would leave the talking to your father. I was telephoned
(lectured) once by Mr Porch. He asked me to explain myself
as to why I was divorcing your father, and that it would be bad
for my children and their schooling. I thought this was a step
well over the teacher/parent relationship, and I certainly wasn't
going to tell him [*exceptionally intimate and shocking details of
our marriage*]. Being talked to in this way by Porch on such
matters, made me feel like a schoolgirl having to explain
myself to the teacher. After that I avoided them both.

Q. What did you think of my school reports?
A. I actually found your reports rather amusing. There was
certainly nothing in them that would worry me. You were not
a great academic. You were an active and well-liked boy, and I
felt that Mr Porch quite favoured you.

Q. What are your thoughts now that you know the truth?
A. If only you had told me. I can't believe you didn't. No
parent would have found this acceptable. I am devastated and
feel a sense of guilt. We would never have sent you to a school
where this went on. I am in shock that such depravity,
perversion and fear was rife throughout the school. I am

disgusted, angry and saddened by what I have learnt. I wish I had never sent you away.

William Say, the head boy who had to endure weekly spankings at 'Sunday Confessions', shared his abuse at Jack's hands with his mother. 'I had absolutely *no* idea, till very recently, that this was going on,' she told me, with feeling. 'It's appalling. I feel terrible – but I saw Mr Porch as being *in loco parentis*, and he had total control over my sons once I'd dropped them at Maidwell.' William's elder brother corroborates this, remembering his mother as being 'scared' of Jack – she'd quickly hand over her boys to him, before beating a hasty retreat from his domain, despite William's tears each time.

'You were a blubber – you blubbed at the start of every term,' William's mother teased him recently, as the three of us had lunch. 'I used to say to you: "We're going to have to get the fire brigade to pump the car out", because there were so many tears.'

Both James's and William's mothers feel guilt at what their sons suffered, but they are as much victims as their sons. Fifty years ago, they felt they had to do the right thing by their social peers – 'the *done* thing', as the British Establishment termed it – and send their boys away, with heavy hearts and foreboding.

It wasn't only the mothers who felt the pain when toeing the line. My former father-in-law Rupert Hutton used to wear sunglasses when driving his children back to boarding school, so they – and the adults present – couldn't see his tears.

And my grandfather noted in his journal, on my first day at Maidwell, how my father came to visit him on his way back to

Park House, 'having first left Charles at Maidwell School, so he was v. depressed – he only stayed a few moments'. My father later said to me that leaving me bereft at Maidwell that September day was his lowest point as my parent.

Perry Pelham told me how he had confronted his mother with the question, why had she sent him to this awful place? He was disappointed that she had hidden behind a defence so predictable, so illogical, as 'Well, it's what parents did back then …' This had left the son's wounds unhealed.

Some have been more fortunate. One of my contemporaries at the school told me recently: 'My parents always thought I was exaggerating – until my sister married a fellow [Maidwell] victim. Both my parents, individually, apologised after hearing our stories.' This made him grateful, but he realises he will never achieve closure, as his Maidwell trauma reverberates on.

The wounds went deep, whether acknowledged or not. Another of my Maidwell friends would listen to my occasional venting about the school's cruel excesses in a quiet trance: he didn't stop me, but he didn't add to what I was saying, except when ambushing me with a quip, in an attempt to make light of it all.

He'd suffered terribly there, being a regular in Jack's Saturday Morning Club for several years, when he was caned for supposedly being idle and dim, while he was neither. Besides the physical pain, he was a vulnerable boy who'd received little encouragement or praise, and who'd been ridiculed in person and in end-of-term reports for being overweight. He'd pretended to take this mockery in good spirits, saying, with a broad but unconvincing smile, 'But it's not fat – it's relaxed muscle!' I found it sad that this intelligent, sensitive man seemed incapable of accepting that he was one of Maidwell's many victims.

Recently he started to peep out over the defences that he'd erected long ago. I was relieved when he told me: 'I know you're right, of course – but I don't want to say any more, because that would mean I was criticising Mummy and Daddy for sending me there.' Like so many who have what psychiatrists recognise as 'boarding school syndrome', he found it hard to face his trauma while his parents still lived.

Later he opened up further when coming to stay with me, as he does every year, telling me that he has only to see the sign to Northamptonshire (the county that houses both Maidwell and my home) to start feeling anxious. By the time he drives past the gateway to Maidwell's grounds, the memory of past distress triggers a sense of panic that makes him shake, and sends him into a sweat.

In the final week of my writing this book he made two additional admissions to me. First, that he still – aged fifty-nine – carries scars on his buttocks from his many canings by Jack. Also, that he remembers half-term breaks from the school – those twice-a-year blocks of a week at home – as traumatic rather than enjoyable, because his brother always spent that precious time sobbing inconsolably at the prospect of soon being forced to return to Maidwell.

His wife prompted him to finally tell his aged parents how bad his Maidwell years had been. It didn't go well. When he shared how miserable he'd been at the school, his parents were incredulous. They told him to 'stop being so wet' and laughed at what they saw as his ludicrous self-pity. What could have been an opportunity for honesty, acceptance and forgiveness instead saw fresh insult being added to ancient injury. My friend hasn't revisited the subject of Maidwell with them since.

I have, though. I told his father how grim it had been at Maidwell and how appalling Jack could be. 'Yes,' conceded the old man, with a jaunty smile, 'but Jack did write such jolly amusing reports!' I conceded his point, but added that I viewed them as works of deep cunning, constructed by a pervert, and designed to distract parents from what was going on at his school. My friend's father made no further comment, looked down and silently walked away.

EPILOGUE

In 1987, I went back to Maidwell as a London-based correspondent for NBC News's *TODAY Show*. My initial brief, before
moving on to assignments around the globe, was to give American
breakfast-time viewers telling insights into Britishness. When I
suggested to my senior producer that I could illustrate the peculiarities of the social elite by doing pieces on Maidwell and Eton
she quickly agreed.

It was strange, returning to Maidwell as an adult, ten years after
I had left it as a boy. Physically, the place had changed barely at
all, and although nearly all of the teachers I had known there had
moved on (Miss Best-Shaw was still dispensing shy kindness in
the seventh form), the members of the backroom staff remained
in place: Annie presided in the kitchen, with the irrepressible May
still lending bustling support, while Frank stoked the boilers and
gang-mowed the lawn.

The tone of the place seemed markedly less formal, and the
pupils looked more at ease than in my day. Jack's departure must
have helped this, of course, but so would the boys' regular contact
with the outside world. While I went on school trips once a year

– to a steam engine rally, to a classmate's wildlife park, to watch Shakespeare's *Henry V* in Stratford-upon-Avon, and on the prefects' tour of Althorp – the late 1980s Maidwellian could leave the school several times each week, if his hobbies included, say, sailing on the nearby reservoir, or riding at a local stables. Indeed, the recreational side of the school week had grown so rich that I had to remind my TV audience: 'This may look like an exclusive country club for very small gentlemen, but it is, in fact, a *school* ...' It was a very far cry from Jack's day, when he kept his boys safely locked up, behind the school walls.

But vestiges of my headmaster's regime still remained. His replacement as headmaster, John Paul, had an authoritative and serious air. I later learned that, while he administered corporal punishment infrequently, when he beat boys, he did so with force. One of my friends, a couple of years younger than me, who straddled the two reigns, told me recently: 'Paul caned me harder than Porch ever did – but only once.'

John Paul was interviewed in the early 1990s, for a BBC documentary about boarding schools. It followed eight-year-olds as they are sent away, giving them a voice, and hearing from their mothers and fathers. Some of the parents were astonishingly callous (a father dismissing the concept of speaking to an eight-year-old son on the phone as absurd – 'they can't express themselves very well'; and a mother claiming she didn't feel she was sending her new boy son to stay with strangers, but with people who'd quickly become 'sort of like best friends'). The programme also heard from middle-aged men impacted by having been sent away to school so young: 'I don't think I ever recovered from that experience, in the sense that it became normal for me to carry around that level of grief and loss – and despair.' Part of them was broken, forever.

The opening sequences of this documentary covered the start of a term at Maidwell: parents' mindless chatter; boys blinking in white-faced shock, struggling to be brave; and the headmaster striving to reassure frightened faces with unfeeling platitudes. Mr Paul used tortured logic to justify the plucking of seven- and eight-year-olds from their homes: 'Well, I'm hard put to think of any boy who, by the age of ten or eleven has not become well used to the concept of boarding, and he's settled in. That doesn't mean to say that he necessarily is going to look back on these as the happiest days of his life. There are boys who will always find school a trauma – whether it be as a day boy, or as a boarder.' You can see in his eyes that Mr Paul knows the preposterousness of his argument – that it *only* takes three years or so to get a child used to boarding – and the illogicality of his conclusion that it's the nature of the boy, not the institution, that determines whether he will be happy as a boarding school pupil or not.

But, while Paul's disingenuousness shows him to come from the same stable as Jack, Maidwell was better under him than in my time there. By the new headmaster's side came a wife, Susan, who had a strong affinity for the pastoral side of the place. 'Mrs Paul has also taught in preparatory schools,' the governors reassured the parents, 'and although at Maidwell she will do no regular teaching, her experience and interest in the younger boys will be of particular value to her in the more general role of headmaster's wife.' The school now had a leading lady, rather than the unwilling extra it had known in Mrs Porch, who had been least unhappy when lurking in the wings.

Some of the parental attitudes that underpinned places like Maidwell continued on in Mr Paul's more temperate governance. On a September day, two decades after my first day at the school, a couple I know very well drove for Maidwell, with their eight-year-old new boy, George, in the back seat. George was aware that he was being taken away to a place where he would be boarding, but wasn't privy to the finer details of the plan.

He remembers trying very hard to be brave, and positive, despite his mounting distress at being sent away from home. It was silent in the car, both parents quietly dreading the moment when they'd have to say goodbye to their gentle, naive son. The mother was only just winning the struggle not to cry.

George's high voice suddenly cut through the charged hush: 'Mama, Papa?' he asked, 'would it be all right if I came home for Christmas?'

It was then that both parents realised with a shock that they'd forgotten to inform their son that the term ahead would last for thirteen weeks, after which he would be home for five weeks' holiday, with the childhood thrill of Christmas at its core.

Both adults have told me how awful they felt at that moment, for failing to furnish their child with such a crucial detail. But, being products of boarding schools themselves, they had just assumed it was obvious. I see all three of them as victims of a system that was, in part, designed to crush normal, family relations.

* * *

Despite what I saw and experienced at Maidwell, I am not against boarding schools. I do feel, though, that sending pre-teen children to them is cruel, unless they truly want to go – as some undoubtedly do.

I have seven children, ranging in age from eleven to their early thirties. Both my sons chose, in their teens, to attend weekly boarding schools (they came home every weekend), while my daughters have, to date, all chosen day schools. I've fully supported all of their decisions, since I agree with George Orwell's summation: 'Of one thing … I do feel sure, and that is that boarding schools are worse than day schools. A child has a better chance with the sanctuary of its home near at hand.'

In the years before my epiphany about the impact of Maidwell on me, my association with the school continued from time to time, mainly because it was down the road from Althorp, which I inherited on my father's death in 1992.

When it launched a co-educational pre-school, in the early nineties, I went to visit it, knowing one of the two female teachers to be exceptionally well thought of. I was relieved to see that this school for very young children was cast in the image of Miss Best-Shaw's seventh form, rather than Jack's abusive operation, and enrolled my daughters there.

But, once I started doing the school runs, I felt very ill at ease, driving in and out of the back gate to the wider school, the setting of so much grisliness from my past. After we separated, my then wife and I were agreed that we would spare our children from a classically English upbringing. We sought a fresh start for them, far from Maidwell, in South Africa. I felt immediately vindicated when the elder three children returned to me after their first morning of nursery school having been set one task: to draw themselves, after which the teacher said to them, 'Now, that is *you* – *your* body – and nobody can ever touch it, except with your permission.' It was a message whose perfection I found thrilling: a total repudiation of Maidwell's culture of physical and sexual abuse.

I returned to live in England several years later, remarried, and had two further children with my second wife. I visited Maidwell, some time around 2008, when the school was hosting a meet of the local foxhound pack. That day I met the then Maidwell headmaster, Robert Lankester, who charmed parents in the front courtyard as Jack had done in my day. I noted further progress, since the boys looked even more at ease with the staff on show, and each other, than in Mr Paul's day.

But, as the foxhounds snuffled busily around the courtyard, I found the pungent scent of past memories flooding my senses. Where I was standing was also where I'd joined in drill, for five years, under Johnno at his most officious – directing the bracing start to yet another Maidwell day with boorish hollering. Straight ahead was the door I had entered as a new boy with my father, before he left alone for home. Meanwhile the side door, fifty paces away, led to the dread corridor that snaked down to the terror of Jack's study.

I have never been back.

* * *

In early 2017, exactly forty years after I left the school, I received a cheery email from an old family friend, informing me that he had recently become a governor at Maidwell Hall, as well as chair of its appeals committee. Could they please use Spencer House, my family's historic home in London, for a launch event?

My reply was courtesy itself until I reached my conclusion, when I felt compelled to speak to the darkness of the past: 'Without wishing to sound rude, I absolutely loathed my time at Maidwell. It is clearly a vastly improved place now, but it was horrific in the mid-'70s. I say that so you know it sadly is not a place that is high on my philanthropic wish list!' They held their event elsewhere.

Today, all but three or four of the staff from my time at Maidwell are dead.

I was on the point of approaching Jack, to ask him why he'd been as he had, when a friend sent me his death notice. This asked for donations to an Alzheimer's charity, so I was probably years late in my quest for answers, even if he had lived further into his nineties.

The last time I can remember hearing from my prep school headmaster was in 1992 after the sudden death of my father. Jack sent his condolences, commending my father as an unusually good and gentle man. 'You should write down all your memories of him now,' he advised, 'so you can one day share them with your children when they want to know more about who their grandfather really was. If you don't do it now, you will forget things.' It was sensible and thoughtful guidance. He'd done the same for his family, he told me, when his father – 'Judy' Porch – had died.

I've never seen the predatory assistant matron since she left Maidwell. While in the very final days of writing this book I rediscovered my 1976 diary in a recess at Althorp, and was rocked by an inscription on its first page that I had no recollection of having seen before. 'Please' had written 'Me', then her home address and phone number, in looping handwriting, where only I would be likely to see it. She had done this, I assume, in the expectation that we would stay in touch, after she left the school. There is something about that word, 'Me', that strikes me now as not only wildly inappropriate, but intensely intimate – and, of course, slyly anonymous.

I've looked her up on the internet from time to time, and last noted her presence at her father's funeral some years back. Further online research has established that she has married at least twice, the first time a year or so after leaving Maidwell, and that she has a middle-aged child, but I can't find where in Britain she might be now. I suspect she either lives abroad or is dead. If alive, she would be in her late sixties. Did she, I wonder, go on to molest other children in subsequent years?

In the wake of the abuse scandals within the Roman Catholic priesthood, twenty or so years ago, private boarding schools in England began to give up their own grim secrets. In early 2015, I contacted a lawyer in London who was in the media as the face of these prosecutions.

Dear [Madam],

STRICTLY PRIVATE & CONFIDENTIAL
I attended Maidwell Hall, Northamptonshire, between
September 1972 and July 1977.

It was a horrific place, overseen by the terrifying
and sadistic headmaster, J.A.H. Porch – known as 'Alec'
Porch.

While physically abused along with all the other boys there,
there are more intimate matters still that I would like your
advice on, with a view to possibly taking legal action.

Yours sincerely,
Charles Spencer

Putting that stark distillation of my time down on paper had a
startling effect on me. I had nightmares about those who'd
corroded a key part of my childhood: the 'intimate matters' of
course related to Please's perversion.

The lawyer replied with professionalism and kindness, but I
realised that pushing ahead with litigation was beyond me then:
'Even contacting you about this stuff has brought a lot of horrible
memories to the surface,' I explained. As I stood down, I promised
her that if anyone contacted her who'd attended Maidwell Hall in
the mid-1970s, with tales of sexual molestation or abuse, I would
be happy to give my evidence in corroboration. I assume none did,
although I recently learned from William Say that he contacted
Maidwell a few years ago, to tell them of his serious abuse at Jack's

hand. The school advised him to take the matter up with the police, not with them – something he has yet to do.

I heard from Mr Maude out of the blue, in 1989. He seemed to have forgotten his dislike for – and his disinterest in – me, during my time at school. There were no apologies for his explosive moods or his terrifying physical aggression.

Instead, in a brazen denial of the past, he wrote to me in a jokey, knowing tone, as if we had been fellow passengers on a blissful ocean voyage long ago, during which we had enjoyed many good times together. He suggested we meet up, but, while I was polite in reply, I was repelled by his invitation. I found his fake bonhomie puzzling at the time, but now see it for the gaslighting that it clearly was. Maude was subjecting me to the charm offensive that had beguiled visiting Maidwell parents, but he was forgetting that I had seen the man behind the wolfish grin for the vicious sadist that he had been, and he couldn't expunge that truth from my mind.

Maude informed me that he was serving as high sheriff of Kent, an ancient ceremonial role in his native county that carries prestige in upper-middle-class circles. I think he wanted me to know that he was no longer treading water as a schoolmaster but had chosen to reclaim the social status that had always been his birthright. This dishonourable aristocrat died in 2018, aged ninety, in the manor house in Kent that he'd inhabited during his long retirement.

I kept in touch with Michael Barker, my favourite Maidwell master, writing to him several times after he moved on to a new teaching position in Oswestry, near the Welsh border.

I was shocked when, some thirty years ago, I learned that Mr Barker had died while still a young man. I can't recall if it was from a heart attack or a car crash, but it was cruelly sudden for his family. I will always be grateful for the way in which he made Maidwell easier for me, and others, to bear.

I have found out nothing about the latter years of Granny Ford, but Cornelius Holland said he had heard from someone he trusted that she had been a big drinker.

'Maybe that explains a very strange time,' I said. 'When I passed her in the corridor after I'd been to the loo, very late at night, and I said "Hello, Please" – she looked straight past me, as if I wasn't even there?' Cornelius said that was most likely the case. 'So many of the staff at Maidwell were drinkers,' he added. 'Perhaps that was their way of getting through working at that place?'

I have heard that Miss Best-Shaw was moved on from Maidwell, against her will, on reaching sixty. Compulsorily retired, she returned to her family's ancestral home, where she passed the remainder of her life quietly with her two unmarried sisters. Her nephew recently sent me a photograph of her in retirement, reading in the garden, and I remembered with a smile how she'd enjoyed sharing books with her boys in the shade of Maidwell's tall trees.

I never followed through with my boyhood promise to myself, that one day I'd track down Goffie and exact my revenge on him. In 2004, I thought of him, and that long ago victory I scored over him by remembering so many of the generals at the Battle of Blenheim, when my account of Blenheim became my first non-fiction bestseller in the UK. Maybe I should have sent him a copy.

However, my anger towards Mr Goffe reignited recently, after I learned that John Hutchinson, a gentle fellow who arrived at Maidwell a couple of years after me, had died in March 2019, aged fifty-three.

I remembered John as far from robust – before joining the school, his fragile legs had required medical support. He also faced learning difficulties, which this typically unevolved 1970s boarding school failed to address. His Maidwell years would have been challenging anyway; but they were made hellish by the likes of Goffie.

John was a sensitive and thoroughly decent boy who was tormented by this shameless, cowardly bully, in a school regime that had a hundred rules, but not one of them proved capable of protecting the most vulnerable in its ranks. What on earth would persuade Goffie – a man, powerful in physique and status – to pick on someone so fragile and defenceless?

As his younger brother recalled in the eulogy that he gave at John's funeral:

At Maidwell John had a tough time, principally because he had dyslexia which was not diagnosed for several years, until age ten. Some bullying teachers accused him of not trying, or of being lazy, neither of which was true. Looking back, John always noted Mr Goffe as the worst offender, a mean teacher who regularly hit his knuckles with a wooden ruler. These constant knockdowns in turn affected John's self-confidence, and he became very shy. But John was always sweet and kind with other boys, never passing on the knocks that were handed out to him.

Aged eleven, John was moved to a school specialising in dyslexia. But three years at Maidwell, being bullied by the likes of Goffie, had changed him. The self-assurance that he'd had as a young boy, before being sent away, was bled out of him. After school he lived the quietest of lives. In adulthood he had no romantic partner or close friends, preferring to sit at home by himself, watching television.

His family background was immensely privileged, but he took humble jobs – helping in a pet store, then a home supplies' warehouse – surprising colleagues at the latter by walking to work on a day when the roads were so clogged with snow that none of them, or any of their customers, made it in.

John died from an intestinal disorder that he had ignored: his family believe that he had lost the instinct for self-care, had failed to get himself to a doctor, and this killed him. He was found dead after failing to turn up for work.

I had not appreciated that the weight of suffering experienced by many of my contemporaries would be so virulent, and so hard to bear. When I read John's eulogy, I cried with pity, and then rage.

I have talked to many of those who survived Maidwell half a century ago and asked them how their years there have impacted them since.

One of these, Thomas Scot, who started as a Maidwell new boy alongside me, has chosen to live abroad, in Sweden – the first country in the world to abolish corporal punishment (and other demeaning treatment) of children. He recognises that the particularly English nature of his boarding schooldays is the reason he has chosen exile overseas. If his native land could condone the cruelty that he suffered, he wanted no home in it.

Recently, when passing Maidwell and finding it was closed and empty for the school holidays, Thomas took his family for an impromptu walk round the school's grounds. For the first time, he recounted some of his grimmer experiences there, and pointed to the spots where they'd taken place. His Swedish wife and children were at first disbelieving, then horrified.

'I suspect,' Thomas has warned me, when learning of this book, 'that there may be pushback from other old boys who have the "It didn't do me any harm" attitude (said through a twisted grimace while throttling a baby rabbit or some other innocent) – so be prepared for that.' But he urged me to continue, as most of our Maidwell classmates have done, because of the damage those years have done to many of us.

Anthony Stapley – who sank to the bottom of the school's swimming pool through Maude's cruelty, and who Jack whipped so hard he bore the scars on his buttocks into middle age – sees the legacy of his Maidwell years as twofold: 'All these experiences we have through our days make us who we are: hardy, tough, resilient, determined', while recognising they've also left us 'wary, untrusting and emotionally retarded/unstable'.

Robert Lilburne, who escaped from Maidwell briefly as an eight-year-old, before being silently returned to the school by his father, says drily, 'It's no wonder some of us struggled a tad after experiencing such an "education".'

Perry Pelham characterises Maidwell as 'This extraordinary place, where it was all about beating, and pain. It didn't matter what you did – drop something, spill water, talk after lights out – you were going to be beaten, and hard.'

Perry remains especially troubled by one, underlying aspect of our schooldays: 'There were actually very few rules – you only really knew you were in trouble again when preparing for the next beating ... It's impacted on the rest of my life, this not really having a clear framework of rules to abide by.'

I recently had lunch with John Okey, who was in my year at Maidwell, to ask him about his recollections of our Alma Mater. We hadn't seen one another for decades, and had never before discussed in detail the private school we attended in the early to mid-1970s.

I was struck by how John remembered everyday details with the same clarity as me. When I mentioned Goffie, he replied at once, with a joyful glint, 'Do you remember that time he got a pea stuck in his beard?'

John summed up Maidwell back then, as 'a *very* strange place indeed'. Jack beat him with the slipper countless times a term, and he recalled being caned so often that he said, 'I always had lines on my buttocks.' This was, I can recall from communal showers after games, no exaggeration. He was one of many who routinely carried the scars of Jack's aggression.

Daniel Blagrave – who'd shared with us his father's belief that women only submitted to the supposed painfulness of sex out of selfless love – got in touch with me after reading two newspaper articles.

The first of these was an interview I'd given to the *Times Educational Supplement*, for one of its regular features: 'My Favourite Teacher'. In it I spoke of how I saw the master Michael Barker as a beacon of warmth in the otherwise frigid landscape of my childhood boarding school. I also mentioned, by way of contrast, that establishment's harsh headmaster. I left both the place and the principal unnamed: they weren't the story. Mr Barker's kindness was.

The following month I was surprised to hear a rebuttal to my assertions, during a rambling interview on a local radio station. The interviewee was Richard Deane, an archaeologist who had been a new boy in my final Maidwell year. Deane had, I learned, become a significant bully after I left the school, his speciality name-calling. One of his victims, a friend who now lives in America, told me how Deane had been his and his brother's 'chief tormentor'. The duo had arrived at the school as gentle innocents, unprepared for its hard edges, or even for its everyday expectations: they started at Maidwell unable to tie their own shoelaces. 'And I used to pick my nose,' my friend confided. 'So, once he had spotted that, Deane had an "in" with his taunting: he forever after called me "Nosepicker" in public and would laugh at me.' He cast his eyes down in humiliation, the embers of that long ago mockery still burning within.

Perhaps Deane needed to defend the ugly environment in which his bullying had thrived, unchecked? Or perhaps he is like a number of my private school contemporaries (none of them from Maidwell) who have sidled up to my wife Karen and asked her to stop me writing about the institution because, in their view,

I'm some sort of class traitor, 'letting the side down'? He tried, in his rebuttal, to vindicate Maidwell and Jack – breaking the anonymity I'd afforded both. Deane presented Jack's frenzied tickling of his pyjama-clad boys, as they shrieked and writhed at his touch, as nothing more than a bit of fun. This, and Deane's justification of other inexcusable aspects of Maidwell's life, persuaded my friend Blagrave to write to me in solidarity:

> The incredible thing is not that you remember [Maidwell] as truly appalling, but more that there are people in this world who seem to think that it was anything more than a gruelling, cold, filthy, stinking cowshed. From the institutionalised violence … to the smell of the pine sawdust used to suck up the ever-present vomit, Jack, [Granny] Ford and their willing henchmen – the place remains etched in my soul … Being prisoners there, I think we were the last of the Victorians in many ways. We were parked there out of tradition, and not for education.

Blagrave said that Deane's 'version of the horror reminded me of Prisoners of War saying, "It wasn't all bad." Of course, it wasn't! The human spirit cannot help but carve something out of any number of vile situations. He seems to think that what we went through was all done with a sense of humour. There was one Easter term where Jack "slippered" us all every day but two. I think you were in that dormitory? There was nothing "funny" about it AT ALL, it was terrifying. Indeed, the school itself was terrifying from beginning to end, full stop. In a way, it's a miracle that Jack's strange predilection for pert, ten-year-old bottoms, slippers and canes hasn't released a deluge of lawsuits ... And to think that all was done in the name of God. Jack's cynical "faith" makes the wretched story even more dark and hard to stomach.'

From the perch of middle age, Daniel looks down clearly on how his years at Maidwell have adversely shaped his life: 'I know that I gave up at the age of eight. I realised that effort was rarely rewarded, and the bare minimum required to get by was going to result in the same amount of pain as trying hard ... It is easy, you will cry, to blame trauma in your childhood for failure in the rest of life, and I would heartily agree. However, in the case of Maidwell Hall, I believe there is an argument to be made along those lines for a lot of children. The danger, of course, is that we are accused of whinging about our silver spoons, however nickel palladium they really turned out to be ...

'The thing we should remember, is that we have had various levels of success in our lives IN SPITE of Maidwell not THANKS to Maidwell, which is what Deane would like the world to think.'

Daniel struggled to understand how one of our schoolmates, now related to him by marriage, could find anything positive in his Maidwell years: 'Tom Wogan's memories are of halcyon days, with a cruel, but fair and adored headmaster. There is no accounting for taste. Then again, perhaps, there were various levels of cruelty and favouritism displayed by the Maidwell establishment that simply passed over our young heads.'

James Temple – fondled and beaten on Jack's pouf – adds: 'It was a school ruled by fear. Where was the word "encouragement"? Where was the nurturing? It was never there. Fear was the cloud that hung over every class.' Remembering the staff, he concludes: 'They were all complicit.

'We have to be honest, Maidwell put us on directions that were very destructive. It destroyed so many of us – burying poison that seeps into your mind and your life. You have to deal with stuff that is ruinous.' James believes he has been impacted particularly in his personal life, and points to a litany of romantic wreckage: 'I can't find love; I don't know what love is' – as well as battles with drugs and alcohol.

So many of the Maidwellians I have talked to have said how their conversations with me have reawakened memories that they'd allowed to lay dormant for half a century.

Isaac Ewer, head boy when I was halfway through the school, was one of these – he remembers Maidwell with fondness, overall: 'I massively enjoyed it, and still see a lot of people from there. I was good at sport, reasonably good-looking and fairly academic, so it was relatively easy for me.' But he conceded that there were things about the school that were, without doubt, 'deeply weird and strange', and 'like a prison camp'.

He quickly rattled off the names of four of his school year there who, he says, remain 'very good friends of mine now. Incredibly good friends – not just because of the brutality.' As he spoke, I remembered them all, two or three years senior to me, in their thirteen-year-old pomp: they were the standout pupils, noted for their sporting prowess and popularity. Jack managed to find excuses to cane them all, regularly.

Isaac's concern now is for the other boys – those who didn't find the place a breeze because of their genetic gifts. They inhabit the same Maidwell school photograph that Isaac treasures, but he can't recall their names. His fear is that they were victims to the dangerous urges that churned deep within the more sinister adults at the school: 'Maybe awful things were happening to the less popular boys. I feel awful about it.'

He believes there was much to be anxious about, when looking in the masters' common room: 'Given the cohort of staff we had, it's inconceivable that there wasn't abuse. We were so much in their care – they could have got away with it.'

Isaac goes on to recall: 'The worst thing you could do [at the school] was show any emotion. If someone cried after being beaten, you ran away from them rather than comfort them. It was too embarrassing to show emotion.' This produced in him, he believes, a positive outcome: 'It made me very robust – compared to our children, I have huge resilience. Someone could stamp on my fingernails, and I wouldn't wince. However bad it was, you just dealt with it. Showing any emotion made it worse.' The lesson from all this? 'If it didn't crush you, it made you very competent.'

In whatever way you viewed Maidwell and its staff back then, it's clear that the school and its ethos remained with you for life.

What effect has attending Jack's Maidwell had on me? There are superficial elements in my life today that hark back to day-to-day living at that school: I dry my hair as Granny Ford prescribed, pulling my towel fifty times each way, left and right. Equally, when I hear anyone count down from ten to zero, I still expect the numbering to descend to 'Going, going, gone, now', as the head boys would shout when chivvying us in the washroom before lunch or tea.

Meanwhile at Maidwell I certainly received the continuation of an excellent academic education. Also, my prep school years were so challenging that they made life at Eton comparatively easy – 'a walk in the park', as one of my fellow Maidwellian-Etonians agrees. Self-dependence from such an early age has helped me to cope with almost any situation, in a cold, functioning way.

On the other hand, I am certain that my life has been shorn of much joy because of my five years under Jack and his henchmen. The happy-go-lucky boy of Park House and Silfield had to grow a hard outer casing, to help survive as a very young child, far from home. Miss Lowe had reported to my parents how, aged six, I was always 'lively and humorous'.

My mother liked to call me 'Buzz', in the years before I was sent away to boarding school, because I had the happy efferves-cence of a bee. But few at Maidwell saw that lighter side of me. As soon as I arrived, in shock and grief, I became watchful and guarded. This was my way of protecting myself in a world domi-nated by a cruel and exacting headmaster, with his entourage of complicit abusers and cowed enablers, supported by a pair of unusually vicious boy bullies.

At Maidwell, I made sure to hide all vulnerabilities, lest they become soft targets. It was best to shield the weak spots, to fit in to the image of the model Maidwellian: unemotional, honest, upright and accepting. And so I became utterly self-reliant – but not always in a good or healthy way.

When looking at the wreckage of my first and second marriages,

I learned early in therapy that being sent away to boarding school at eight years of age meant that I had next to no understanding of intimacy. It is an almost inevitable consequence of the trauma of which homesickness was the most obvious symptom. Equally, I became highly reactive, so that any slights or threats of abandonment jolted me into 'fight or flight' survival mode. This unwanted legacy has proved hard to shift, even in the face of decades of therapy.

It's of course easy to look for reasons why things have not worked out, yet very hard to know for sure how far apart catalyst, cause and chance stand. But I am certain that some things died for me between my eighth and thirteenth birthdays, when in Jack's care. Innocence, trust, joy – all were trampled on and diminished in that outdated, snobbish, vicious little world that English high society constructed, endorsed and then handed over to the care of people who could be very dangerous indeed.

It amazes me still that I – always a stubborn child – meekly succumbed to the misery of the bleak path chosen for me. It just didn't occur to me to rebel – to insist that I wouldn't go to that very private school which encapsulated many of the worst failings of the boarding tradition. My disappointment in myself, for this unconditional surrender, has only grown as I've aged.

This memoir is, I now see, my attempt to right that wrong, some five decades on. I've retraced the steps of the boys who walked beside me then, and have tried to make sense of the failings of those adults who let us down so terribly.

Along the way, I have to say, with surprise as well as relief, that I feel I have reclaimed my childhood.

ACKNOWLEDGEMENTS

My first and fullest thanks go to the many Maidwellians who shared their experiences with me with bravery and generosity. Thank you, gentlemen.

I wrote more than half of this book before any publisher had sight of it. Thank you to William Patrick and my old friends Karen Stirgwolt and Doug Segal for making some helpful suggestions as to direction and form during these initial phases, and for giving me American perspectives on a very English tale.

I am – as ever – extremely grateful to my UK editor, Arabella Pike, of William Collins, for her light touch and wise counsel. I know how lucky I have been to have such a distinguished professional in the background, while completing a work that I have found uniquely demanding. Thank you, too, to Arabella's colleagues Iain Hunt and Katherine Patrick for their enormous hard work.

Many thanks to Aimée Bell, of Simon & Schuster, who fully grasped the aims of this book from when it began to take shape in my mind five years ago. She has backed it with her customary flair, intelligence and energy. I am also grateful to her boss, Jennifer

Bergstrom, for endorsing Aimée's judgement in pursuing this work. Sincere thanks, too, to Jennifer Long, Sally Marvin, Jennifer Robinson and Sierra Fang-Horvath of Simon & Schuster.

My literary agent, Caroline Michel, of PFD, has been a fabulous support, while her experience and sophistication have been especially invaluable to me. Thanks, too, to Kieron Fairweather, who so ably assists her.

Deborah Klein, Sally Wilcox and Howie Saunders – my Los Angeles lawyer, agent and manager – proved wonderfully supportive while I needed this book to be secret. They believed in me, when I had no other professionals to rely on.

I am also grateful to Fiona McMorrough, of FMcM, who has given me such stalwart literary PR advice – as she has, on and off, for more than a decade and a half.

My *Rabbit Hole Detectives* podcast cohosts (and friends) Dr Cat Jarman and the Rev. Richard Coles each gave thoughtful and helpful pointers at crucial phases. I love how we support each others' many creative projects.

Final thanks go to my family who have often had to put up with me at my most distracted, tetchy and wrung out during the past five years. Catharsis has perhaps not been obvious to date, but hopefully it will be achieved now that this work – in many ways, the book of my life – is finally done.

CS